QUEEN

OF THE

SEA

A HISTORY of LISBON

BARRY HATTON

First published in the United Kingdom in 2018 by
C. Hurst & Co. (Publishers) Ltd.,
41 Great Russell Street, London, WC1B 3PL
© Barry Hatton, 2018
All rights reserved.
Printed in the United Kingdom by Bell & Bain Ltd, Glasgow

The right of Barry Hatton to be identified as the author of
this publication is asserted by him in accordance with the
Copyright, Designs and Patents Act, 1988.

Distributed in the United States, Canada and Latin America by
Oxford University Press, 198 Madison Avenue, New York, NY 10016,
United States of America.

A Cataloguing-in-Publication data record for this book
is available from the British Library.

ISBN: 9781849049979

This book is printed using paper from registered sustainable
and managed sources.

www.hurstpublishers.com

For Carmo, who makes things possible.

"A culture, we all know, is made by its cities."

— Derek Walcott

CONTENTS

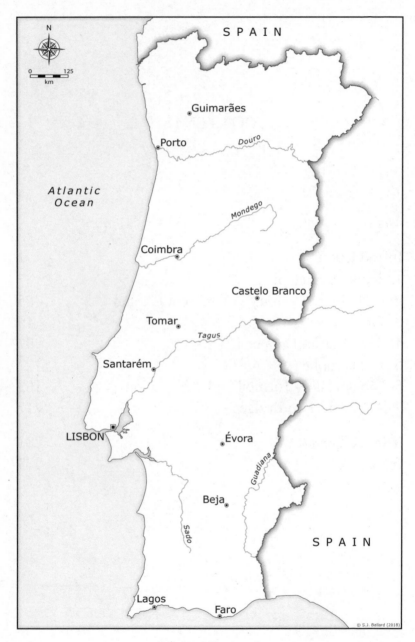

Map of Portugal

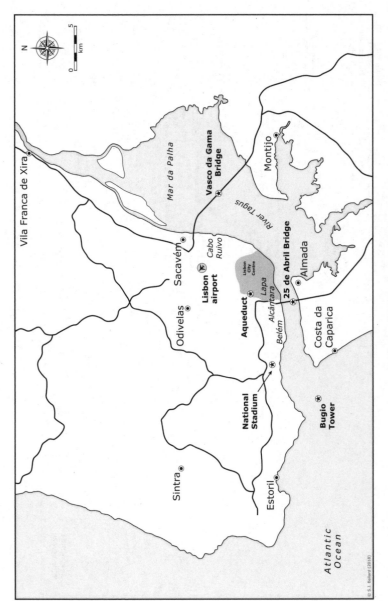

Map of the Lisbon Region

© S.J. Ballard (2018)

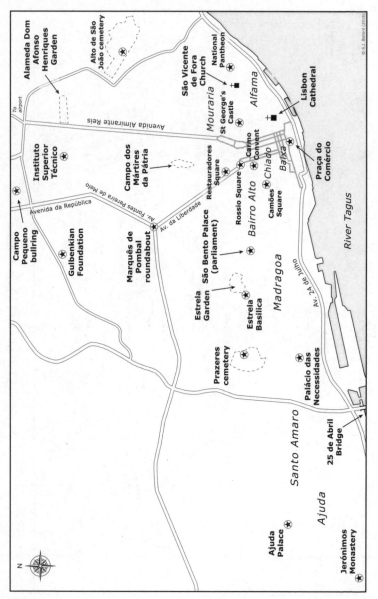

Map of Lisbon

© S.J. Ballard (2018)

INTRODUCTION

Jan Taccoen was captivated. The Flemish nobleman had stopped over in Lisbon in 1514 on his voyage to Jerusalem, and in his nine days in the Portuguese capital he repeatedly came across three elephants with their handlers proceeding through the city. Taccoen was astounded by the rich variety of life he witnessed on Lisbon's streets—not just people from other European countries, but also from the distant and exotic lands of Africa and the Orient. "You can see many animals and strange people in Lisbon," he remarked in a letter home.

The Portuguese king's cortège at the time was a remarkable sight. It was led by a rhinoceros which was followed by five elephants rigged out in gold brocade, then an Arabian horse, a jaguar, and finally the sovereign and his court. The same year Taccoen disembarked, King Manuel I sent a white Indian elephant as a present to the pope. His flaunting of wealth and national adventure had royal precedents. Before King Manuel, Prince Henry the Navigator had sent an African lion to his representative in Galway, Ireland "because [the king] knew nothing of its kind had ever been seen in those parts," according to the fifteenth-century Portuguese chronicler Gomes Eanes de Zurara.

These exotic animals were the trophies of a conquering country. In the early sixteenth century, Portugal projected its power across two oceans, to three continents. After the Portuguese spent decades exploring the West African coast, Bartolomeu Dias was the first European to round the southernmost tip of Africa, in 1488, and enter the Indian Ocean. Adam Smith, the eighteenth-century political economist, judged that milestone to be one of "the two greatest and most important events recorded in the history of mankind", along with the discovery of America. Vasco da Gama followed in Dias' footsteps, finding his way to India and its spices, in 1498. Two years later, Pedro Álvares Cabral placed a *padrão*—a stone marker—for Portugal on the coast of what would become known as Brazil. In the East, the Portuguese pushed on to the South China Sea, where they were the first Europeans the Japanese encountered. Technical ingenuity, geopolitical guile and daring ambition drove the empire. The Portuguese were full of élan. They were conspicuous operators on the world stage and played a prominent role in bringing about the early modern period of history.

The fabulous wealth Portugal harvested during those electrifying days of empire was concentrated almost entirely in Lisbon. This seat of imperial power grew into one of the busiest ports in Europe and one of the continent's biggest, wealthiest and most famous cities. Lisbon was an Aladdin's Cave of "exotic" goods. The cargo holds of the returning ships contained slaves, gold, silk, jewels, sugar and spices. The wares attracted buyers to the Portuguese capital from across medieval Europe. Lisbon was where you could purchase, along a single street, Chinese porcelain, Indian filigree, bolts of silk and other fine cloth, incense, myrrh, precious gems and pearls, pepper, ginger, cloves, cinnamon, nutmeg, saffron, chillies, ivory, sandalwood, ebony, camphor, amber, Persian carpets and handsomely bound books.

Those days of splendour, however, were numbered. Dark chapters lay ahead in Lisbon's history. After one catastrophic eighteenth-century event, the city was almost moved somewhere else.

Barely a month after the Portuguese capital was wrecked in 1755 by what is believed to be the strongest earthquake ever to strike modern Europe, followed by a tidal wave as high as a double-decker bus and a six-day inferno that turned sand into glass, the king's chief engineer had already sketched out a handful of suggestions for rebuilding the city. Manuel da Maia, an eminent military engineer with heavy jowls who was born in 1677 and was seventy-eight years old when the quake hit, laid out the options as he saw them in a celebrated official report, known as his *Dissertação*.

One of the possibilities was to abandon the ancient city and relocate Lisbon to an area 10 kilometres further west, nearer the ocean. There, foundations built into solid limestone rock had mostly spared buildings from the earthquake. For a people traumatized by one of the continent's deadliest catastrophes, the proposal was reasonable—as well as plausible—considering the scale of the destruction and necessary rebuilding.

But Maia also saw amid the devastation a chance to introduce a degree of eighteenth-century urban renewal in the tightly wound medieval city. King José I had previously expressed enthusiasm for such modernization. The monarch became known as "the reforming king" for his efforts to adapt Portugal to changing times. He and his influential secretary of state Sebastião José Carvalho e Melo eventually opted for Maia's suggestion to keep Lisbon where it was—with a twist. They approved a rebuilding project that swept away the downtown's medieval shape and replaced the sinewy streets with an airy, gridiron pattern more typical of northern and central Europe. The two epochs contributed different weaves to the city's pattern. The organic, anarchic muddle of the medieval part and the scientific sanity, uniformity and formality of the eighteenth-century rebuild furnish one of those contrasts that keep a city interesting.

A phrase recurs in Portuguese histories of Lisbon when they describe places or buildings: "Before the earthquake, this was…" Because in Lisbon's life there will always be a Before and After that watershed event. The earthquake stripped the city of many riches it had accrued during the Age of Expansion. There are still emblematic national treasures, such as St George's Castle and the Jerónimos Monastery, though even they had to be partly rebuilt. The bottom line is that there is not such a variety of sights for visitors in Lisbon as might be encountered in cities elsewhere on the continent. Rome, it isn't.

Lisbon's special appeal lies elsewhere. Its secret is in the mix. There is an afterglow of Lisbon's imperial history, when the city was the nerve centre for Portugal's extensive colonial possessions in Africa, South America and the Orient. That cosmopolitan legacy endows Lisbon with an intriguing, exotic flavour that is unique in Europe. Lisbon, for all its loss, still engages the imagination.

Lisbon—one of the European Union's smaller capitals in a largely unsung country on the bloc's fringe—is closer to Africa than the EU Brussels headquarters, and not only in a geographical sense. Foreign university students call Portugal the "Morocco of Europe", and they mean it as a compliment. In its scale, Lisbon is down-to-earth, charming and close. While more celebrated cities can be haughty, unpretentious Lisbon opens its doors. It is part of the city's charm. Walking though some of the older parts of the city can feel like wandering through a kasbah. Lisbon is a mood, and that cannot be captured in a travel brochure or photographs on a website.

This hilly city is heaven for the *flâneur*. As you walk through it, sudden, arresting vistas pull you up, hold your gaze and make you feel proud to have found them, no matter how long they have been there. The Portuguese name "Lisboa", with three syllables, is more musical than the clipped "Lisbon", and the city's melody is captured in the leisurely, graceful pace of the canary-yellow trams that scoot up and down its many hills and the orange-and-white ferries that sedately score the River Tagus with lines of foam.

This book is for anyone who shares my affection for Lisbon, or who is willing to be seduced. And, truth be told, it's not hard to be seduced by Lisboa, Queen of the Sea.

ONE—TRIPLE ATTRACTION

You could be forgiven for thinking that the residents of Lisbon's Alfama quarter all have bulging thighs like downhill skiers.

Hiking up and down the medieval neighbourhood's often steep and slender streets to reach the hilltop castle isn't just a walk through Lisbon's history. It is also a physically demanding, delightful and vicarious exercise. More than that: going up to St George's Castle and standing on top of its Ulysses Tower is the best way to figure out the why and the how of Lisbon. The view from the battlements is not only thrilling. It also provides a vivid sense of why a city took root on this spot.

The site ticks three important boxes: a high, steep-sided hill for defence; a broad and bountiful river; and a large natural harbour on the Atlantic coast. The hilltop, like a crow's nest, is the north bank's trump card against the almost flat south bank of the River Tagus. This hill, archaeologists say, received Lisbon's first settlers. Phoenicians fortified a settlement here in the seventh century BC, when it was already a lively port, and over the following centuries Romans, Barbarians, Moors (Muslims of North African descent) and newly minted Portuguese followed suit.

For a long time there were some doubts about the scale of the Phoenician presence. Archaeologists had found in Lisbon only broken bits of pottery with Phoenician lettering, which could have meant that the Phoenicians just passed through. But a dig in 2014 unearthed convincing proof that a substantial community of Phoenicians dwelt here. A heavy Iron Age gravestone, more than 70 centimetres tall, was found. It had a seventh-century-BC inscription in Phoenician, indicating a Phoenician cemetery and, therefore, a permanent settlement. It was one of the early twenty-first century's most spectacular archaeological finds in Lisbon. The excavation was by the downtown riverside, in what is nowadays the Rua do Cais de Santarém, where a quay once stood.

The Alfama district captures the flavour of Lisbon's more recent past. In Moorish times, when its distinctive labyrinthine layout took shape, this south-facing hillside was an aristocratic area. It had a pretty view of the river and was rendered safe by stout city walls. Alfama, the city's oldest *bairro* or neighbourhood, maintained an air of distinction for centuries until people with money departed after the 1755 earthquake and the poor used the rubble to rebuild on the same foundations in the familiar style. In a 1954 letter about her trip to Portugal, the American writer Mary McCarthy reported to her friend and political theorist Hannah Arendt that in the Alfama neighbourhood below the castle she had encountered "plenty of medieval poverty, like Africa".

Alfama is no longer in the grip of poverty. In fact, it is increasingly gentrified. Even so, it has maintained a coarse, earthy edge and is mostly a low-income part of town. Its alleys and roofs that almost touch help conjure up what the entire city looked like until the mid-eighteenth century. The

Panoramic View of Lisbon, an anonymous sixteenth-century depiction, now in the library of Leiden University in the Netherlands, shows that the entire city was just such a maze of streets. Alfama is a relic of that period—the medieval city preserved in miniature.

Alfama is a warren, at times murky and grubby, of cobbled streets. It is a jumble of little houses with low doors and tiny windows, punctuated with little greengrocers, bars, cafés and restaurants that can make it feel like a souk. Washing often billows from lines stretched over the pavements, forcing passers-by to push it from their faces like an overlong fringe. As McCarthy noted, it can feel here like every day is laundry day. Such scenes are a staple of black-and-white Portuguese films of Lisbon in the last century. Under António Salazar's twentieth-century dictatorship, the custom was not regarded as exposing poverty, but as evidence of wholesomeness. Today, Lisbon is one of the few European capitals where you can spot underwear hanging out to dry close to the city centre.

Wandering through Alfama, voices and TV sounds can be overheard behind net curtains. Faces linger at small windows as locals watch the world go by. Unattended barbecues smoke outside doors, and smells of cooking drift slowly down streets. Jesús, a friend from Goa, the former Portuguese colony in India, once stole a sardine from one of these barbecues when he was a hungry young boy and had just arrived in Lisbon. He tried to run off with it but it was piping hot and he dropped it. As he fumbled with the steaming sardine, its owner appeared in her doorway and shouted to him. She wanted to know if he was hungry, because, if so, she would give him some food. He warily walked back to her, expecting to be slapped around the head, but she sat him down and fed him. "That's when I knew I would spend my life in Lisbon," Jesús says. It is the kind of conduct Alfama is proud of.

Alleys branch out from Alfama's Rua de São Miguel, including Beco da Bicha, which is just a few feet wide. A typical sixteenth-century building, with protruding green shutters over the windows and the top floors jutting out, overlooks Largo de São Miguel. In Largo de São Rafael, part of the old city wall stands in line with modern buildings. Roofs meet over the Beco do Carneiro. There are deep shadows and windows that never receive direct sunshine in this sunny city. Flowering trees overhang the street, and sudden splashes of purple and orange bougainvillea surprise the walker. The overall effect is enchanting. Getting lost is easy and agreeable.

Dona Fernanda lives in one of Alfama's typical small and snug dwellings, in her case a 3-metre-wide house. It looks as if it is being squeezed by the slightly higher neighbouring buildings. Her house is bonny. Its windows have a dark green trim, and a flower bed outside has red roses, purple hydrangeas and pink geraniums. But life is hard for the widow. The house is quaint but it has never had a bath or toilet. She uses a chamber pot and bathes at a local day-care centre. Dona Fernanda is ninety-four years old and has lived in this house for seventy of those years. It stands across from Santiago Church, which has a cypress tree outside it and a sign stating, *Aqui começa o caminho* ("Here begins the Way"), with a red arrow pointing north towards Santiago de Compostela in Spain and a plaque reading "610 kilometres". Dona Fernanda, once a handbag-maker at a local factory, pays just 28 euros a month in rent. Her great regret is a lost sense of community in Alfama, where tourists and executives are increasingly bedding down. "All those old habits have gone—

saying good morning to your neighbours, getting your bread and milk delivered," she says.

Dona Fernanda's house is a short walk from Lisbon's cathedral, which was built on the site of a mosque the Moors used. The cathedral was badly damaged by earthquakes in 1337, 1344 and 1347, and then in 1755, and was repeatedly repaired and rebuilt. Ordered built by King Afonso Henriques after his army conquered the city in 1147, it is a national monument and one the country's most important examples of medieval architecture. But it is an underwhelming building. The unimpeachable *Guia de Portugal* (Guide to Portugal, published over the twentieth century) speaks, in a sorrowful tone, of "regrettable patching-up" and "architectural chaos". It is perhaps best remembered as the place where, on 6 December 1383, Bishop Martinho Anes was thrown from the north tower by angry locals for supporting a Spanish claim to the Portuguese throne.

This area stood inside the medieval city walls, which are known as the Cerca Moura (Moorish City Wall) or Cerca Velha (Old City Wall). The wall is a national monument and parts of it can still be glimpsed amid Alfama's jumble of buildings. Historians believe that the wall's original foundations went up during Roman times, around the fourth century AD, and were improved by the Moors after their arrival in Lisbon in 714. Augusto Vieira da Silva, an engineer who published a book on the Moorish wall in 1899, calculated it was about 1,250 metres long and up to 2.5 metres thick. That suggests that the walled city, at its late eleventh-century zenith, sat on about 30 hectares—say, about thirty rugby pitches. Other dwellings were scattered over 15 hectares outside the wall. Lisbon's population at that time is estimated at anywhere between 5,000 and 20,000 people.

"The topographical layout of medieval Lisbon was above all Islamic," wrote António Oliveira Marques, one of Portugal's leading twentieth-century historians.

We don't know what the Roman one looked like, because the entire outline has vanished over time. Primitive Lisbon probably grew up on the southern slope of the castle hill, with a *castrum* on top and a series of buildings going down to the Tagus. The result was an almost triangular area, so typical of Mediterranean cities and, also, Islamic cities.

Even the *reconquista* did not fully remove that Moorish influence. The Moors still feel present in Alfama. Indeed, they left their stamp on Portuguese culture, in sometimes subtle ways. Portuguese words beginning "*al*"—such as Alfama itself, derived from the Arabic word for baths or drinking water—are inherited from the Islamic occupation. Portuguese hand-painted tiles, called *azulejos*, are another legacy. And people in Porto, Portugal's second-largest city and the capital's great rival 300 kilometres to the north, mock the people of Lisbon by calling them "Moors," as if they aren't "real" Europeans.

The castle overlooking Alfama and the rest of the city is perhaps Lisbon's most emblematic landmark, and the view it offers is staggering. As the sun sets over the Atlantic—if you sailed that way, the first land mass you would come to is North America—the electric blue sky shifts through a kaleidoscope of colours. The sun fades to apricot, followed by more delicate hues: candy-pink and lilac, before a triumphant dying blast of violet, magenta and crimson.

Such Lisbon charms have inspired poets. Miguel de Cervantes, describing the arrival of a group of pilgrims in Lisbon in the seventeenth-century *Works of Persiles and*

Sigismunda, has a cabin boy exclaim, "land, land … though it might be better to speak of sky because we undoubtedly have come to the famous anchorage of Lisbon." Lord Byron, in his eighteenth-century *Childe Harold's Pilgrimage*, wrote, "What beauties doth Lisboa first unfold! … That, sheening far, celestial seems to be…"

The castle is closely associated with Portugal's early history. It became the political and military heart of the country in the twelfth century after the Portuguese wrested it from the hands of Moors in the momentous Siege of Lisbon. Two centuries later, following a landmark battlefield victory, King João I was inspired to name the castle after the chivalrous warrior and early Christian martyr St George. The king was stirred to the grand gesture by his epic military success in the 1385 Battle of Aljubarrota, 130 kilometres north of Lisbon, when some 6,000 Portuguese soldiers aided by English long-bowmen defeated an invading army of around 30,000. That kept the Portuguese kingdom from the clutches of neigh-bouring Castile, the powerful Iberian kingdom that would form the core of Spain. The war cry used by the Portuguese at Aljubarrota was "Portugal and St George!" Indeed, that remains the Portuguese army's war cry seven centuries later, and St George is the army's patron saint.

The castle grew out of a stronghold erected around 1050 by the Moors, who governed most of the Iberian Peninsula from the eighth century. The Moorish fortifications were improved by the Portuguese, who added an ample royal palace as well as a bishop's residence and the royal archive. The palace was the birthplace in 1455 of King João II, later one of the driving forces behind the Age of Expansion, and in 1502 of João III, who became king aged nineteen and whose thirty-six-year reign was impressive for its longevity as well as the capture of new lands in western India, including Bombay, from *Bom Bahia* or "Good Bay" in old Portuguese. The castle was also the birthplace of Portuguese drama, with the first performance of Gil Vicente's *Monólogo do Vaqueiro* (Cowherd's Monologue) in 1502, and it was where Vasco da Gama was received on his 1499 return from his voyage to India that opened a new chapter in world history. They were the castle's glory years.

Though earthquakes over the centuries caused considerable damage to the castle, and razed its most recent additions, this national monument still impresses. The castle has ten square towers and sits within a moat. It forms roughly a square, measuring some 50 metres on each side, and its yellowish stone gives off a soft glow in the morning and evening sun. The walls measure up to 10 metres high and 5 metres thick. It would serve admirably as a set for a medieval-themed film.

Up to the end of the fourteenth century the whole city could be seen from the castle's towers, with dwellings spilling down the hill to the river in a patchwork of overlapping rooftops. It is still a picturesque spot, though being so exposed it can be windy and cool even in summer when a *nortada* (north wind) blows up. The lawns shaded by contorted olive trees and bushy stone pines make excellent places to rest from the uphill climb. Medieval jousting tournaments are held here, and the guided tours include a night-time visit to catch glimpses of the bats that call the castle home. Among the prize sightings, according to the enthusiastic organizers, are the European free-tailed bat, the common pipistrelle, and Daubenton's bat.

Though visitors nowadays come in their droves—more than a million a year—the castle was not always a centre of

Lisbon's attention. Its upkeep was often neglected. More dramatically, in the nineteenth century a military barracks and other administrative buildings were built over the castle, virtually concealing it from view. It was astonishingly insensitive, in architectural and cultural terms. The carbuncle was removed only in the 1940s, when the government spruced up the site and embellished its medieval complexion.

Looking up to the castle from Lisbon's downtown, the Portuguese flag and Lisbon's black-and-white insignia fly side-by-side from the battlements. From the top, the downtown is so close that you feel you could lob a stone and it would land in a busy square. These hillsides were too steep for medieval siege machines, such as towers and catapults, to reach the castle. Furthermore, the castle's defensive design was shrewd. Like a Russian nesting doll, the castle has inner and outer walls with narrow zig-zagging passages that herded invaders into crossfire zones and had tight corners to prevent a battering ram being brought through. St George's Castle holds a record envied by any stronghold: it was never overrun.

For a long time threats to Lisbon's security came by sea. Since the seventeenth century the first sight encountered when approaching Lisbon from the Atlantic has been the Bugio Tower, which stands like a lonely and defiant sentry in the mouth of the Tagus. Seen from the city, it sits like a button on the horizon, silently flayed by waves, its round fort typical of the Renaissance period. But defending the way into Lisbon had already become a pressing concern from the fifteenth century onwards. The booty that came with Portugal's foreign conquests was widely coveted. The initial response to that threat was to anchor a large warship in the mouth of the river and, as later with Bugio, to use it to establish a crossfire with forts on land. One of these gate-keepers was the fearsome galleon *São João Baptista*. It is reckoned to have been the world's most powerful battleship when it was built in 1534. Its hundreds of bronze cannon earned it the nickname *Botafogo* (Spitfire).

The Bugio Tower was decreed obsolete in 1945 and handed to the Navy Ministry's lighthouse service. Bugio roughly marks the end of a spit of sand, flecked with foamy waves, which reaches out from the south side of the mouth of the Tagus. It is possible to make out the sandbank at low tide, and pleasure boats go out to it, but it is treacherous for shipping. Bugio's lighthouse, though not part of the original monument, today stands 14 metres high and indicates to ships which side to pass by blinking its green light every five seconds. It is tempting to imagine a Portuguese Gatsby watching from the riverbank.

The Tagus has a gaping mouth, 10 kilometres across. This is where one of Europe's longest rivers meets the world's second-largest ocean. From that open-armed welcome the mouth quickly tapers, like a funnel, to its narrowest point at just 2.3 kilometres wide. That is where the first bridge across the Tagus was built in 1966. Its resemblance to the Golden Gate Bridge in San Francisco is uncanny.

After that, the Tagus yawns wide again. The *Mar da Palha* (Sea of Straw) estuary is more than 20 kilometres across at its widest point and up to 46 metres deep. Lisbon looks out over this huge lake and sees the moods that play on its surface. The Sea of Straw can be a lively cobalt-blue, with low waves that glint like fish scales, or it can brood with a silty brown colour, choppy and irritable in the wind. The provenance of the estuary's name is uncertain. Some say it refers to straw that used to float downstream from farmland further north. Others say straw once commonly loaded onto German ships at Lisbon would fall into the water. And others maintain it refers to the colour when the sun at a shallow angle reflects off the water.

Though the people of Lisbon are very fond of their *Rio Tejo*, they have not always taken good care of it. Up to 2013 the effluent from more than 100,000 Lisbon residents was flushed untreated into the Tagus. That was roughly the same amount as polluted the river in the sixteenth century. (In 1989, during an election campaign for Lisbon's mayoralty, the Social Democrat candidate Marcelo Rebelo de Sousa—who more than twenty years later would become Portuguese president— swam in the Tagus as a political stunt to get his name more widely known. The general reaction was, "Yuck!")

The river water is salty up to Vila Franca de Xira, 40 kilometres from the mouth. Going further upstream, the Tagus Valley broadens into a fertile alluvial plain that has long fed Lisbon. The Tagus stretches back deep into Spain. Its source is in the Sierra de Albarracín, in Aragon, a few hundred kilometres east of Madrid.

When Filipe II of Castile became king of Portugal in 1580, he eyed the Tagus and wondered how far upstream it might be possible to sail. Perhaps he could get home that way. He charged royal engineer João Baptista Antonelli with finding out. The conclusion was that the river was navigable from Lisbon to Aranjuez, about 40 kilometres south of Madrid. After some improvements on the river, vessels began moving between those two points. Indeed, much of the marble used in the building of the Escorial royal residence came from quarries in the Portuguese town of Estremoz and was transported up the Tagus.

The Tagus is the longest Iberian river at just over 1,000 kilo-metres, and more than half of it is in Portuguese territory. It has been Lisbon's lifeblood. Strabo, the geographer of antiq-uity, noted that the Tagus "contains a lot of fish, and is full of oysters". In the Middle Ages, the people of Lisbon used to say that the Tagus was two parts water, one part fish. Nowadays, in the early morning, the mouth of the river is often speckled with tiny fishing boats riding the current. The rhythm of their outings is dictated by the tide tables of Lisbon's Instituto Hidrográfico. But unpredictable forces also come into play. When there is heavy rain, or dams upstream open their sluice gates, the currents in the river mouth can be tricky, flowing one way at the surface and in the opposite direction on the river-bed, fishermen say. Fishing was good up to the end of the twentieth century, when overfishing and illegal fishing started taking their toll. The river has not just nourished the city; it has helped protect it. For the celebrated nineteenth-century histo-rian Oliveira Martins, the Tagus was "a splendid moat".

Lisbon's name can be reliably traced back as far as Roman times, as is the case with many old European places. The con-jecture that the city was founded by Ulysses after the Trojan War, when he lost his way in the Mediterranean, is not so much mythical as whimsical. The name Alis Ubbo, supposed to have been given by the Phoenicians and meaning "gentle cove", has won wide currency as the city's supposed *ur*-name. But the revered *Grande Enciclopédia Portuguesa e Brasileira* (Great Portuguese and Brazilian Encyclopaedia) thinks that is tosh, describing it as a "poetic yet pointless invention".

The Romans used Olisipo, which under the Moors became Al-Uxbuna. The Christian conquest brought Lixboa.

* * *

Where does the special quality of Lisbon's light come from? It is a question so often asked and for so long that it has become something of a parlour game.

The light in Lisbon is something to marvel at, even beneath winter clouds. It is not so much a feature of the city as a hallmark. It is a textured brightness, a creamy glow, at once vivid and silky.

Some people believe that Lisbon's orgy of light is a consequence of the broad estuary, or the river or the ocean, or all three. Others put it down to the city's closely packed white buildings and terracotta roofs, or attribute it to a happy blessing of latitude. And some say it is a legacy of the Romans.

Traditional Portuguese pavements, called *calçada portuguesa*, are unique. They are made of fist-sized cubes of limestone and basalt, with black stones used to weave patterns in the mostly white paving, like a mosaic. The technique was thought up in the 1840s by a military engineer called Lieutenant General Eusébio Furtado. He was familiar with— and inspired by—Roman paving techniques. Luisa Dornellas, the head of Lisbon City Council's training department, which schools workmen on how to lay the paving, has no doubt about its importance: "What sets apart Lisbon's lustre, compared with other cities, is this light that comes from the ground," she says. Like elsewhere in the bygone empire, vestiges of Roman rule have mostly sunk deep below the surface of the city streets. In Lisbon, part of this legacy is right beneath the soles of your shoes.

Lieutenant General Furtado was governor of St George's Castle from 1840 to 1846. The parade ground of the 5th Light Infantry Battalion was inside the castle walls, and it was bare earth. The governor decided in 1842 to do away with that and replace it with paving and flower borders punctuated by trees. He came up with the Roman-inspired paving scheme and found some cheap labour to do the back-breaking work of laying it: convicts. They turned out in chain gangs and became known as *grilhetas* after their *grilhões* (chains).

The black-and-white paving pattern made quite a splash, according to accounts in city newspapers of the time. People reportedly flocked to the castle to witness the novelty. The City Council noticed it, too, and in 1848 Furtado's proposal for the Roman-style paving of Rossio Square in downtown Lisbon was given the go-ahead. Finished in 323 days, the Rossio's wavy pattern was called *Mar Largo* (Broad Sea). It is still there today.

The Portuguese took *calçada portuguesa* across their empire, perhaps to help them feel at home. It can be encountered in Macau, near Hong Kong; in Luanda on Africa's tropical west coast; and in Rio de Janeiro, where the Copacabana's *calçadão* is famous. Wherever it is found, take pity on whoever laid it. The *calceteiro* spends his working day squatting on a tiny stool, bent over with a hammer as he chips away at the cubes to make sure they are a regular shape and then nestles them in a sandy base layer. It is the kind of toil that deserves a statue, and in 2007 one was erected in downtown Lisbon.

The Portuguese are tremendously proud of their *calçada*. But there is a terrible truth that was long unspoken: it is lethal when wet and after a while walking on it is terribly hard on the soles of your feet. The then-mayor of Lisbon, António Costa, committed heresy in 2014 when he publicly expressed such thoughts to justify cutting back on the expensive business of laying Portuguese pavements. He noted that he did not have at his disposal the free labour of convicts, and added: "Let's be honest, it's nice to look at but it's terrible to walk on. It's slippery, it's uncomfortable." The council decided to maintain it in tourist areas but phase it out elsewhere in the city.

Evidence of Rome's six-century presence in Lisbon is, otherwise, thin. And it took an earthquake and a giant underground boring machine to disinter much of what can be seen nowadays.

Roman Lisbon stretched from the second century BC to the fifth century AD. In 195 BC Romans led by Cato the Elder put down an uprising in Spain, and a stone inscription that once existed in St George's Castle suggests that he came through Olisipo too. Olisipo was incorporated into the Roman Empire in 138 BC. Military commander Decimus Junius Brutus Callaicus added fortifications to the hilltop where the castle now stands and used the site as a base for Rome's efforts to tame peninsular tribes. Julius Caesar fully conquered the province of Lusitania, on the western edge of the empire, only around 60 BC.

Under Emperor Augustus, Lisbon's political and administrative stature grew. It was renamed Felicitas Julia Olisipo and oversaw an area that stretched beyond the south bank to the Arrábida hills, visible about 50 kilometres away. Olisipo had three main zones: the *oppidum*, or fortified settlement, on top of the hill; the town area built over the south slope of the castle hill; and the riverfront beaches where fishing and trading boats came ashore.

After the Roman conquest of Britain, Lisbon's status surged once more because it was a stopover on the Atlantic shipping route from the Mediterranean to northern Europe. Olisipo became a hub of Roman trade and industry. The fertile upstream plains provided farm produce and, as Strabo noted, the river was teeming with fish. That made it ideal for brewing and exporting *garum*, the smelly fish sauce used by Romans as a condiment and sent around the empire in amphoras, some of which were manufactured on the south bank of the Tagus. Still today, fatty fish such as sardines, sprat or mackerel are plentiful off Lisbon's Atlantic coast. Those fish, including their entrails and eggs, are ideal for making *garum*, which is concocted by mixing the fish with salt and herbs, leaving it in the sun to ferment, then stirring until it becomes a liquid. A grand industrial complex of *garum* fermentation tanks existed along Lisbon's riverside, including up to the downtown area called the Baixa. A Roman cemetery in Rua dos Corrieiros, discovered beneath a modern bank, existed until the first century AD when it was relocated to Praça da Figueira to make way for more fermentation tanks.

Lisbon's new-found wealth paid for thermal baths, underground galleries, a theatre and a hippodrome. These trappings of a thriving city lent Lisbon new imperial prestige. These 1,000-year-old remnants were hidden from view until the 1755 earthquake cracked open the earth and excavations unlocked their secrets. The public baths were built in 44 AD. A Latin inscription, painted in red, was found on a buried wall and commemorates the renovation, in 336 AD, of the original *Thermae Cassiorium*. The Cassian Baths, named after one of the city's prominent families, were properly excavated only in the early 1990s. They are in Rua das Pedras Negras, but no museum yet stands on the site.

The purpose of the Roman galleries, unearthed in the current downtown area in 1771 as post-earthquake rebuilding progressed, has long been debated. The likeliest explanation is that these underground arches were installed to provide a solid platform for buildings above them, including possibly a forum. This part of the old town sits on rivers and streams with sandy beds that flowed into the Tagus until the fifteenth century. Geologically, the area is a steep valley, and the galleries allow underground water to run off. These galleries usually have water about a metre deep inside them, but they are pumped out twice a year—in April and September—for public visits. Visitors queue along the Rua da Prata and, through a manhole in the middle of the street as cars and buses drive by, proceed gingerly down steep steps into Lisbon's distant past.

The Roman theatre, located down the hill from St George's Castle, was a prominent landmark for anyone arriving in Olisipo by river. To that end, it was built—unusually for a Roman theatre—facing south. It demonstrated the power and the privilege of the city's rulers. This large, imposing building's terraced amphitheatre on three levels could hold around 3,000 people for its hours-long performances. Built in the time of Augustus, it was later remodelled under Nero.

The theatre was discovered only in 1798. Italian architect Francisco Xavier Fabri drew what he encountered at that time and campaigned to preserve the ruins. His appeal fell on deaf ears, however. Homes were built over the site, though Fabri's drawings have survived. The first scientific excavations took place in the 1960s, when seven buildings on the site were purchased and four were demolished so archaeologists could get down into the theatre, 9 metres below ground level in Alfama's Rua de São Mamede. Apart from being built-over, the theatre's heavy stones and pillars had been cannibalized for use in the constructions standing over it. Despite the building's deterioration, authorities have made a laudable effort to reconstruct the monument. The theatre's museum includes Iron Age artefacts encountered during the dig.

Some 200 years after those finds, as Lisbon spruced itself up to host the last World's Fair of the twentieth century, huge tunnelling machines expanding the city's underground train system burrowed back in time and threw up long-lost treasures. A dramatic discovery was made in the downtown area: a Roman hippodrome where chariot races like those portrayed in the film classic *Ben Hur* were staged. The arena was discovered 6 metres beneath the surface of Rossio Square, in the heart of the city's shopping district. The racetrack, at least 190 metres long, was among the biggest built in the Roman Empire. The discovery that Lisbon possessed two Roman entertainment amenities on a grand scale—the theatre and the hippodrome—cast the city in a different historical light. "We had thought Lisbon was relatively unimportant in the Roman Empire, being merely a trading post," said Ana Vale, an archaeologist monitoring the tunnelling work, "but in fact it was a city of note."

Such magnificence was not to last. Rome's decline and departure opened the door to Barbarian rule, which lasted for three centuries until another advanced civilization arrived in Lisbon: the Moors.

TWO—A DIFFERENT COUNTRY,
A DIFFERENT CAPITAL

When a European coalition army assembled outside Lisbon in 1147 on a mission to snatch the city from the Muslims who had called it home for five centuries, their squabbling almost doomed the enterprise before it began. Gathered for battle, these crusaders from northern Europe became involved in a heated row over how to proceed against the infidels. Their host, Portugal's King Afonso Henriques, bent over backward to accommodate their demands and reconcile their interests. It brings to mind modern-day NATO conferences on the Middle East.

The allied attacking forces finally came to an arrangement, and what would become the famous Siege of Lisbon began on 1 July. However, the bickering resumed after the conquest, almost seventeen weeks later. Even so, capturing Lisbon and claiming it for Christianity would be recorded as the high-water mark of the Second Crusade, which otherwise was a wretched endeavour.

The fullest surviving record of events in medieval Lisbon through those summer months and into the early autumn is an English crusader's letter home. The original manuscript is held at Corpus Christi College, Cambridge. The letter's authorship has long been the subject of scholarly debate. The most widely accepted explanation is that it was sent by an Anglo-Norman priest called Raol, who signed it simply "R", to Osbert of Bawdsey in Suffolk, in the east of England. There are other candidates for the author's identity, however, including Robert, an Anglo-Norman cleric who later became dean of Lisbon cathedral.

The letter is in Latin. It was first published by the Lisbon Academy of Sciences in 1861 and translated into English by Charles Wendell David in his 1936 work *The Conquest of Lisbon*. The celebrated nineteenth-century Portuguese writer Alexandre Herculano drew on it liberally in his *História de Portugal* (History of Portugal), a ground-breaking work because it harvested evidence from original sources and exploded some national myths.

The letter is known as *De expugnatione Lyxbonensi*—"The Storming of Lisbon". The great appeal of this dispatch is that it is a relatively detailed eyewitness account of the fighting by someone who had access to the siege leaders' inner circle. On the other hand, it should be noted, it is also the winners' version of history.

A crusader fleet making its way to the Holy Land stopped off in Porto, in northern Portugal, where the local bishop's eloquence persuaded the force to help the Portuguese monarch defeat the Saracens in Lisbon before proceeding to the Middle East. Lisbon, the letter to Osbert notes, was "very rich and prosperous". That cannot have failed to bring a glint to the eye of the warriors bent on collecting booty as well as spreading the faith.

King Afonso Henriques' army, meanwhile, was flushed with success. In March it had swiftly overrun the castle at

Santarém, a significant Moorish city on the fertile plain 80 kilometres to the north-east of Lisbon, in a daring night-time surprise attack, and the monarch was keen to press his advantage. But Lisbon occupied an enviable defensive location and was the Moors' mightiest city in western Iberia. It was plugged into a trade network with North Africa and was generously furnished with cereals, olive oil and wine. Another surprise attack was impossible because an approaching force could quickly be detected from the city's hilltop fortress.

Afonso Henriques was squaring up to Al-Uxbuna for a second time. He had tasted defeat there in the early 1140s, also with crusader help, after failing to break through the city's strong defences. His force retreated that time, but not before destroying crops and razing the homes located outside the city walls.

For his second bite at the apple he could now marshal a larger force. Al-Uxbuna is described in Raol's letter as "a very well-fortified stronghold", with a circular fortress and walls down to the Tagus protecting the triangular-shaped city. What Afonso Henriques needed was sheer might, and the Second Crusade's army provided him with his best chance so far. There were roughly 12,000 crusaders, made up largely of English, Scottish, French, German and Flemish warriors, in about 170 ships. The king, who had about 5,000 men, just had to make sure his allies stayed the course.

The monarch and his troops marched to Al-Uxbuna where they met the crusaders arriving by sea from Porto. Afonso Henriques was soon confronted with disputes among the foreigners. Some argued over how, and whether, to proceed and under what terms. They were, the letter to Osbert recounts, "unwilling to bear the expense of a long labour in the siege" and wanted to go swiftly to the Mediterranean where they could "extort much easy money" from African and Spanish merchant ships. Others disagreed, and the letter reports "everybody all around shouting". The tension subsided after Afonso Henriques pledged to let the crusaders have the spoils of the city, including prisoners for ransom, before he raised his flag over it. The leaders swore oaths to observe the pact.

The allied forces made camp on three hilltops looking across to the city. Al-Uxbuna had a gate on each of its eastern and western sides and another on the riverfront. It is clear from the abundant insults hurled between the attackers and defenders that the fighting was at close quarters. The sneering can seem slightly comical in our post-Monty Python world, though the chronicler of the action does not shirk from detailing what was said—by the Muslims, at least:

> While we kept watch, meanwhile, under their walls through the days and nights, they heaped derision and many insults upon us. They taunted us with the many children who were going to be born at home while we were gone and said that our wives would not be anxious about our deaths, since home was well supplied with little bastards.
>
> They showed to us, moreover, with much derision the symbol of the cross. They spat upon it and wiped the feces from their posteriors with it. At last they urinated on it, as on some despicable thing, and threw our cross at us...

After some early feints and skirmishes to gauge the city's defences, the attackers got down to business. They built two huge siege towers, 30 and 25 metres tall and protected by wicker and hides, as well as battering rams and catapults. The two catapults, with 100 men on each machine working in shifts, were said to rain 5,000 stones an hour down on the city.

Not surprisingly, those inside the city "were greatly harassed by this action". But almost all of the machines burned to the ground, while a remaining siege tower became stuck in sand and was trapped by the rising Tagus tide. (At that time, as in Roman days, the river often flooded the city's lower parts. A Tagus tributary now flowing underground through Lisbon's Baixa district comes from the confluence of two other streams that run beneath two of the modern city's main avenues: Avenida da Liberdade and Avenida Almirante Reis. Heavy downpours still occasionally flood riverside areas.)

Stalemate ensued, and allied spirits flagged. Some of the frustrated attackers spoke of moving on, abandoning Lisbon to Islam. The turning point came when Moors who were captured as they tried to escape the city were found to be carrying letters pleading for help from Muslim leaders further south. The pleas told of acute food shortages and misery inside the city walls. The Portuguese and the crusaders were choking the city to death. They just didn't know it. The revelation stiffened their resolve. They beached their ships in a pointed sign to the city defenders that they were hunkering down to prolong the fight through the approaching winter.

The siege moved up a gear. A fire was lit in a mine dug under the city wall, and part of the wall collapsed. The defenders, alarmed, dashed to the breach. The attackers swarmed around the hole, firing so many arrows into the gap that the Moors' shields bristled "like hedgehogs". Then the remaining siege tower, freed from the mud, moved ever closer to a different place along the wall as the military initiative swung decisively in the attackers' favour. The desperate defenders hurriedly reinforced that second spot and flung down burning pitch and oil and stones. The attackers thronged behind the tower, firing arrows and bolts up to the battlements. It was a dance of death. The Moors were heroically defending their city and fighting for their lives. The attackers were undeterred as victory—more than four months after the siege began—finally came into view.

The letter is an at times thrilling account of a medieval siege, especially at the crescendo: as the remaining tower moves ever closer, to within a metre of the city wall, and just as it is about to extend a bridge onto the battlements the Moors throw up their arms in surrender.

The Muslims opened the gates of Lisbon to the Christians on either 23 or 24 October—it is unclear which—and the occupants began leaving their homes on Saturday 25 October. The conquerors raised a cross on the fortress' highest tower, and King Afonso Henriques walked around the battlements. It is not hard to imagine his pride and sense of achievement as he looked out over the city, the river and the ocean.

An Englishman, Gilbert of Hastings, was picked as Lisbon's first bishop after the reconquest, and he stayed in the post until 1162. Some of the crusaders were not very pious, however. The success sowed dissent, with arguments breaking out over how to divide up the spoils. A "renegade priest" from Bristol, according to the letter to Osbert, stirred up some of the men. Some Rhinelanders and Flemish, unable to wait for their share of the loot, reneged on their pre-battle oath and rushed into the city, which they mercilessly pillaged and ransacked.

The medieval thuggishness aside, some crusaders believed that dying in battle against infidels was not just heroic but conferred a kind of martyrdom. Certainly, remembrance and veneration of fallen knights was significant among the common people. Take Henry of Bonn, who died in the Lisbon siege. A palm tree that sprouted from his Lisbon tomb was said to cure illness, and a cult arose. Portugal's sixteenth-century poet Luis de Camões devoted a stanza to Henry in his epic Renaissance poem *Os Lusíadas* (The Lusiads), one of the landmark works of Portuguese culture. Camões attributed the palm tree's healing properties to a miracle and called Henry "a martyr of Christ".

Lisbon's São Vicente de Fora Church is bound up with this cult, which faded after the Middle Ages. The church and an attached monastery, which are among Lisbon's most stately buildings, stand on high ground where King Afonso Henriques' army pitched camp during the siege. The sovereign ordered their construction after he captured the city. For centuries they remained Lisbon's biggest structure and a city landmark. In 1582 the old buildings were demolished and a church built in their place in Renaissance style, being completed in 1629. The church was badly damaged by the great storm of 19 November 1724 and then by the 1755 earthquake. Its bright white limestone, like marble, still lends it a regal presence amid the tight-packed modern buildings. Inside, tile panels depict the taking of Lisbon and Santarém. And, in a chapel off the nave, a discreet marble plaque indicates that *os ossos do cavaleiro Henrique Alemao* (the bones of Henry the German) are buried in the monastery.

Apart from the monarch the best-known Portuguese participant in the siege, and a name that most Portuguese recognize, was a knight known as Martim Moniz. Except that his story is a myth. Legend has it that he led his men in an attack on one of the city gates and managed to force it open. Though mortally wounded, the story goes, he threw himself into the breach so that it could not be shut and the Christians could enter the city. A downtown Lisbon square is named after him, and its underground train station has marble friezes of him and his fictional feats on its walls, though they are largely lost on hurried commuters.

The fine line between fact and exaggeration, or blatant medieval invention, is something Portuguese Nobel literature prize winner José Saramago played on in his 1989 book *The History of the Siege of Lisbon*. Historical and literary mischief was a Saramago trademark. In the novel, a Lisbon proof-reader impishly inserts the word "not" into a text on the siege, thereby fictionally altering the course of European history with a stroke of his pen. The story weaves between the past and present, between the real and the imagined.

In 1998 Saramago became Portugal's second Nobel laure-ate after António Egas Moniz, who shared the 1949 prize for physiology or medicine after pioneering lobotomy procedures at Lisbon University's Neurological Institute. The novelist moved with his dirt-poor family from the farming area around Santarém to Lisbon when he was a small child. Many memorable scenes from his books were set in the capital, including in one of his best works *Baltasar and Blimunda*, another historical fantasy. In that novel, the eighteenth-cen-tury city is portrayed as filthy and its citizens enthralled by the Inquisition's bonfires.

Saramago ended up falling out with Portugal's political elite and moving to Spain in the 1990s. He regretted the late twen-tieth-century modernization of Lisbon, where property specu-lation and public works disfigured some of the picturesque older *bairros*. Even so, he remained fond of the cultural toler-ance he witnessed in the city, which for centuries has mixed the blood of Christians and Muslims, Africans and Jews, Indians and Chinese. Saramago wrote that "the spirit of Lisbon lives on, and it is the spirit that makes cities eternal."

Saramago's ashes are buried next to an olive tree outside the Lisbon foundation that carries his name. The foundation is housed in the upper floors of the riverside Casa dos Bicos, one of the city's few remnants of the sixteenth century, though much changed from its original form. The building is a peculiarity of Lisbon architecture. The symmetrical, pointy stonework on its facade make it appear studded with diamonds. Indeed, it was inspired by a similar building in Ferrara, Italy, called the Diamond Palace. The Lisbon version was built by Brás de Albuquerque, son of Afonso de Albuquerque, a great military chief who consolidated and extended Portugal's conquests in the East. A once popular expression was *ter a Casa dos Bicos* ("owning the Casa dos Bicos"), indicating someone who possessed a fortune.

The capture of Lisbon was a pivotal event for the fledgling Portuguese kingdom, which was barely four years old. Lisbon gave Portugal ballast and made the country a feasible project. The historian Oliveira Martins said taking the city "wrote out the nation's birth certificate". It also constituted an important milestone in the Iberian *reconquista*.

Crucially for King Afonso Henriques, and his successors, conquering Lisbon opened a door to the south. It would take about another hundred years for the Portuguese to completely drive the Moors out of the southern Algarve region. Once that was accomplished the country's geographical and economic centre of gravity shifted. Keeping the capital in Coimbra, an inland city to the north, amounted to an anomaly. The Lisbon siege created a new country. Lisbon's growth and importance as a port eventually eclipsed other cities, and in 1256 King Afonso III moved his court there. It was the new capital.

* * *

The first icon of Portugal's traditional and distinctive *fado* music was not someone you would want to cross.

The early nineteenth-century Lisbon singer Maria Severa flouted convention. She smoked, drank and rolled up the sleeves of her dress. She had fiery eyes and a sharp temper and reputedly was a great beauty. The poet Raimundo Bulhão Pato, later quoted in Júlio de Sousa e Costa's 1936 book *Severa*, said she was:

> haughty and impetuous, as generous as she was ready to smack someone in the face if they were up to no good! She was brave, deeply considerate toward those she held dear, just as she was vulgar toward her enemies. She was no ordinary woman, you can be sure of that.

Severa performed in sleazy Lisbon venues notorious for drunkenness, violence and prostitution. In those places, the new musical form of *fado* was born and blossomed. Severa's mother owned a tavern and was known as *A Barbuda*, meaning "The Bearded One", though we can perhaps rather infer, more charitably, that she had a dark complexion. The house where Severa lived is in the narrow, shadowy Rua do Capelão, where a plaque on a wall commemorates her. It is in the Mouraria district, at the foot of the castle hill. This is the area where King Afonso Henriques allowed the defeated Muslims to settle—outside the city walls—after his triumph. It was long known as a poor, scruffy neighbourhood and an infamous gathering place for ne'er-do-wells.

Afonso Henriques had not taken leave of his senses by allowing his adversaries to sleep on his doorstep. For the Portuguese, the Muslims were not strangers. They were familiar, and had been for at least four centuries. Afonso Henriques negotiated truces with some of the Muslims' other Iberian leaders before attacking Lisbon, thus ensuring the besieged city would not be relieved. Christians, called Mozarabs after an Arabic word, and Jews had lived inside the Muslim-held city. Such tolerance has endured and is a Lisbon hallmark. The historian Jaime Cortesão, wrote that, on the peninsula, Portugal constituted "a region of transition and hybridism of cultures where, like nowhere else, the influences of Christianity and Islam converged."

Mouraria (from *Mouros*, the Portuguese word for Moors) is perhaps the quarter where Lisbon's fluid blend of cultures has been most evident. It remains the city's most ethnic neighbourhood, where Christians, Muslims, Hindus, Africans and Chinese live cheek-by-jowl along cobbled streets that, as in Alfama, recall medieval times. In 2014, people of more than fifty different nationalities lived in the Mouraria melting pot. The sinewy Rua do Benformoso was brought back to life by mostly Bangladeshi shopkeepers in 2014 after becoming largely derelict during a three-year economic recession. Chinese shopkeepers drag bulging black plastic bags and cardboard boxes heavy with assorted low-priced wares into their stores at a shopping mall overlooking Martim Moniz Square. The stores have names like Grande Mundo (Big World), and their employees have lunch at local eateries where the menus are only in Chinese. Other restaurants offer stodgy West African fare from Cape Verde and Guinea-Bissau. Grocery stores sell exotic fruit and vegetables that can be hard to identify, and enticing aromas of Indian spices drift up the steps from the underground station. Martim Moniz Square is a popular summer venue for outdoor music concerts showcasing little-known world music bands.

In the early 1800s the rich cultural broth in this part of town, along with the Alfama district and the docks, gave birth to *fado*. Its stylistic origins are uncertain. It blended rhythms from distant outposts of the Portuguese Empire, from Latin America to Africa and the Orient, while the innumerable foreign sailors passing through Lisbon threw their own sea shanties and folk tunes into the mix. *Fado* blended musical forms the same way as its birthplace blended people.

Among *fado*'s distinguishing features in its infancy was that it was played in Lisbon's seedier bars, and Mouraria was its heartland. It was also closely associated with the lower classes. It was performed by, and often sang about, people who are down on their luck. It was also cheap to put on—all you needed was an acoustic guitar and a singer. The oft-mentioned similarities with the Blues are clear. *Fado*, meaning fate or destiny, speaks of life's trials and torments, but with passion. It can come across as a chafing, woe-is-me lament but, like the Blues, it is lyrical, heartfelt, and sometimes funny.

The *Grande Enciclopédia Portuguesa e Brasileira* explains that *fado* cannot be taught in music schools. That is because *fado* comes from the gut. "It is an extremely personal and expressive type of song. You can tell the importance of the performer's personality," it says. "It is a trait of a real *fado* singer that they never sing the same thing the same way twice. They bring it to life differently each time they sing." The bottom line is, you have either got it or you haven't. And Severa had it, in spades.

The taverns-cum-brothels where Severa sang were rough places. The famous Portuguese artist José Malhoa captured something of the grimy, sordid flavour of early *fado* in his painting *O Fado* from 1909 which hangs in Lisbon's Museu da Cidade (City Museum) and occasionally at the city's Museum of Fado. It was a work that, for the artist, was at times maddening.

The painting shows a man sitting on a chair strumming a guitar, next to a woman who is also sitting but who has her face turned away from the viewer. They both look the worse for wear. There is an almost empty bottle on their table, and the woman is smoking a cigarette. The man is the well-known Mouraria delinquent Amâncio. He kept getting thrown into jail for disorderly conduct, repeatedly compelling Malhoa to postpone his painting plans. The woman is Adelaide, also infamous and known in Mouraria as *Adelaide da Facada* (literally, Adelaide the Knife Slash) because she had a long scar on her left cheek, which she turns away. The work was badly received because of its unconventional, if colourful, subject matter and was exhibited in Lisbon only in 1917. Before that, it was admired where it was shown abroad, including in Paris where it was called *Sous le charme* and in Liverpool where it was titled *The Native Song*.

Some of the capital's aristocracy was drawn to the lewd and garish *fado* venues. Severa had an affair with the Count of Vimioso, making her much gossiped about. But few reliable facts are available, beyond that she died aged twenty-six and single. Even a photograph of Severa published on the front cover of Lisbon *fado* magazine *Canção do Sul*, in issue 234, of 1 September 1939, turned out to be a fake. A true depiction of her was further muddied by the novel *A Severa*, published in 1901 by Júlio Dantas, which in any event did not aim to be an accurate historical portrait. It was a big hit, though, and was turned into a hugely popular play, still performed today, and a 1930 feature film that was the first talkie by a Portuguese director.

The play, which debuted in 1955, had in the starring role a young woman called Amália Rodrigues. She would become the first *fado* diva. Her star outshone all her rivals as she took *fado* from the Portuguese capital to the world stage and became the best-selling Portuguese musician in history.

Severa and Amália could hardly have been more different, though they both came from poor Lisbon families. Severa was bawdy and coarse and didn't shrink from violence while Amália, who died in 1999, was elegant and sophisticated and hated swearing. Amália, popularly referred to by her first name, had no formal education beyond primary school. She started working early to help support her family, becoming a seamstress' apprentice and selling fruit on Lisbon streets.

Amália made her professional debut in 1939 at the Retiro da Severa, a popular downtown Lisbon restaurant with *fado* music, where she stayed six months and was paid unprecedented wages for a *fado* performer. She had strong, handsome features and a charismatic stage presence. She introduced customs to the genre that have endured: performing in a black dress and shawl and positioning herself on stage in front of the accompanying guitarists.

Amália's supple, limpid voice captivated audiences, as did her emotionally charged performances. From the 1950s, she spent long months on the road, taking the Lisbon music to places such as Algeria, Caracas, Leningrad, Japan and Australia. In 1952, she performed for fourteen straight weeks at La Vie en Rose in New York. The following year she was the first Portuguese artist to appear on American television. Amália counted Charles Aznavour and Anthony Quinn among her fans and friends. Quinn, speaking to Portuguese television channel SIC in 1996, said of Amália, "She is full of womanhood. She is like a tree trunk—she is delicate and wonderful and full of femininity … She's just one of the great human beings worth knowing."

After decades on tour, Amália's next solo performance in Lisbon would not be until 1985. Still, she found time to unveil the plaque commemorating Severa in Rua do Capelão. In 2001 Amália's remains were transferred to the National Pantheon in Lisbon, where illustrious figures from Portugal's past are laid to rest.

Despite its central place in Portuguese culture, *fado*'s tendency towards sombre sentimentality and gloomy laments turned many people off. For years, *fado*—looking inwards and backwards—breathed stale air. Then along came Mariza and blew away the cobwebs. Daughter of a mother from Mozambique and a father from Portugal, Mariza grew up in Mouraria in the 1980s and 1990s. Her somewhat irreverent nature led her to perform *fado* songs with catchy melodies, and her willowy figure with honey-coloured skin and platinum hair ensured that she got noticed. Her foot-tapping tunes broadened *fado*'s popular appeal and allowed a new generation of performers to break through. Some people in traditional, conservative *fado* circles—where making a noise while *fado* is being sung merits a sharp rebuke—frowned at Mariza's modern style. For them, it was "*fado* lite". She, however, could point in her defence to *fado*'s beginnings as an adaptable and robust form. In the end, her record sales and international acclaim spoke louder than the grumbling in Lisbon *fado* houses.

Stardust falls on the top women singers, but the men on guitars are more than just a backing group. They can stand alone as performers. Even Amâncio, in Malhoa's painting, could probably play very well, despite having no formal musical education or even classroom instruction. More recently, Carlos Paredes stole the limelight. He became known as *o homem dos mil dedos* (the man of a thousand fingers) for his mesmerizing solo instrumental performances on the Portuguese twelve-string guitar. His 1983 live album *Concert in Frankfurt* is guaranteed to give you goosebumps, and it sold handsomely. The music was in his blood—his father and grandfather were *fado* guitarists, too. Despite his success, Paredes worked for most of his life in the X-ray archives of Lisbon's Hospital de São José. He was born in Coimbra, and played a Coimbra-style guitar, but he spent most of his life in the capital. "It fit my imagination, my sense of poetry," he said of Lisbon.

* * *

The most powerful Portuguese man who ever lived could give orders to crowned heads of Europe and start intercontinental wars, but he was only able to do so for eight months.

Pedro Julião was born in Lisbon in the early decades of the thirteenth century. On 20 September 1276 he was elected pope. Better known to the Portuguese as Pedro Hispano, details of his life are sketchy, including his date of birth. His unfortunate death, in May 1277, in the former papal city of Viterbo in central Italy, is properly documented, however: he was crushed to death in the papal palace when a roof collapsed.

The only Portuguese pontiff in history is believed to have been baptized at Lisbon's Igreja de São Julião, which was the official residence of the head of the Portuguese Church from the thirteenth century and possessed a fabled opulence. It was another casualty of the 1755 earthquake. A church of the same name was built nearby, next to Praça do Município (City Hall Square). The future pope studied at Lisbon's cathedral before attending the University of Paris. His learning and writings, especially on philosophy and medicine, earned him a reputation as one of the most scholarly popes. As leader of the Church, he sought to mend relations with Constantinople and was a determined foe of Islam.

His unexpected election, after a stretch as Pope Gregory X's personal physician, was likely an attempt by those casting ballots to avoid upsetting the political balance of power in Viterbo, and it went ahead despite Portugal's King Afonso III being excommunicated in a row with the Church over taxes. Hispano's selection, on the other hand, reflected Portugal's increased stature.

King Afonso Henriques' defeat of the Moors had generated a new spurt of growth for Lisbon. The city's population expanded from around 5,000 inhabitants in the twelfth century to some 14,000 in the thirteenth. The conquest did not remove threats, however. As well as keeping an eye on Castile's ambitions, Lisbon still had to fight off Muslim corsairs who repeatedly harassed the burgeoning city. A saying still used in Portugal is *Anda Mouro na costa* (literally, "there are Moors off the coast"). It indicates that trouble is afoot, and is something a father might say if he suspects his young daughter is being courted without his knowledge. King Afonso III finally cleared out the Muslims in 1249 when he took Faro, their last Algarve stronghold.

King Dinis, the next monarch, was still concerned enough about safeguarding what had been accumulated by his ancestors that before the end of the thirteenth century he bulked up Lisbon's defences with a new wall, 1.6 metres wide, along the riverfront. That wall, like so much else, vanished in 1755. But a 31-metre stretch of it re-appeared in 2010 when the Bank of Portugal was digging around its vaults. An exhibition centre was built to house this national monument.

With corsairs and Castile regularly menacing, Lisbon residents needed to be on their guard. At 64 Rua da Mouraria stands an orphanage founded in 1273 by Queen Brites, wife of Afonso III. Though run-down and rebuilt after 1755, the six-storey building is a gem that Lisbon so often conceals and surrenders only if you are brazen enough to lean your weight against the door. The walls of its stone staircase are lined with hand-painted Portuguese blue-and-white tiles in rococo style that depict biblical scenes, thirty-two from the Old Testament and nine from the New Testament. Every day people walk past the building and have no idea this astonishing work of art is here. Senhor Carlos, a janitor who also serves as a makeshift custodian of the building's memories, might take visitors up to the roof where a thick metal plate with a plant pot on top of it covers the entrance to an escape tunnel. It leads up to the castle, a stone's throw away. He won't let anyone go down the tunnel. It is thick, he says, with rats the size of cats.

King Dinis was a modernizer, and his policies added momentum to Lisbon's increasing prosperity. He improved the streets, building Rua Nova dos Mercadores—the city's longest and straightest street at around 200 metres, which would blossom into a colourful international emporium during the Age of Expansion. He developed Portuguese agriculture, earning the nickname *O Lavrador* (The Farmer), and gave a tonic to Portugal's national and international business by expanding local markets and signing a trade treaty with England in 1308. To help police the realm and its long coastline, King Dinis needed to reorganize the Portuguese fleet. To achieve this he picked a skilled Genoese seafarer called Manuel Pessanha, who in 1317 established one of the world's first permanent naval fleets at the service of the Crown and laid the foundations for Portugal's later naval might. Pessanha became admiral of the fleet as well as the monarch's trusted right-hand-man. In return, he was granted the fiefdom of Pedreira, a district between Rossio and Chiado in what is now downtown Lisbon, plus a handsome annual retainer.

Nevertheless, bigger walls, and another siege, awaited Lisbon in the following century.

* * *

The weathered stone pillars and stark, soaring arches of the fourteenth-century Carmo Church stick out of Lisbon's downtown district like the ribs of a skeleton. The roofless ruin, quiet amid the bustling modern city, has an eerie feel inside, like the eye of a storm. This peaceful spot is where, momentously and astonishingly, the man who was perhaps the greatest military leader in Portuguese history and the country's second-richest man after the king retired to a monk's cell after hanging up his sword and giving away his fortune.

It is hard to exaggerate the role Nuno Álvares Pereira played in Portugal's national narrative. Fernando Pessoa, in his celebrated 1934 collection of poems called *Mensagem* (Message), said Álvares Pereira's sword "lit the way" for his country, when it was in perhaps its darkest hour. Pessoa called him "Saint Portugal". And, indeed, Álvares Pereira would attain sainthood.

The *Grande Enciclopédia Portuguesa e Brasileira* declares him to be "one of the most wonderful and mettlesome figures in Portuguese history". His feats were of popular renown, complete with the inevitable myths and exaggerations, and his deeds were dramatized by the playwright João Almeida Garrett in a play first performed at Lisbon's Condes Theatre in 1842.

Álvares Pereira took his place on the Iberian stage when Portugal's independence looked like a lost cause during what the Portuguese refer to as the Crisis of 1383–85. Despite the successful taking of Lisbon, Portugal as a national political project almost fizzled out. It burst back into life with Álvares Pereira who helped put King João I on the throne. That monarch would then place Portugal on a path to global greatness.

The problems which Álvares Pereira would eventually be compelled to confront took shape during the reign of King Fernando I. As Lisbon spread in the fourteenth century, swelling to around 35,000 inhabitants, Fernando ordered a bigger city wall to be built, enclosing an area six times larger than that within the Moorish wall. It is called the Cerca Fernandina, and one of its towers stands neglected beside Martim Moniz Square. The nearby Rua das Portas de Santo Antão in modern Lisbon is named after a gate through that wall.

The on-off wars with Castile that punctuated Portugal's early history, with three conflicts during his own reign, weighed on King Fernando. He was right to worry. The Iberian tension peaked after he died without heirs, and the widowed Queen Leonor Teles supported the claim of their only daughter Beatriz and her Castilian husband, Juan I. In essence, that would hand the kingdom to its powerful neighbour, which the Portuguese had held at bay for so long at the cost of so many lives.

The prospect split the aristocracy and angered the people. Álvares Pereira took a gamble and threw in his lot with Dom João, a bastard child of King Pedro I. Álvares Pereira, whose father was a prior and mother a nursemaid at court, had known João since they were young. Álvares Pereira's unwed father had thirty-two children, according to calculations by the historian Oliveira Martins. Nuno was the thirteenth.

The legal argument supporting João's claim to the throne was thin, he being the deceased King Fernando's half-brother. But he trumped Juan by being Portuguese born and bred. He was also a very hesitant person, however. Álvares Pereira and other conspirators had to egg him on, assuaging his crippling doubts with assurances that the people were with him. At the same time, the scheming and widely hated Count João Andeiro, suspected lover of Queen Leonor, was doing his best to deliver Portugal into the hands of Castile.

Amid the intrigue and national uncertainty, the do-or-die moment came at a palace in the celebrated Largo do Limoeiro (Lemon Tree Square), in Alfama, on 6 December 1383. There, the future King João I drew his sword and cut down Count Andeiro, though he needed assistance from two cohorts to finish off his victim. The result: within two months of King Fernando's death, João was acclaimed in Lisbon as defender of the realm and moved into St George's Castle.

Portugal's neighbour was unimpressed. Castile's forces laid siege to Lisbon the following May, by land and sea. Its army camped on a hill which is nowadays the Bairro Alto quarter, popular with tourists for its hip bars and restaurants. (It was a popular spot for sieges, too: in 1589, an attacking English force would also camp here.) Álvares Pereira was dispatched to the border where more Castilian forces were entering Portugal. There, at the Battle of Atoleiros, he earned his spurs. Leading his men from the front, in a helmet without a visor, Álvares Pereira inspired his army to a watershed victory over a larger force. Thanks to his astute tactics, deploying his men in defensive squares and using pikes against horses, for the first time in Iberia an army mostly on foot defeated an army boasting heavy cavalry. The triumph galvanized the Portuguese. It encouraged the notion that God was on Portugal's side and showed the Portuguese they had the mettle and the ingenuity to fell bigger adversaries.

The psychological effect was lasting. The following year the Portuguese army, again under the shrewd tactical leadership of Álvares Pereira, won another major battle at Aljubarrota despite being outnumbered once more. Meanwhile, Castile lifted its siege of Lisbon after just four months due to an outbreak of plague. Álvares Pereira was, militarily, the second-in-command after the monarch and held the formal title of *condestável*, a kind of lord high constable of the time. The auspicious campaign against Castile sharpened Portugal's sense of national identity and also lent credibility to the wearer of the contested crown. The grateful king showered Álvares Pereira with properties, making him the country's biggest landowner. He was one of the wealthiest men on the peninsula.

Befitting a man whose grandfather was an archbishop and father a prior, Álvares Pereira was a deeply religious man. As thanks for his good fortune he ordered the building of the Carmo Church and Carmelite Monastery on land purchased from Admiral Pessanha. The site overlooked, and the building outshone, Rossio Square. Started in 1389, it was one of the biggest architectural projects Lisbon had ever seen. It partially collapsed twice during construction. Álvares Pereira said that if it happened a third time, he would have the foundations cast in bronze. It was completed only in 1423. The church was huge, with three naves, and richly decorated.

By the time it was finished, Álvares Pereira's wife, two sons and daughter were dead. With the monastery completed, the eminent patriot and medieval military genius shared out his vast wealth among his family and the Carmelites and swapped his armour for a monk's habit on 15 August 1423. He died in one of the monastery's cells eight years later, at the age of seventy.

Pope Benedict XVI canonized Álvares Pereira in 2009. The Portuguese Episcopal Conference saw in his life a lesson for today, remarking—with a dig at modern politicians—that his example encouraged "more sober and benevolent lifestyles that are more conducive to sharing what we have. [His life is] also an appeal to exemplary citizenship and a powerful entreaty to dignifying political life as an expression of humanism at the service of the common good."

The rebuilding of the church and monastery began three years after the 1755 earthquake but was never finished. The ruins possess an elegant beauty, though. Inside, there is an eclectic museum that includes a pair of Peruvian mummies from the fifteenth century, as well as the tomb of King

Fernando I, which is remarkable for its size and the detail of its stonework.

The triumph over Castile, after vanquishing the Moors, allowed Portugal to spread its wings. It became predator instead of prey. King João I's marriage to England's Philippa of Lancaster, daughter of John of Gaunt, produced children who would become known as Portugal's *ínclita geração* (illustrious generation). It included Henry the Navigator and set the stage for the world's newest, and unlikeliest, empire.

THREE—GOLDEN YEARS

Queues are a common sight outside the midnight-blue doors of the Antiga Confeitaria de Belém (The Old Belém Confectionery), in the Lisbon riverside district of the same name. Inside this café, some very special pastries are on sale. Only three members of staff possess the secret recipe for the sweet custard tarts produced there since 1837, and they say the bakery in the back produces on average 40,000 of them a day in the peak tourist season. The tarts are called *pastéis de Belém* or *pastéis de nata*. They offer light, crispy pastry cupping a silky, vanilla-flavoured custard that is slightly charred on top. Each tart comes with miniature sachets of caster sugar and cinnamon to sprinkle over them. And, in their sprinkling, the twenty-first-century customers unwittingly join up more than 500 years of Portuguese history.

The café lies close to the spot from where, during the Age of Exploration starting in the fifteenth century, Portuguese sailing ships that were among the biggest on the seas were seen off on their sometimes years-long voyages. The king and his court, church leaders and crowds of local people gathered for the annual departures. The Portuguese Discoveries delivered a giddy period of milestones in world history. It was a flush of genius and enterprise never witnessed again in Portugal. The

Portuguese, wrote the historian Jaime Cortesão in his 1960s work *Os Descobrimentos Portugueses* (The Portuguese Discoveries), "set in motion a world revolution" by leading Europe out of the Mediterranean and into the Atlantic and beyond, creating new horizons. Portugal connected continents, bringing "new worlds to the world," wrote the poet Camões. The Portuguese, in great wooden ships called *naus* (carracks) that were furnished with unrivalled artillery, projected their power across the Atlantic Ocean, the Indian Ocean, the Red Sea and beyond. The country's reach was unparalleled.

Back in Lisbon, it rained money. At least, it did if you were plugged into the intercontinental trade that to a large degree was run as a monopoly by the Crown. The fabulous wealth Portugal harvested during those days of empire was concentrated almost entirely in the capital. Cosmopolitan Lisbon was the place to be if you wanted news or gossip about what was happening across the globe. The success of the explorations and the bounty they fetched meant not only that the machinery of state had to be repurposed for empire. It also demanded that the capital be reshaped and made fit to reflect its new status. Portugal went from European minnow to big fish. And Lisbon outgrew its clothes.

At first glance, Portugal's accomplishments seem to be one of world history's unlikeliest feats. Lisbon may occupy an enviable spot, but political geography was unkind to the country. Small and boxed into a remote corner of south-west Europe by its burly rival Castile, Portugal was trapped, so to speak, between the devil and the deep blue sea. The Portuguese chose, *faute de mieux*, to get wet. Portugal availed itself of that which had appeared to be a handicap and, driven by such legendary pioneers as Henry the Navigator and Vasco da Gama, headed out to sea. The Portuguese, in the end, were like a canny mouse cornered by Castile's overfed cat.

The cross and the Crown went together on the explorations around Africa, and across to India and the Arabian Sea, the Persian Gulf and the South China Sea, and also in the other direction to what would become Brazil. The departing fleets were blessed in Belém—Bethlehem in Portuguese—which is now a riverside suburb but at that time was a significant distance outside the city. The ceremonies were held on a beach called Praia do Restelo, whose broad, shallow disposition made it suitable for the regal and religious fanfare that accompanied each departure. Boats ferried the crews from there out to the anchored ships.

The adventure was supercharged: the voyages of conquest were seen as a divine mission against infidels and as opportunities for royal glory, wealth and power. Beyond the horizon, the Portuguese demonstrated bravery verging on recklessness. Their achievements are venerated, even if their pugilistic approach in the lands they encountered sometimes resulted in massacres and merciless slaughter (details that are conspicuous by their absence from Portuguese school textbooks). Though it occasionally looked as if Portugal's reach around the globe might be greater than its grasp, the seafarers brought back to Lisbon riches on a scale that Europe had seldom witnessed.

A Portuguese battle fleet that sailed out of the Tagus on 25 July 1415 turned left toward North Africa and its target: Ceuta. The successful attack on that Muslim stronghold was the starting gun for the Age of Exploration. The Portuguese inched down the West African coastline, growing bolder and bolder, until King João II hatched the *Plano das Índias* (the Indias Plan) later in the fifteenth century. The scope of his ambition was staggering: to divert through Lisbon the trade in lucrative spices from the Orient to Europe. At that time the spices, used by Europeans in cooking and by apothecaries for medicines, came overland to Alexandria and then by sea to Venice, from where they were sold across Europe. This audacious Portuguese monarch wanted to cut out the middle man and bring them from India straight to Lisbon by ship. And he did.

The *carreira da Índia* (India passage) amounted to a round trip of more than 30,000 kilometres, and at least six months, which was fraught with danger. The rhythm of departures was synchronized with the Indian Ocean's monsoon season, and the fleets of up to half-a-dozen carracks left Lisbon each March. Fewer than 2,000 men went on each voyage, most of them in the service of the Crown. They included nobles seeking honour and fortune, the country's best captains and navigators, soldiers, stonemasons and carpenters and other skilled tradesmen, and convicts and slaves.

Portugal may nowadays be a laggard in developing new technology but in the Age of Discovery it was far ahead of the field, often thanks to Jewish scholars. The quest was, as far as was possible, a covert operation. A cloak of official secrecy veiled Portugal's technological advances in naval architecture, navigational aids and seafaring know-how, such as tides and prevailing winds on the high seas. In 1504 King Manuel I prohibited the drawing of precious maps or globes except for official use. Portuguese ships called caravels were the fastest craft on water, and their sale abroad was forbidden without royal approval. Also, ship captains, pilots, carpenters and sailors were prohibited from working for foreign countries. That did not deter foreign spies from prowling around Lisbon's murky medieval streets, however—especially those working for archrival Venice.

Dreaming big paid off, in a big way. By virtually cornering the European market in goods from the East and Africa, the Portuguese kingdom became cash-rich. Pepper cost the Portuguese two cruzados a sack in Cochin, on India's west coast, and they sold it in Lisbon for thirty cruzados. With that steep mark-up, Lisbon prospered and a degree of euphoria took hold. The Portuguese were, said Oliveira Martins, "intoxicated by the scale of the wealth". Damião de Góis, one of Portugal's outstanding Renaissance figures who by royal appointment chronicled the reign of King Manuel I, reported that he often saw at the riverside Casa da Índia (India House), where the arriving goods were inventoried and stored, "merchants with bags full of gold and silver currency to make payments [but] officials told them to come back another day because they didn't have time to count it all."

The flourishing economy propelled Lisbon's urban expansion. The city dilated, in buildings and population. Plague, drought and hunger drained the countryside, and peasants converged on the capital in hope that the wealth might trickle down. (Here lie the seeds of Portugal's long-standing macrocephaly, with Lisbon's disproportionately dominant head casting a long shadow over the country.) The population swelled from around 70,000 in 1528 to some 120,000 by the end of that century. King Manuel ordered that the city's extensive olive groves be cut down to make way for new buildings.

It was a time of plenty for the Catholic Church, too. Lisbon became sown with grand religious monuments.

Convents, monasteries and churches flourished in the city's soil. By the second half of the sixteenth century, Lisbon had more than a dozen substantial convents and monasteries. The religious orders often grabbed the most prominent hilltop locations, such as Graça, Nossa Senhora do Monte, Santana, Pedreira, São Vicente and Penha de França, and these new buildings gave birth to new neighbourhoods in their vicinity. A new architectural scale took hold, exemplified by the immense Hospital Real de Todos os Santos (Royal All Saints Hospital) and the spectacular Jerónimos Monastery.

Vasco da Gama's 1499 arrival back in Lisbon after two years at sea, during which he found the sea route to India, provided one of the last major royal occasions at St George's Castle. Caravels went out to meet Gama in the mouth of the Tagus and escorted his two surviving, battered carracks into port. Local people crowded the riverbanks to cheer his triumph, and church bells across the city rang out. King Manuel and Gama, side-by-side, went on horseback up to the castle as people crowded along the streets and waved from houses.

The castle was their destination, but the king had something else on his mind—something that would change Lisbon forever. He had already set his master plan in motion, clearing land by the river from 1498 onwards. In 1500 construction of a new palace began, and several years later the monarch moved in.

King Manuel I's decision to abandon St George's Castle and switch the court to a magnificent new royal palace by the river was a milestone that reflected Lisbon's deep political, administrative, economic and cultural changes. The move added momentum to the reshaping of the city by shifting its centre of gravity from the hilltop down to the river. The relocation also carried a heavy symbolism, pulling back the curtain on a new era that wedded Portugal's destiny to the sea. The Portuguese monarch went from being a crusading warrior king who had conquered the castle to a trade king who had conquered international commerce.

With its overseas triumphs Lisbon grew in confidence and burst out of its medieval defensive boundaries, spilling into surrounding land. Not everyone was impressed, however. France's King François I looked down his nose at Portugal's commercial success. He sniffily referred to King Manuel as *Le Roi Mercier* (The Grocer King).

King Manuel's construction of the new palace, called Paço da Ribeira, set off an urban revolution in the early 1500s. It provided a cue for the riverside area, which had been growing in importance since the previous century, to finally take precedence as the city's commercial and administrative heart. The name of the new royal residence is often translated into English as Riverside Palace. That may be misleading, however; as some point out, although a *ribeira* can be a riverbank, it can also indicate a large stream or small river, and the palace was perhaps named after the Ribeira da Valverde, one of the tributaries flowing down what is now the Avenida da Liberdade and into the Tagus where the palace stood.

The palace was "the richest, the most luxurious, the most stunning Portuguese dwelling ever seen," according to historian Paulo Caratão Soromenho. The building was rectangular, at a right angle to the river and had a stone bulwark over the water. The opulent rooms were on three floors, with arcades at street level. Over the coming years the palace was improved and stocked with sumptuous riches, including rare jewels, great tapestries, works of art by old Masters, a royal library containing some 70,000 books, and an elaborate royal chapel.

The huge space cleared along the riverfront, in addition to the simultaneous landfill operation that reclaimed land from the Tagus in a major engineering operation, was intended for more than just a big new palace. The palace itself occupied the west side of what became known as the Terreiro do Paço (Palace Courtyard), a public area. This broad square still exists and is known as the Praça do Comércio (Commercial Square). The palace's main entrance, decorated with marble balconies, was on the northern side away from the river.

The area around the palace came to include the India House, the royal mint, the royal armoury, royal warehouses and royal shipyards. King Manuel could admire from his window the evidence of his power. This part of the city was the heart of Portugal's military-industrial complex and ground zero of Portugal's imperial might. It bore comparison with the Arsenal of Venice, regarded as the most significant centralized production complex of pre-industrial Europe.

The Lisbon armoury, according to Góis, stored a huge quantity of infantry armour as well as armour plate for 2,500 cavalry, many heavy and light artillery pieces, arquebuses, pikes, lances and a large number of crossbows. The beach on the western side of the palace, called Ribeira das Naus, was used as a shipyard. The carracks and other vessels were beached there for cleaning and repairs. New ones were built, too. By the mid-sixteenth century, the biggest ships had grown to as much as 600 tonnes. Several hundred caulkers and carpenters were employed full-time. Many of them lived in a new quarter up the hill named Bairro Alto. Some Bairro Alto streets were named after the tradesmen. There was, for example, Rua dos Calafates (Caulkers Street), now called Rua do Diário de Notícias. Some 200 caulkers lived there in 1551 and some earned well enough to have a servant. There were also hundreds of jobs in allied industries such as making rope, sewing sailcloth and forging metal as the Crown concentrated all essential production in a single area.

King Manuel could watch from his palace the loading and unloading of the ships after he built the Cais de Pedra, a stone quay jutting out into the river from the vast courtyard. He was also close to the Armazéns da Índia (India Warehouse), located on the opposite, eastern side of the square from the palace, which took care of naval logistics and provisioning.

The nerve centre for the India operations was right under the monarch's nose, in the India House. It was set up on the ground floor of the palace and was in charge of the administration and management of trade throughout the empire. It weighed cargoes, logged deliveries and kept ledgers. Ships had their own storage rooms there. Góis described the Casa da Índia as an "emporium of aromas, pearls, rubies, emeralds and other gems that year after year are brought from India." That wasn't all. It also piled up bags of pepper, cinnamon, nutmeg, cloves and other spices. It took receipt of porcelains, silk, incense and myrrh, too, and it stored the copper and tin and other metals that would be taken by the ships to foreign lands as barter. The India House was the marrow of Portugal's success, and King Manuel went down to visit it every day.

But being wealthy wasn't enough. In Renaissance Lisbon, you had to be seen to be wealthy, and the monarch was no exception. The showiness and pageantry of the royal entourage was legendary.

The first elephants seen in Europe since Roman times were unloaded in the Portuguese capital in the early sixteenth century. These gifts from India for King Manuel performed tricks, bowing on command and blowing water, and delighted the courtiers and the inhabitants of Lisbon. Other arrivals were an African rhinoceros, gazelles, antelopes, monkeys, parrots and a jaguar. They were the trophies of a conquering country.

The animals made up the monarch's cortège whenever he proceeded through Lisbon. Góis described the procession: it was led by the rhino, followed at some distance by five elephants rigged out in gold brocade, then an Arabian horse, the jaguar, and the king and his entourage accompanied by the beat of drums and the fanfare of trumpets. It is not hard to imagine what a stir the extravaganza must have caused, with people likely running to gawp at the spectacle. Oliveira Martins asked, "Was this a European king? Was it an Indian raja? Or a sultan from Babylon?"

The exotic animals were kept on the palace's ground floor, in barred rooms. The king fancied seeing a fight between an elephant and a rhino, so the two were brought together in an interior patio, with members of the court hanging out of the windows to watch the whimsical spectacle. The entertainment was brief, however. The elephant soon turned and ran, smashing through a door and running into the street, eventually reaching Rossio Square several hundred metres away before it came to a halt.

King Manuel wanted the rest of the continent to know about his affluence. In a flamboyant gesture, in 1514 he sent to Rome a white Indian elephant as a gift for the new pope, Leo X. An elephant was a fitting symbol for Portugal and the pontiff, possessing power, longevity and stoutness. The animal certainly made a splash in Renaissance Europe, hungry for novelties. Transported by ship from Lisbon, it took several weeks for the elephant to be led from the Italian coast to Rome, because so many people crowded around to see it. The first elephant in Rome since Hannibal was a great success. Pope Leo X was enthralled by the animal and very fond of it. He named it Hanno, after Hannibal, and Portugal was the talk of the town.

The following year King Manuel sent a 2-tonne rhino called Ganda to Rome. It wore a green velvet collar embroidered with golden roses. The ship had to stop off in Marseille so that King François I, intrigued, could see it. The adventure went awry, however, when the carrack was shipwrecked off the Italian coast and the rhino, chained to the deck, died. When it later washed up on shore, King Manuel had it stuffed and taken to Rome anyway. The German artist Albrecht Dürer never saw the rhino, but his woodcut of it became more famous than the animal itself.

Even charitable work had to be ostentatious. The Hospital Real de Todos os Santos, erected in the centre of Lisbon between 1492 and 1504, was the biggest hospital ever seen in Portugal. It—pointedly—rivalled hospitals in Spain and Italy. It was run along the same lines as the Hospital de Santa Maria Nuova, in Florence, with specialized medical staff tending the sick and observance of rules on hygiene and diet. More agricultural land was swept away to make room for it, roughly along Rossio Square. It was another grandiose example of the emergence of the modern state. Some even say it was the beginning of Portugal's national health service. It was certainly the country's most important hospital up to the eighteenth century.

Its facade, around 100 metres long, had thirty-four arches. At its centre stood a church and tower, with three wings leading off to form a crucifix shape. The hospital was on three floors and contained large infirmaries which were divided into three wards—two male and one female. It could cater for about 250 in-patients. It also had kitchens and a dining hall, quarters for about fifty staff, operating rooms, an emergency room, a section for the mentally disturbed, and private quarters for nobles. Góis, impressed, remarked that it had "very clean bedding".

The lavish spending extended to projects that were intended to magnify King Manuel's accomplishments, emphasize his piety and immortalize his reign. It was also an example of the extravagance that absolute power and mega-wealth invite.

The greatest expression of that temperament was the Jerónimos Monastery, in Belém. It is regarded as a masterpiece of what would later become referred to as the Manueline style of architectural ornamentation. Completed 100 years after it was begun in 1502, the building was the monarch's biggest prestige project. Having survived the 1755 quake mostly intact, the national monument is one of Lisbon's signature buildings and one of Portugal's gems.

After its completion, the Jerónimos Monastery was the city's most important religious monument. It replaced the monastery at Batalha, about 100 kilometres to the north, as the resting place of royalty. Marble tombs resting on—inevitably—elephant figures hold the remains of King Manuel and his Spanish queen Maria, and of his son King João III and his queen Catherine of Austria. Elsewhere at Jerónimos stand the tombs of Vasco da Gama and Luís de Camões, placed there in the nineteenth century, of nineteenth-century novelist and historian Alexandre Herculano, and of the twentieth-century poet Fernando Pessoa.

The building was not intended, as is often claimed, to commemorate Gama's accomplishments. King Manuel requested the papal bull for its construction in 1495, two years before Gama's departure for India. The monarch, whose three successive queens were Spanish, named it out of a keenness to bring closer together the neighbouring Iberian kingdoms. The Spanish royals were fond of the Order of Jerónimos, and this Lisbon project was intended to be one of twelve Jerónimos Order monasteries in Portugal for which Manuel requested the pope's blessing. He, like other Portuguese royals, had an elusive dream: a single Iberian country, with a Portuguese monarch at its head.

Belém in those days was little more than a medieval village. The monastery's scale, muted nowadays by the modern city's dimensions, was staggering. Artistic renderings of the time show the vast building sitting amid desolate land. Construction began on the symbolic date of 6 January—the Feast of the Epiphany, more commonly known in Iberia as Three Kings' Day. The initial architect was Diogo de Boitaca, with João de Castilho later taking charge. They both were authorities on the Manueline style.

Jerónimos was paid for by a generous donation from the Florentine banker and slaver Bartolomeu Marchione as well as a 5 per cent tax levied by the Crown on the trade in spices, gems and gold, known as the *vintena da especiaria, pedraria e minas*. An old saying had it that Jerónimos was "built by pepper".

The monastery and its church stand parallel to the Tagus, so that anyone passing on the river can see a lot of its 300-metre length. It fired a cultural broadside, so to speak, at anyone sailing into Lisbon. Then, as now, it was a look-at-me building, with its south-facing walls of local limestone reflecting the sun. Jerónimos sent a message. It said, we are very wealthy and very pious.

The ornate and elaborate Manueline style was inspired by Portugal's associations with the sea. It is intricate and busy— like the times that gave birth to it. Maritime motifs in stone capture, Medusa-like, the paraphernalia of the adventures, featuring ropes and knots, anchors and navigational equipment, as well as religious flourishes. The enchanting Jerónimos cloisters on two floors are richly sculptured, like stone filigree. Statuettes depict great historical figures. In the south portal, for example, Prince Henry the Navigator is portrayed as bearded and wearing armour and holding a sword and shield. The church's vaulted ceiling, 25 metres high, is dizzying. Octagonal pillars soar up to the webbed dome. The *Guia de Portugal* says the effect is less like that of a cathedral than of a giant cave punctuated with stalactites. The stained-glass windows are, disappointingly, from the 1930s.

Equally representative of the Manueline style is the nearby Torre de São Vicente, better known as the Torre de Belém (Belém Tower). This unusual military building rendered in thick blocks of stone was originally 250 metres out into the river and formed part of the Tagus defensive system. Changing currents and sedimentation have filled in the gap to the shore. It is a boxy, odd-looking structure, with two distinct parts: a square tower, in a palatial style with ceremonial rooms and featuring a Venetian-style veranda with river view; and a bulwark with positions for seventeen cannon and a magazine beneath it.

The building, completed in 1521, is utilitarian while capturing in its details a Manueline ornateness, with that style's Islamic flourishes. Its turrets imitate Koutoubia, the largest mosque in Marrakesh where the man appointed to oversee the Torre de Belém's construction, Francisco de Arruda, had worked for two years. On the north-west corner, one of the gargoyles is a rhino's head, thought to represent Ganda.

Another, more modest, monument close to the Belém Tower also captures a sense of Portuguese adventure and triumph, though it came 400 years later. In 1922, pilot Artur de Sacadura Cabral, aged forty, and fifty-three-year-old navigator Carlos Gago Coutinho set off from Belém on the first flight across the South Atlantic, linking Lisbon with Rio de Janeiro. The endeavour, however, was not only about the route. It was also conceived as a way of testing a novel piece of navigational equipment. Coutinho had developed a new sextant, called a precision sextant, which measured the altitude of a star without recourse to the horizon. It was a breakthrough that was in the great tradition of Portuguese navigators. The 19 April 1922 edition of the newspaper *Diário de Notícias* reflected the jubilant national mood. It dedicated most of its front page to the news that the pair had made it onto Brazilian soil and were heading down to Rio. "Long live Portugal!" said its banner headline. "The Portuguese race returns to its epic days. Once again, our tiny land imbues the world with its generous heroics!" That little Portugal is undeservedly overlooked by the rest of the world is an article of faith among the Portuguese.

The intrepid duo took off from the Tagus at 7:00 a.m. on 30 March, in the centenary year of Brazil's independence, on board a specially built 350-horsepower Fairey seaplane. It was christened *Lusitânia* in a nod to Portugal's deep history. Three Portuguese Navy support ships had left five days earlier. The pioneering journey lasted seventy-nine days, though that was with stops in the Canary Islands and Cape Verde, before reaching Brazil. Actual flying time for the 8,300-kilo-metre crossing was sixty-two hours and twenty-six minutes. In the end, it was accomplished in three different planes after the pilots twice ditched into the ocean and were rescued. Dating from 1991, the modern Belém monument by archi-tects Martins Bairrada and Leopoldo Soares Branco and sculptor Domingos Soares Branco is an inox replica of the original Fairey seaplane, set on a plinth. Busts of the aviators are inside, depicted in the leather helmets they wore in the open cockpit across those thousands of kilometres.

In sixteenth-century Lisbon, the buzzword among the elite and contemporary authors was "grandeur". That was the word they wanted associated with the city. After all, what else would a capital of a country with an intercontinental empire merit?

Damião de Góis set a high bar for uncritical praise with his *Urbis Olisiponis Descriptio* (Description of the City of Lisbon), a rhapsody penned in 1554. Written in Latin so that foreign-ers would be able to read it, the book flatters the city—and, by implication, the king. It is not unlike a modern-day travel brochure listing Lisbon's unmissable attractions. The Portuguese historian José Sarmento de Matos called it "a book of propaganda". Góis wrote that only Lisbon and Seville could compete for the crown of "Queen of the Seas" (Lisbon, in the end, comes off best in his telling). He painted a splendid picture of the city, its broad and busy streets, its fine buildings, the riches kept at India House, and a city wall with twenty-two gates giving onto the river and sixteen onto land. He also mentions the old chestnut about Lisbon being founded by Ulysses.

While Góis talked up the city, Francisco de Holanda, one of Portugal's leading Renaissance figures, thought it was severely lacking and demanded better. He grumbled about the lack of grand monuments. Lisbon deserved a statelier, commanding presence, he believed. His 1571 book called *Da Fábrica que Falece à Cidade de Lisboa* (On the Public Works that Lisbon Needs) put forward bold proposals for gargantuan—some said megalomaniacal—building projects he felt would give the capital more architectural cachet and international prestige. Holanda wanted a grander royal palace, bigger city gates, a rebuilt castle, huge ramparts and giant bulwarks, a city park, paved streets and the rebuilding of three Roman bridges over the Tagus north of Lisbon.

An architect and painter, Holanda went as a young man to Italy to draw its grand buildings. He studied there for almost ten years and was a friend of Michelangelo. He earnestly wanted his home city to harness the same kind of architectural greatness he had witnessed in Rome, Venice and Naples. Holanda was learned and passionate but not very practical in his aspirations for a kingdom that was overspending and, despite its vast income, getting into debt. In the end, his ambition was greater than the royal coffers, and he found no takers for his proposals.

One of his suggested improvements, however, was exceedingly practical. But it would not take shape for another 150 years. Holanda complained that Lisbon was "dying of thirst"—an exaggeration, but one that would have earned the blessing of locals—and proposed a system of aqueducts, reservoirs and underground pipes to supply the city like the Romans had once used.

The people of Lisbon got their water from wells or public fountains called *chafarizes*, which were supervised by city authorities. These fountains were for centuries a feature of the city, as were the *aguadeiros* (water-sellers). The *chafarizes* were the office water-coolers of their day—places for gossip while doing chores. They were also popular spots for children to play, though a 1432 city by-law prohibited children from playing with cork boats and throwing stones into one fountain where presumably this had become a problem.

The Chafariz del Rei (King's Fountain), on the riverfront below Alfama, was possibly the first in Lisbon and the biggest up to the mid-sixteenth century. It had bronze spouts, as many as nine of them. To help stop fights from breaking out, a 1551 by-law assigned each spout to a particular trade. One was used to fill water barrels for ships heading out on the explorations. Damião de Góis praised the fountain's marble structure and its abundance of clean water. "Sometimes it sends out hot water; then it rests for a moment before spurting out very cold water that is a pleasure to drink," he wrote. The fountain still exists, next to a busy street, with the current façade dating from 1864.

Only the poorest people fetched their own water from the *chafariz*. Better-off households had servants to get it, and others bought it from barrels carried by the water-sellers who roamed through the city. Some of these water-sellers had reputations as rogues, charging whatever price they felt they could get away with and defying official attempts to regulate their business.

Despite the urban constraints, Lisbon had a spring in its step. Merchants from across Europe sought it out and marvelled at what was going on in the city. Cristóvão Rodrigues de Oliveira, in his *Lisboa em 1551—Sumário* (Lisbon in 1551—Compendium), published three years after that date, tallied more than 500 ships each day sailing into Lisbon and dropping anchor in the Sea of Straw. The Tagus was also busy with river traffic, bringing downriver cargoes such as farm produce and charcoal for the burgeoning capital.

Lisbon's bounty drew merchants from northern Europe, including England, France, Flanders and Germany. They plugged a gap, because Portugal lacked a mercantile middle class similar to those found further north. Portuguese society was split between peasants and nobles, with little in-between. The shrewd Fugger family, keen to plug into the riches, set up a branch in Lisbon. It was where the money was. This German trade and banking dynasty of the fifteenth and six-teenth centuries commanded immense financial power and political clout. In the Portuguese capital, the Fuggers' repre-sentatives bought spices and sold metal from their central European silver and copper mines.

The Lisbon streets were a spectacle. Black people from Africa mingled with people from the East and blue-eyed, blond-haired sailors from northern Europe. There were sea-soned prostitutes and novice nuns. There was a bewildering mixture of tongues. It was almost the known world in minia-ture. Portuguese historian Jorge Fonseca comments that for visitors from northern Europe, Lisbon must have seemed like "an intermediate zone … between the normal world and barbarism". It inspired a sense of wonder. And any foreign power desiring news from across the seas needed eyes and ears in Lisbon.

This Renaissance melting pot buzzed with energy, and most of it was focused around the shops of the celebrated Rua Nova dos Mercadores. "This was the beating heart of the capital, made from luxury and devotion; this is where people from far away, brought by the conquests, crossed paths in their variegated, colourful dress," wrote Oliveira Martins. Running behind the Palace Courtyard, it was one of the city's broadest and longest streets. It was paved with granite and was an emporium of exotic wares.

This opulent bazaar offered Chinese porcelain, Indian filigree, bolts of silk and other fine cloth, incense, myrrh, precious gems and pearls, pepper, ginger, cloves, cinnamon, nutmeg, saffron, chillies, ivory, sandalwood, ebony, camphor, amber, Persian carpets and handsomely bound books. The colourful market also sold parrots and monkeys that sailors brought back from the jungle in the hope of making some money. A Venetian called Alvise Cadamosto, who went on some of the Portuguese voyages to Guinea in the fifteenth century, said one caravel he travelled on had about 150 parrots on board, even though it carried only about twenty men and the ship was only 25 metres long and 7 metres wide. It must have been the noisiest ship on the high seas.

The Rua Nova contained about twenty draperies, thirty stores selling silk and other cloths, thirteen selling groceries and spices, nine drugstores, eleven bookshops, and more than fifty haberdasheries and goldsmiths, according to Oliveira Martins. Two late sixteenth-century paintings of Rua Nova dos Mercadores were identified in 2009. They were at an Oxfordshire manor house and belong to the Society of Antiquaries of London. The works by an unknown Dutch artist are detailed and contain dozens of figures, many of them dark-skinned, with a row of buildings in the background. The buildings were up to five floors high with stores at street level under arcades. One of the paintings features an area that is fenced off with iron railings. That was Rua Nova dos Ferros, on the eastern end of Rua Nova dos Mercadores.

Within it, tradesmen and money-changers had a semi-private area to do business. On the western side of Rua Nova dos Mercadores, Rua Nova del Rei led up to Rossio Square.

Those streets were Lisbon's busiest thoroughfares, though the area around the palace was also lively. In a 1535 letter from Garcia de Resende to Francisco de Castelo Branco, master chamberlain of King João III, the poet describes "the elegant riverside with its labyrinth of different women selling and big new streets with such grand merchants and so many officials and so many handsome women and so many foreigners".

But, on the whole, Lisbon was a filthy city. The majestic palace and elegant churches rubbed shoulders with misery and squalor. With no proper city sanitation and rare indoor plumbing, effluent commonly ran in the dark, narrow—and smelly—streets. The contents of chamber pots would be flung into the street, with a shouted warning of *Água vai!* (Here comes water!). Otherwise, black women slaves carried it in pots balanced on their heads and threw it in the Tagus. There were plenty of dogs and mules in the streets, too. Not surprisingly, Lisbon repeatedly had to endure outbreaks of typhoid, diphtheria and other illnesses, as well as the black plague which spread quickly in the cramped streets and crowded homes. Poor building quality offered little protection from cold or heat.

Most people remained untouched by the fruits of the Age of Expansion. Their stories went largely untold. Those people cheering the king and Vasco da Gama along the streets possessed little. They were the have-nots, and the haves passed them by. Beggars in rags, Oliveira Martins recounts, crossed paths with *fidalgos* in silk on the streets of Lisbon. The *fidalgos* were an invented class. The term was introduced during the thirteenth century, borrowing from the Spanish *hidalgo*, to distinguish between knights of noble pedigree and those of untitled, lower standing. *Fidalgo* comes from *filhos d'algo* (literally, "sons of something"). These men dwelt in the royal penumbra and commonly lived off an allowance granted by the Crown. They were sometimes scorned as what would nowadays be termed freeloaders or hangers-on.

At court, the ostentation and luxury extended to the dining table. Beef, the most expensive meat and out of the reach of most people, was the main dish. In 1524 the palace pantry received 3 tonnes of it, compared with half a tonne of pork, according to modern research by Maria José Azevedo Santos. The common people mostly made do with boiled fish and bad wine. The European overseas exploration changed royal eating habits: the palace pantry now featured tomatoes, chocolate, potatoes and pineapples. The sugar cane planted in Madeira in the fifteenth century brought another cultural shift. With sugar abundant in Lisbon, the Portuguese invented all kinds of new desserts. At convents and monasteries, after egg whites had been used to make wafers, or starch clothes, use was found for the yolks by dreaming up a wide variety of puddings which came to be called *conventuais*. Some of the names they were given are mischievously comical: nun's belly, nun's kisses, abbot's ears and blessed mothers.

Living conditions for most people in the city were squeezed, to say the least. People from around Portugal and from abroad continued to pour in throughout the sixteenth century. To ease the overcrowding, King Manuel ordered the demolition of balconies and verandas, which were occupying up to one-third of streets, and allowed people to build upward, adding extra floors.

A slice of this Lisbon life was depicted in a twelve-page letter written by Flemish nobleman Jan Taccoen van Zillebeke, who disembarked in the Portuguese capital on 11 April 1514 on his way to Jerusalem. He spent nine days in Lisbon and provided a snapshot of the city as it grew at full bore. Taccoen was visiting his son, almost certainly one of the many Flemish traders residing in the Portuguese capital to buy goods and ship them to northern European markets.

Taccoen was astounded by how much building was going on. "Lisbon, I am told, was very different thirty or forty years ago, when it was little more than a small city," he wrote. From what he saw, including a "magnificent hospital," he added: "Lisbon, in the future, will be a big, wealthy and powerful city, because it is impressive to see how many new houses are under construction."

Lisbon had its shortcomings, however. "When it rains it is hard to walk. There is only one street that is properly paved," Taccoen observed, probably referring to Rua Nova dos Mercadores. He recorded that the streets were "narrow, with very few gardens and houses very full of residents". The number of people living in Lisbon was "startling". "The houses are tall and made of stone and with white plaster. They are flat on top and covered with a kind of tile that acts as a gutter. Three or four families live in each one, on top of each other."

He did not miss the insalubrious aspects of the city either, as he describes daily routines:

> In most [houses] there are no chimneys or toilets. People usu-
> ally light a fire in a fire-pan, over which they stew or grill, or
> do so in a fireplace. When they go to bed they take chamber
> pots ... and their slaves, first thing in the morning, carry them

on their head down to the river. For men, though, there is a good big toilet next to the river; anybody can go and there are at least 100 holes.

At the same time, Taccoen was alert to the manifestations of wealth. A barrel-maker from Bruges, called Gilles de Backere, took care of Taccoen's lodging in Lisbon. Backere had changed his trade and was now a merchant. "Every day he uses silver platters, salvers and plates and many gold goblets that are so beautiful they must be very valuable," says Taccoen, wide-eyed:

> On holidays, on the sideboard there was a lot of china, goblets, jars, decanters, bowls for washing your hands, all in gold, of great value, and the entire living room was covered in tapestries. The woman who runs the boarding house was at least sixty years old; she wore a gold bracelet on each arm, seven or eight rings on her fingers, and two or three necklaces.

The city intrigued Taccoen. He was amazed by the number of Africans and Orientals on Lisbon's streets. Most were slaves, but some were of good standing and were invited to the empire's capital to foster good relations with the distant lands, especially the Congo. He describes three distinguished men from India who had come to be baptized: "They had in their cheeks many gems, as they did in their chins, and in their mouths, on their lips, two long teeth of precious stones."

The Flemish visitor was thrilled by three elephants he saw several times in the street during his stay:

> I saw them pick up something the size of a coin with their trunk and place it on the head of their handler or whoever was in charge of them. When they go before the king, they bend down and make a bow ... Their driver used to take them to drink at a fountain and there were lots of naughty

boys who pulled their tails. So the handler said to the elephant, "Douse them"; it filled its trunk with water and sprayed the one who had done it harm.

Taccoen also relates a scene of the monarch dining in his riverside palace:

> He sits alone in the middle of the table. After washing their hands, five priests ... say grace. There are five servants who wait at the table, cutting the meat and performing other duties. There are eight or ten pageboys standing near to him, and one on each side as well, with a long rod and a silk streamer on the end which they use to swat flies away.

The monarch drank only water with his meals, according to Taccoen. "When the king wants a more festive meal, he orders brought into the hall large tables full of expensive china and girls who dance while he eats."

Lisbon was a secure, confident capital, basking in Portugal's status. The city gates are not locked—and do not even have locks, Taccoen reports. "This country is full of soldiers and artillery," he adds.

Despite Lisbon's seductive lustre, Taccoen sensed a shadow. Toward the end of his account, he tells of a gallows that stood by the river, close to where ships docked. He witnessed there the hanging of two women who had "misbehaved" in their marriage. He describes what would happen at a Lisbon hanging:

> When they are taken to be executed they—both men and women—wear just a shift that reaches down to the ground, with nothing else and no shoes, with a hood at the back, and that's how they are hanged. When they are strangled, the hood is pulled over their face, so that they are not recognized, and the shift is rolled up between the women's legs. Then a

small pot is placed in their hand. People drop money in it and kiss their hand, because they are hanging just 2 feet off the ground.

After that gruesome description, and apparently moved, Taccoen abruptly ends his letter: "I don't want to write anything else about Lisbon, because otherwise my readers will stop reading me."

Lisbon, indeed, had a dark side, whose harrowing consequences are another city hallmark.

* * *

On Easter Sunday, 1506, with Lisbon in the grip of the black plague and tormented by food shortages, the city's churches were crowded with people craving comfort. At a service in the chapel of the São Domingos Monastery, next to Rossio Square, someone exclaimed that they could see "a sign" on a crucifix. "It is a miracle!" people declared. One man demurred: it is the reflection of a candle, he said. His casual remark triggered a pogrom that would become known as the Easter Massacre and leave a stain on Lisbon's history.

The dissenting voice in the chapel belonged to what was called a New Christian. These people were also referred to as *marranos* (swine). They were Jews who had been forcibly converted in the final years of the previous century, their faith sacrificed to political schemes occupying Iberia's royal houses. Despite the brutal conversions anti-Semitic sentiment still simmered and, on that Easter Day, it boiled over. People in Lisbon went berserk. When the days of bloodletting ended, around 2,000 New Christians—men, women and children—were dead, killed in cold blood.

Damião de Góis provided an account of the slaughter. He says that some men "of low standing" dragged the New Christian out of the chapel by his hair, killed him and set him on fire in Rossio Square. A crowd gathered, and several friars appeared with a crucifix crying "Heresy!" It was a word heavy with meaning and designed to fire people up against the Jews. Locals and foreign sailors started killing all the New Christians they could find and burning them on pyres they lit in Rossio and on the riverfront. Slaves and house-boys obligingly brought firewood, Góis says. More than 500 were killed that day as the mobs ran amok, urged on by two friars carrying a crucifix.

The next day, the account continues, the mobs of more than 1,000 men acted "with great cruelty". Góis says that:

> when they couldn't find any more New Christians in the streets, they broke into the houses where they lived and dragged them out with their children, wives and daughters, and flung them all together, dead or alive, onto the pyres without remorse. The cruelty was so great that they even slaughtered young children and infants, dashing their head against walls. And they didn't forget to plunder their homes and steal all the gold, silver and possessions they could.

Góis explains that more upstanding members of society—those who might have restored order—were out of the city owing to the plague. Upon hearing about the horrors King Manuel, who was 150 kilometres away in Avis, sent envoys with special powers to punish those who perpetrated the slaughter. Many were arrested and hanged. The two friars were burned to death.

Anti-Semitic tensions had been felt in Portugal for decades, and the situation in Lisbon in April 1506 was particularly combustible, but Jews had for a long time before that lived peaceably in the capital. When King Afonso Henriques and his Christian allies captured the city, they encountered Jews living within the walls cheek-by-jowl with the Muslim majority. From the twelfth to the fifteenth centuries Jews made up a small but significant portion of the Portuguese population and provided some illustrious statesmen. Yahia Ben Yahia was the finance minister of Portugal's first king, Afonso Henriques, and Isaac ben Judah Abravanel was the treasurer for King Afonso V in the early fifteenth century. Jewish mathematicians, astronomers such as the illustrious Abraham Zacuto, cartographers and merchants stood at the vanguard of the Age of Expansion. The Jews also produced an intellectual elite. In 1489 Rabbi Eliezer Toledano published the first two books printed in Lisbon—one a commentary on the Torah and the other Joseph ben David Abudarham's commentary on the synagogue liturgy in Seville. Rabbi Guedelha Palaçano was a prominent physicist and astrologer at Afonso V's court.

Jews found a warmer—or, at least, less hostile—welcome in Portugal than in other European countries, according to historian João Silva de Sousa. He counted the number of Jewish communities in Portugal at twenty-three in the fourteenth century and 139 in the fifteenth, amid mounting persecution in other peninsular kingdoms. The Lisbon community was the biggest. Even so, Jews had to live within certain bounds and under specific laws that were intended to prevent an occasional coolness in relations building into outright hostility. Jews could not, for example, have Christians working for them and were barred from some official posts. They were also highly taxed. On the other hand, they were judged according to their own laws and by their own magistrates, and could circulate freely and observe their faith unmolested.

The areas where Jewish communities lived were called *judiarias* and were mostly located inside city walls. Under fourteenth-century King Pedro I, those areas were ringed off and had gates that were closed at dusk and reopened at dawn. The Lisbon community was, over the centuries, located in four *judiarias*. Augusto Vieira da Silva, a venerated expert on Lisbon history, produced the most exhaustive cataloguing of these neighbourhoods in works he published in 1899 and 1901. The oldest *judiaria* was in the Pedreira neighbourhood, roughly where Largo do Carmo is now, from 1260 up to 1317. The Judiaria Velha, also known as the Judiaria Grande or Little Jerusalem, from the time of thirteenth-century King Afonso III, was the most populous one, in what is now the city's downtown Baixa area. A synagogue was built there in 1307. King Dinis cleared away the *judiaria* in Pedreira so he could grant the land to Admiral Pessanha, and the residents there moved to what became known as the Judiaria Nova, or Judiaria Pequena, which probably occupied just one downtown street though it also possessed a synagogue. The Judiaria de Alfama, in the neighbourhood of the same name, is the only one that still offers evidence of what once existed on the site through the name of one of its streets: Rua da Judiaria. This old Alfama Jewish quarter was small but had its own synagogue. It opened in 1374, without royal assent, which briefly caused tension between Jewish leaders and the monarch. It was at No. 8 in Beco das Barrelas. Life in this neighbourhood, and during the Easter Massacre, is vividly captured in Richard Zimler's 1998 novel *The Last Kabbalist of Lisbon*. The city's Jewish cemetery was close to where Rua do

Benformoso is nowadays. It flanked the Judiaria Grande and the Moorish cemetery.

The three creeds—Christian, Jewish and Muslim—traditionally existed freely in Lisbon. But the peninsula's political complexion changed at the end of the fifteenth century and brought a stunning reversal in Jewish fortunes. When Spain momentously drove out Jews in 1492, Portugal's King João II took in tens of thousands of them—in return for a cash payment. But Manuel I, his successor, in order to achieve his ambition of cementing ties with Spain, aimed to marry Isabella, the eldest daughter of Ferdinand and Isabella, Spain's Catholic rulers, and Isabella's parents had a condition: Manuel must expel infidels from his kingdom. The sovereign wrestled with how to achieve this without heavy loss. He knew how valuable the Jewish experts and financiers were for his ocean exploration. He contrived a plan to compel the Jews to convert or face expulsion. When thousands of Jews gathered on the Lisbon quayside to sail out of Portugal in 1497, most were brutally and ruthlessly subjected to forced baptism. It was called *uma conversão em pé* (a standing conversion). It was public and deeply traumatic. It is thought that this episode gave rise to the saying *ficar a ver navios* (left looking at ships), in reference to the want-away Jews who could see their ships in the river but couldn't reach them. The phrase signifies someone who has been duped.

Some Jews managed to get out before things turned nasty and fanned out across the world. More than 500 years later, in 2015, Portugal sought to make some degree of amends. It passed a law granting citizenship rights to the descendants of these Sephardic (Iberian) Jews who had once lived in Portugal. That came with a potentially useful European

Union passport. The applicants had to demonstrate their centuries-old Portuguese heritage and, astonishingly, many could. They swiftly received a lesson in Portuguese bureaucracy, however. The application process was expected to take four months, but after eighteen months fewer than 300 of more than 3,500 applications had been reviewed.

On paper, Jews no longer existed in Portugal after 1497. The same fate befell Muslims. From that year on, there could be only Old Christians and New Christians in the country. King Manuel gave the land of Lisbon's Jewish cemetery to the City Council for building, and the gravestones were used in the construction of the Hospital de Todos os Santos. Despite the new status quo, vexations that had occasionally punctuated Jewish life in Portugal grew increasingly common. The New Christians were made scapegoats for people's hardships. They were the easy targets of religious antagonism and economic jealousy, or were subjected to attacks motivated by petty rivalries. In 1630, in Lisbon's old Santa Engrácia Church, the tabernacle was broken into. Simão Pires Solis, a New Christian, was blamed for the sacrilegious burglary and burnt alive. Later, he was found to be innocent. It emerged that he had bravely refused to speak during his interrogation so as not to give away his amorous liaison with a nun. The ensuing scandal led to the church's closure and demolition, with the current Santa Engrácia built in its place. It took so long to build that *obras de Santa Engrácia* (Santa Engrácia construction work) became a modern saying for something that seems never-ending. It was finally finished in 1966.

As well as public prejudice, the Jews also fell prey to a more sinister and more sophisticated enemy: the Inquisition. Between 1536 and 1821, the Inquisition directed its efforts against heresy in Portugal and hunted down New Christians suspected of concealing their true faith. The suspicion was sometimes confirmed. Many Jews continued to practise their faith behind closed doors, using secret rooms and nooks for meetings and hiding their Torah scrolls. The inquisitors and their staff set up their national HQ and Lisbon tribunal at the Palácio dos Estáus, on the northern side of Rossio Square, close to the São Domingos chapel where the Easter Massacre began. The palace, from 1451, began life as a residence for visiting dignitaries. From 1570, it was adapted for the Inquisition, complete with lodgings for inquisitors and cells for suspects. Rebuilt after 1755, it burned down in 1836. Ten years later, the National Theatre opened in a new building on the site which still stands.

To escape the menace of the Inquisition some Jews preferred to get out with whatever they were able to carry, quietly selling whatever assets they could—probably at knock-down prices—including their homes. Because of the way the Inquisition worked, the Jews were vulnerable. Their enemies, rivals and debtors could tip off the inquisitors and remain anonymous. It was as if the Inquisition invisibly stalked the streets, haunting the city. The inquisitors demanded that the friends and relations of suspects inform against them, either in writing or in person, telling about their religious conduct so that the court might decide on the extent of their guilt. Nevertheless, the Portuguese, as French historian René-Aubert Vertot would later remark in his 1747 study *History of Portuguese Revolutions*, were "more superstitious than devout."

Thousands of Inquisition processes are recorded in the files of the Torre do Tombo national archive in Lisbon. The number of burnings at the stake which took place in Lisbon is unknown, though estimates fall in the range of several thousands. Considering the extended length of time the Portuguese Inquisition operated, that number is perhaps surprisingly low. It seems the *autos-da-fé*, as the burnings were termed in Portuguese, were largely held *pour encourager les autres*.

But the Inquisition knew how to break lives in other ways. It kept people incarcerated at its whim and tortured them as it saw fit; it had the power to ruin reputations. And it was not only Jews suspected of camouflaging their true faith that the inquisitors were after. Their investigations later extended to other supposed sinners, of varying social rank. The early twentieth-century scholar and head of the national archive António Baião listed some examples of the accused from the late sixteenth and early seventeenth centuries: Diogo Mendes, a New Christian, who said in a rage that he had no soul; a man called Gaspar, accused of sodomy with the master of an Italian ship; Diogo de Sousa, reported for cursing; Pedro Carneiro, reported for bigamy; and Bartolomeu Fernandes, who was denounced by his wife for denying the virginity of Our Lady.

Lisbon, it must be remembered, was a pious city. It could also be sinister and brutal. Taccoen recounts two indelible memories. On the Thursday before Easter he watched a torchlight procession. Ahead of the priests, some 100 hooded people went, bare-chested, flagellating themselves with rope that was studded with gold and silver spurs. After a while they were drenched in blood, but on they slowly walked and chanted in unison, their identities concealed by the dark hoods. Taccoen also witnessed an execution where monks went to the condemned man's prison and served him food and wine. Then, carrying a raised crucifix, torches and holy water, they accompanied him to the place of his public hanging in the Ribeira. In the ghoulish night-time procession were small children, brought to pray for the man's soul.

Not even the great names of the Portuguese Renaissance were safe from the tentacles of Persecution Inc. In the case of the great botanist Garcia de Orta, the Inquisition even reached beyond the grave. Orta was the son of Jews expelled from Spain who settled in Portugal and were probably forcibly baptized. Orta became a respected doctor, was given a chair at Lisbon University and appointed King João III's personal physician. The Inquisition kept a close eye on prominent, educated New Christians like him. Though he had the protection of powerful allies at court to keep the inquisitors at bay, Orta decided to depart for Portuguese India in 1534. There, his renown as a pioneering scientist grew, especially in the fields of botany, tropical diseases and the oriental use of medicinal plants.

But the men of the Inquisition were not ones to let bygones be bygones. A year after his death in Goa, in 1568, his sister Catarina was interrogated there and burnt at the stake as a practising Jew. Several other relatives were arrested, tortured and persecuted. In 1580—a full twelve years after his death— the Inquisition exhumed Orta's remains and burnt them at the stake for his observance of the Jewish faith. It was a remarkable display of vindictiveness. For the Inquisition, revenge was a dish best served cold.

The celebrated seventeenth-century Jesuit priest António Vieira also enjoyed the monarch's favour but it was not enough to keep the Inquisition at arm's length. Vieira, though, relished the battle. He travelled widely and possessed many talents, including fabled eloquence. He is considered one of Portugal's greatest orators and prose-writers. The poet Fernando Pessoa called Vieira "the Emperor of the Portuguese language" and said he delighted in the "cool perfection of [Vieira's] syntactical engineering" that made him "quiver like a branch in the wind". Vieira performed duties as a missionary, diplomat, philosopher, writer and teacher. He was close to King João IV, becoming one of the monarch's advisers and being invited to give sermons at the royal chapel in the Paço da Ribeira. His sermons, often political and using vernacular language, drew large audiences in Lisbon. Despite his popularity he was jailed by the Inquisition, pending trial, in October 1665, when he was fifty-five. He had drawn the Inquisition's wrath by defending tolerance toward Jews. He also argued for the rights of colonized indigenous people and opposed slavery.

The Inquisition accused Vieira of "heretical, foolhardy, malicious and scandalous proposals". At his trial, he refused to recant, even though he faced a sentence of being burned alive. Instead, he rebutted their arguments. The Inquisition's decision was published more than two years later, two days before Christmas Day in 1667. Its reading took more than two hours. Vieira stood facing his accusers the whole time. The sentence: he was forbidden from preaching, was to remain within the walls of Jesuit premises, and ordered to sign a written pledge never to repeat, orally or in writing, the ideas that led to the charges. The Jesuit order subsequently asked the Holy Office of the Inquisition to pardon Vieira. He was summoned to the Palácio dos Estaus on 30 June 1668 to hear that the pardon had been granted. He then left Lisbon.

Good connections at court could not keep Damião de Góis out of the Inquisition's clutches, either. Góis had been a pageboy of King Manuel I and was sent by King João III to be a royal representative in Antwerp, one of Portugal's main trading partners, in 1523. In 1545 João III appointed Góis the official teacher of Prince João Manuel. Góis was unable to take up the post, however, because he was denounced by a former colleague to the Inquisition for heterodoxy. Years before, Góis had spent four months in Freiburg with the elderly Erasmus. His prestige ensured his safety that time. But the Inquisition waited twenty-six years before striking again. Old and sick, and by then without friends at court, Góis was arrested in 1571 and condemned the following year as a heretic and a Lutheran. His possessions were confiscated and he spent twenty hard months in prison. His death two years later was mysterious. He was found lying in a hearth and was judged to have collapsed. When his remains were exhumed in 1941, however, a large hole was detected in his skull. It was unlikely to have been caused by a fall.

These distant events are unanimously viewed as blots on Portuguese history, and modern leaders have strived to set things right, as far as they can. In 1988, then-president Mário Soares met with members of Portugal's Jewish community and formally apologized for the Inquisition. In 2000, the leader of Portugal's Roman Catholics issued a public apology for the suffering imposed on Jews by the Catholic Church, and in 2008 a monument to the dead flanked by an olive tree was erected outside the São Domingos Church. Portuguese authorities announced in September 2016 that a long-planned Jewish Museum would finally be built in Lisbon. It was due to open in late 2017, in the Largo de São Miguel, in the heart of Alfama's old Jewish district, but legal disputes postponed the plan. Lisbon

Mayor Fernando Medina said the museum would "recall the cultural diversity of our history, without hiding the fact that the Jewish presence was made up of periods of light and darkness."

* * *

After centuries of sometimes skittish relations and occasional deadly conflicts between Iberia's neighbours, a quixotic young sovereign's unwise military adventure in North Africa handed the keys of the Portuguese kingdom to Spain. Three generations of Habsburg kings, hundreds of kilometres away, came to rule Portugal from 1580 to 1640—six decades being a lifetime in those days. Lisbon went from seat of the royal court and glorified capital of empire to provincial Iberian city. The days of elephants in the streets were over. Many nobles, sensing the balloon had popped, elected to go and live on their country estates.

King Sebastião acceded to the Portuguese throne when he turned fourteen, in 1568, and reigned for only ten years before his death on a distant battlefield. The youthful king was seduced by tales of chivalry and the glorious feats of his royal ancestors. He ordered the rebuilding of the old royal quarters in St George's Castle and was the last Portuguese monarch to sleep there. Sebastião was also headstrong. To raise an army to fight the infidels, he dug the kingdom deeper into debt. His *conselheiros* counselled him against engaging the powerful North African and Turkish armies. He went anyway.

Sebastião may have been encouraged in his folly by Camões and his epic poem *Os Lusíadas*. Camões dedicated the work to the boyish Sebastião, seen by many as the country's great hope for the future at a time when Lisbon's early sixteenth-century surge in prosperity was subsiding. The poet praised the king, who returned the favour with a small pension, and encouraged the monarch to attack the infidel at the gates of the Portuguese kingdom, just across the Mediterranean.

Luís Vaz de Camões was not yet the hallowed figure who would later be put on the same shelf as Cervantes and Shakespeare. But his work, in 1,102 rhyming stanzas, was compelling. It recounts Vasco da Gama's dramatic first voyage to India. Within that storyline Gama narrates Portuguese history, going back to before Roman times. The work expresses at once the romantic lyricism and the practical ambition of the Age of Expansion. It captures the breadth of the enterprise and of the era. It is also deeply patriotic in its portrayal of Portugal's destiny.

The epic begins, in the translation by William Julius Mickle:

Arms and the Heroes, who from Lisbon's shore,
Thro' seas where sail was never spread before,
Beyond where Ceylon lifts her spicy breast,
And waves her woods above the wat'ry waste,
With prowess more than human forc'd their way
To the fair kingdoms of the rising day:
What wars they wag'd, what seas, what dangers pass'd,
What glorious empire crown'd their toils at last,
Vent'rous I sing, on soaring pinions borne,
And all my country's wars the song adorn;
What kings, what heroes of my native land
Thunder'd on Asia's and on Afric's strand:
Illustrious shades, who levell'd in the dust
The idol-temples and the shrines of lust:
And where, erewhile, foul demons were rever'd,
To Holy Faith unnumber'd altars rear'd:

Illustrious names, with deathless laurels crown'd,
While time rolls on in every clime renown'd!

This celebration of the deeds of the Discoveries featured two fictional characters that remain cultural touchstones: the Adamastor, a mythical monster and metaphorical hurdle which the Portuguese overcome with their stout-heartedness, rendered nowadays in a statue in the Bairro Alto quarter; and the Cassandra-like Old Man of Restelo, who warns of misfortune and folly when Gama sets off from the beach in Belém.

Very little is known for certain about Camões, but his life was undoubtedly colourful. He is believed to have been born in 1524 or 1525, possibly in Lisbon. The date of his death is accepted as 10 June 1580—a date that is still a public holiday called the Day of Portugal, Camões and the Portuguese Diaspora. However, a Lisbon gravestone was once found that stated that he died a year earlier than that. Camões survived close scrapes and poor luck. Perhaps his greatest misfortune was that his most celebrated work gained fame and sold well only after he had died.

Camões is likely to have belonged to the impoverished nobility, given his evident education in the Classics and the empty pockets that grieved him all his life. He was jailed after a street fight in Lisbon and, probably as penance, sailed on the king's ships to Africa and Asia. He lost an eye in battle in Ceuta, was shipwrecked in the mouth of the Mekong River, and had passionate affairs of the heart. ("Love is a fire that burns unseen," he wrote in one sonnet.) In between were long periods of penury when he survived on his friends' generosity. He returned in 1569 to Lisbon where he tried to get *The Lusiads* published. It eventually came out three years later.

Such was the poet's obscurity that he was buried in the graveyard outside the church of Lisbon's Santana Convent along with other paupers. The church and convent stood near where it is said the poet's mother lived. Camões' friend Gonçalo Coutinho made the effort—belatedly—to properly mark his grave. Coutinho had the remains moved inside the church and had a marble tombstone placed there. The inscription read: "Here lies Luís de Camões. Prince of poets of his time. He lived in poverty and misery and that is how he died in 1579." The tomb and headstone were lost in 1755.

Camões' reputation reached its zenith in the nineteenth century, when he was romanticized by officials and in the public mind. João Almeida Garrett's poem *Camões*, published in 1825, is considered the dawn of Romanticism in Portugal. Someone put up a plaque around that the time on a house on the corner of Calçada Santana and the Escadinhas de São Luís, claiming that Camões had lived there, but there is no documentary evidence to that effect. In 1854 the government set up a committee to find out what had happened to his remains but, after some suspense while it examined the rebuilt Santana Church, the investigation drew no conclusion. Officials did not leave empty-handed: they took some bones to the Jerónimos Monastery for an official tomb there. That is where visiting foreign heads of state nowadays lay a wreath as part of diplomatic protocol. In downtown Lisbon, in the Camões Square, there is a bronze statue of the poet on a pedestal holding a sword and a cape. The *Guia de Portugal* describes the statue as "slightly ridiculous, unworthy of the glory of Camões", which seems rather harsh.

Portugal was orphaned at the Battle of Ksar El Kebir, also known as the Battle of Three Kings. King Sebastião died, aged twenty-four and heirless, in the unforgiving August heat of Morocco. It was a calamity. The Portuguese throne came up for grabs, and the crisis of succession would last two years. There were six pretenders.

The 1580 Battle of Alcântara resolved the dispute in favour of Spain, which had long coveted its neighbour. King Felipe II of Spain was a grandson of King Manuel I. His mother was Isabel, one of Manuel's Lisbon-born daughters. Felipe paid influential Portuguese nobles to support his claim to the Portuguese throne and was declared King Filipe I of Portugal on 17 July 1580. The people weren't behind him, though. Popular support lined up behind António, Prior of Crato—a Portuguese claimant who headed a Catholic military order. Filipe flexed his muscles. He dispatched across the border one of his best generals, the Duke of Alba, at the head of an army to ensure that events developed to his advantage.

The Spanish force met serious resistance only when it got within 10 kilometres of the capital. The showdown came at Alcântara, nowadays a busy city suburb, on 25 August. The Spanish force of some 20,000 men advanced on the city from the west, bombarding coastal fortifications into submission and sowing disarray among the defenders. The Spanish army was led by veteran officers who were commanding some of the best-trained and best-armed troops in Europe. The Portuguese defenders, numbering around 8,000, were motivated but poorly organized. They made a stand at the river flowing through Alcântara to the Tagus. They dug trenches and set out their artillery but the Spanish force crossed the river further north and outflanked them. A Spanish cavalry charge scattered the Portuguese, who were routed. Nothing now stood between Filipe and Lisbon. Coming after Ksar El

Kebir, Alcântara was the second catastrophic battlefield defeat in two years. King Manuel I's dream came half-true: Iberian union was accomplished, but it was led by a Spaniard.

Even so, and despite past antagonism, Portuguese nobles anticipated improvements under Filipe. The Portuguese Crown's resources had become depleted due to cavalier spending. Amid the opulence and grandeur, expenditure had been outstripping revenue for years. The empire was hugely expensive to run and maintain. Hangers-on like the *fidalgos* drained the royal coffers. The result was heavy debt, much of it held abroad. There were other difficulties, too. Two ambassadors from Venice, known only as Tron and Lippomani, travelled to Lisbon to compliment King Filipe soon after he sat on the Portuguese throne. They walked through Rua Nova and were taken aback by its variety of foreign goods. But they also noted that prices had shot up recently for three reasons: the plague that had gripped Lisbon; the pillaging committed by the Duke of Alba's men, even though it was expressly forbidden; and that the fleets had not come from India for the past two years, leaving some shops poorly stocked.

Furthermore, trade in the East, where the Portuguese were thinly spread, was under looming threat from English and Dutch encroachment. The nobles wished for a return to the times of plenty, but the new reality dulled Lisbon's shine. Many Portuguese left for Brazil, which was closer than India and promised to be the next El Dorado, to seek their fortune.

Meanwhile, Portugal surrendered its long-standing neutrality in European affairs by coming under the umbrella of the Spanish royal house. It became fair game for Habsburg's enemies. England was among them, even though it had been Portugal's ally since the Treaty of Windsor in 1386. Filipe I, however, was bent on restoring Catholicism in England. He assembled the Invincible Armada, which gathered in the Tagus and set off from Belém on 27 May 1588. It contained 130 ships, twelve of them Portuguese, and around 30,000 troops. After its defeat in the English Channel, Portugal felt a backlash. A naval force led by Sir Francis Drake and General John Norris bore down on Lisbon the following year but was unable to make a dent on the city which had improved its river fortifications.

The geopolitical changes also hurt business. The English Navy hunted Portuguese ships, knowing their cargoes on the return from India were likely to be valuable. The huge *Madre de Deus* fell into an English trap near the Azores in August 1592. The English were astonished by the size of the carrack and by what is was carrying. It had seven decks, 1,600 tonnes of cargo, thirty-two cannon and more than 600 people on board. Its cargo included jewels, pepper, cloves, nutmeg, cinnamon, ginger, camphor, silks, calico, carpets, incense, pearls, ivory, Chinese porcelain, ebony and animal skins.

The Spanish monarchs never made a permanent home in Portugal, nor did they form any apparent sentimental attachment to it. Indeed, while the expectation might be that the Portuguese would march to the beat of a different drum under Spanish rule, the Filipes largely left Portugal to its own devices. They had more pressing affairs to tend to on the wider European stage. The footprint in Lisbon of those six decades is slight.

Filipe's oath during his first and only visit to Lisbon set the tone. Filipe I of Portugal made his grand entrance into the capital on 29 June 1582. It was one of the most sumptuous festive occasions the city had ever seen. Triumphal arches in timber were erected in the streets, and there were cannon salutes by Portuguese and Spanish ships anchored in the Tagus. Filipe agreed to a series of undertakings, including to respect local customs and privileges, leave all legislation in place and keep Portuguese as the official language, among other things. Filipe stayed in Lisbon for just over two years, with his troops barracking in St George's Castle and flying his flag over it. The Duke of Alba died in the city in 1582.

Filipe I set about putting his mark on Lisbon. He wanted to draw a line under Sebastião's reign and he figured out a way to do that in one fell swoop. Sebastião had started building a church named after himself in the Terreiro do Paço riverside square. Filipe summarily scrapped that project. He had the foundation stones dug up and sent to his pet project: the São Vicente de Fora Church and Monastery. Filipe also invested in a display of his earthly power. On the river's edge, on top of the bulwark of the Paço da Ribeira, he built an enormous tower. It dominated the cityscape from the Tagus and became the square's distinguishing feature and a landmark. It was an eloquent symbol. While São Vicente de Fora gave a nod to the Catholic Church, this project served a military purpose. It had openings for cannon, and underlined the king's status with its Sala dos Embaixadores (Ambassadors' Hall) on the top floor featuring a domed ceiling, plush furnishings and a magnificent view. It was like a New York penthouse for that time. It was in these years that Cervantes, then in his thirties, visited Lisbon. Seeking to endear himself to the monarch, he wrote flattering reports about life in the city.

But Filipe's most emblematic, and enduring, project was the major rebuilding of São Vicente de Fora. The complex had been begun by King Afonso Henriques after his successful siege of Lisbon, and was later improved by King João III, who died in 1557. Filipe's choice of this eye-catching project made something emphatically clear: a new dynasty was in charge. The authorship of the São Vicente de Fora's ambitious refashioning has long been disputed, but most scholars suggest that the architect was Juan de Herrera, the great sixteenth-century Spaniard famed for completing the El Escorial royal retreat near Madrid, while the hands-on management fell to the Italian Filippo Terzi. The massive rebuilding project was completed only in 1629. By that time, a Portuguese architect had also had a hand in the endeavour— Baltazar Alves, who oversaw the work from 1597 and is regarded as the brains behind the majestic façade as well as the tactful adaptation of the Mannerist style to local tastes.

Filipe I symbolically appropriated the São Vicente de Fora project. He knocked down the previous royal versions of the building that were linked to the founding of Portugal. In that way, he hoped to affirm his own local dynasty. São Vicente de Fora was the biggest construction project of his reign and was designed to impress. The church's façade possesses two towers, as if it were a cathedral, to lend it dignity and prestige. The sober, elegant building was a massive physical presence at the time and a work of recognized quality. King João V secured some measure of Portuguese revenge in the eighteenth century for Filipe's presumption. A staggering collection of Baroque hand-painted tiles (*azulejos*) at São Vicente de Fora, which are rivalled only by those at the Convento de São Francisco in Salvador de Bahia, Brazil, depict scenes from Portuguese history. The collection of monarchs conspicuously does not include the Filipes. It was as if João V wanted to rewrite history and erase those six decades.

Despite its lower rank on the peninsula under Madrid's rule, Lisbon was still one of Europe's largest cities by population. The nobleman Luís Mendes de Vasconcelos, in his 1608 book *Do Sítio de Lisboa* (On the Place of Lisbon) sought to persuade the next Habsburg in line, Filipe II of Portugal (Felipe III of Spain), to make Lisbon the capital of Iberia. The city, he wrote, "not just because of its natural layout, but because of its exceptional perpetuity … is worthy of being the head of the empire of the whole world."

But it would be another ten years before Filipe II even deigned to travel to Lisbon, and then only in order to get the Cortes to recognize his son as the successor to the Portuguese throne. His arrival on 5 June 1619 brought another great city celebration. The Spanish sovereign arrived at Terreiro do Paço on a royal barge rowed by 600 men. Ships and forts along the Tagus fired their cannon. Boats went out to greet him. The quayside was decorated with flowers, and Filipe II received two golden keys to the city. He rode in a carriage which is now the oldest on display at Lisbon's National Carriage Museum. It is open-sided with a red velvet interior and black leather roof.

Filipe II spent about three months in Lisbon. The conduct of the Spanish courtiers and nobles accompanying him hinted at dark clouds on the horizon. They were accommodated and took meals at Lisbon monasteries and other respectable institutions but behaved abominably. They were arrogant and insolent. They stole plates, china and tablecloths and brushed aside protests. Complaints by locals to Filipe II fell on deaf ears. Relations soured, though they had never been very warm. It was a legal union, not an emotional one.

Through the early seventeenth century relations between Portugal and Spain were calm and stable. Madrid helped out with military expenditure to protect Portugal's trade in the Orient, which kept Portuguese nobles' income safe, and invested in the local Catholic Church. But as Spain's prosperity waned amid European wars, the Spanish monarchy increased taxes in Portugal. Portuguese commoners became unhappy, and rebellions erupted in rural areas. Spanish nobles began to be appointed to official positions in Portugal. When Portuguese nobles were asked to fight in Madrid's war against Catalonia, it was the final straw.

A group of forty Portuguese conspirators began to convene at the palace of Antão de Almada, close to Rossio Square. A pavilion in its garden was the meeting place for the coup planners who are known as *Os Quarenta Conjurados* (The Forty Conspirators). They risked their heads by plotting against the king. On 1 December 1640 they held a last meeting in the garden before proceeding to the Paço da Ribeira royal palace, where they forced their way in. The viceroy, Margarida de Saboia, Duchess of Mântua, hid in a cabinet while her secretary-general, Miguel de Vasconcelos, was defenestrated by the assailants. The conspirators proclaimed King João IV, a descendant of Manuel I, as the new monarch amid cries of "Freedom!" The royal house of Spain, at grips with the Thirty Years' War and trying to put down the Catalan uprising, did nothing. It was a swift palace coup and one of the most momentous days in Portuguese history.

Independence wasn't theirs yet, however. Still to come were twenty-eight years of sporadic battles with Spain, mostly near their land border, in what was the longest military conflict in Portuguese history. The Treaty of Lisbon, mediated by King Charles II of England, ended the fighting and recognized Portugal's independence. It was signed at

Lisbon's Santo Elói Convent in 1668. The stately home belonging to Antão de Almada became known as the Palácio da Independência and is today a public building. In 1886, a 30-metre-high monument to those who restored independence (the *restauradores*) was inaugurated in a Lisbon square of the same name. 1 December remains a public holiday, the *Dia da Restauração*.

FOUR—THE AFRICAN CONNECTION

On Sunday, 17 September 1882, at 8:30 p.m., the doors opened on a lavish gala at a grand house in Travessa do Outeiro, a street not far from Lisbon's Estrela Garden and the Basilica da Estrela, the city's magnificent Late Baroque church. Newspaper advertisements, posters and flyers had announced the event. They promised that it would be "dazzling". The entertainment included rides in a tethered balloon, and there were salutes fired by mortars followed by "a splendid ball". The occasion merited extravagance. It was the coronation ceremony of the new queen of Kongo, Amália I. It would, the advertisements declared, be a "great party of the Congolese court to mark in a solemn manner such a majestic and august day".

The coronation in nineteenth-century Lisbon of a West African queen is not as puzzling as it might at first appear. From the fifteenth century onward the Portuguese went to Africa, and Africa came to Portugal. Most Africans came as slaves, and in large numbers. By the mid-sixteenth century, there were almost 10,000 black slaves in Lisbon, representing around 10 per cent of the city's population. It was a remarkable number that distinguished the city from the rest of the continent. People of African heritage are a common sight in

post-colonial Western Europe today, but in the sixteenth century, they weren't. Vivid traits of Africa have been a Lisbon
hallmark for centuries, and remain so. "The city's history
cannot be told," says Angolan novelist José Eduardo
Agualusa, "without talking about those thousands of Africans
who over the centuries have settled in the Portuguese capital,
enriching it and reinventing it."

On their voyages during the Age of Expansion the
Portuguese made friends where they could. Apart from the
slaves they brought home, some Africans stepped onto the
Lisbon quayside as free men and women. The Portuguese
especially sought to educate in Lisbon indigenous people who
might return to Africa as clergy. German physician
Hieronymus Münzer, visiting Lisbon in 1494, reported young
black men being taught Latin and theology. The goal was to
send them back to Africa as missionaries, interpreters and
envoys of the Portuguese Crown.

The distinguished visitors to Lisbon from distant outposts
of empire included royalty from the then Kingdom of
Kongo, in west-central Africa, now partly Angola and the
Democratic Republic of the Congo. The Portuguese explor-
ers reached Kongo in 1483 and forged alliances. Eight years
later, Kongo's tribal leader Nzinga a Nkuwu was baptized
and took the title João I of Kongo. His son, and eventual
successor, Mvemba a Nzinga also took the sacrament and
later became Afonso I of Kongo. Their ambassadors and
family relations travelled freely to the Portuguese capital.
Several centuries later, princesses from these lands still had a
residence in Lisbon, in a quarter called Mocambo that had a
strong African presence. They held balls at which dishes from
both Europe and Africa were served, according to Isabel
Castro Henriques, a Lisbon University historian.

Queen Amália I's coronation party was advertised in the weekly Lisbon newspaper *O António Maria*. As well as entertainment, the ceremonies included "the granting of honorary distinctions, commendations, titles, etc". That detail was not as innocent as it seemed. The queen's trip to Portugal and her sojourn in Lisbon were a drain on the royal Kongolese purse. Her retinue was composed of a private secretary, six high dignitaries with their consorts, and a cook. As a consequence, not only were the titles and commendations for sale, but an entrance fee was charged at the door.

The newspaper advertisement was appropriately egalitarian. "All Portuguese and others are invited to join the party, thus deepening the ties of friendship and fraternity with the subjects of the new queen," it said. Above this phrase was a sketched silhouette of a plump African woman wearing a crown and with two attendants. At the bottom was a similar sketch in negative, showing a portly male figure—bearing a resemblance to King Luís I of Portugal—and two attendants, white on a black background. Beneath it was the phrase, "Black or white, all courts look alike."

Queen Amália's story has a twist in the tale. She eventually gave up the throne and ran away with a wealthy Portuguese farmer to the country's southern Alentejo region, near Évora. She reportedly bore many children and lived to the age of eighty-two. Lisbon City Council named a street after her, Rua Rainha do Congo, in 1989. The plaque describes her as a "celebrated personage".

Queen Amália, however, was one of the exceptions in the frequently grim narrative of Africans in Portugal. The Portuguese were the world's biggest slavers. They trafficked around 5.8 million across the Atlantic, mostly from Africa and mostly to the plantations and gold mines in Brazil, between 1501 and 1875, according to data gathered from original archive sources in a dozen countries by Emory University in Atlanta, Georgia. That was almost double the total of Britain, which had the second highest count. It is a dark side of the voyages of discovery, and a truth that is seldom spoken in Portugal. There is no slavery museum in Lisbon like the one in Liverpool or at the Museum of London. A memorial to slaves was planned for the riverside area in 2018, however, after the project won enough votes in the City Council's annual participatory budget, which balloted local people on how they wanted part of Lisbon's revenue spent.

The first major delivery of African slaves in Portugal—and perhaps Europe—occurred along the southern Portuguese coast, in Lagos bay, on 8 August 1444. The arrival of the 235 slaves was watched by Prince Henry the Navigator, mounted on a horse. The scene was memorably recounted by chronicler Gomes Eanes de Zurara, who wondered, "What heart, however hard, could fail but to be stung at the sight of such an event?" In Africa, the slaves were commonly exchanged for glass beads or tin or copper baubles.

A papal bull of 1454 required slaves to be baptized. They were then given Christian names. Following King Manuel I's 1512 decree that slaves could be offloaded only in the port of Lisbon, centralizing the trade in the capital city, they were baptized at the Igreja da Conceição, behind Terreiro do Paço. The church stood on the site of Little Jerusalem's one-time synagogue. The church is still there, pinched by the heavy downtown traffic, though little more than its elaborate Manueline-style doorway survived the 1755 earthquake.

The church's location made it convenient to serve the profitable sixteenth-century West African slave business. The Casa dos Escravos (Slave House) was a department of the Casa da Guiné (Guinea House), which stood on the nearby riverbank. That was where the slave registrar had his office, as well as two large, lockable rooms for the latest batch of arrivals. Norms written in 1509 established procedures for new arrivals: a detachment of royal officials went out into the river to inspect arriving slave ships. The slaves were brought onto the deck and counted. They were then taken to the Casa dos Escravos, where they were physically assessed. A price was written on parchment and hung around their neck.

They were sold in public, usually in the square called Largo do Pelourinho Velho, by Rua Nova dos Mercadores, though sometimes they were paraded through the city streets and sold to whoever made a bid. Sales were overseen by a licenced "trader in beasts and slaves". The sale and the owner's name were recorded at the Alfândega (Customs House) on the other side of the square, though those duties later moved to the new Casa da Índia (India House). The Crown levied a 25 per cent tax, known as a *quarto*, on sales.

Foreign visitors to Lisbon recorded these scenes, and some didn't have the stomach for them. Taccoen, the Flemish nobleman, wrote that while he was in Lisbon a ship docked that was loaded with spices and carrying around 300 black prisoners in its hold—men, women and children. They were completely naked when they were taken off the ship. On the quayside, in the open air, they were given food. It was a kind of gruel, served in larges dishes. "They surrounded each dish on their knees and ate like that, without spoons, scooping up the food in their hands, and there were so many dishes that each one got a share," Taccoen reported:

Afterwards they were made to wash the dish and it was filled with drinking water. They knelt down and drank it, as if they were animals. And they are sold on the spot by their owners when the merchants arrive. The buyers check their mouth, to see if they have good teeth, and between their thighs as well as making them move their arms. They make the men and boys run up and down. When a price is agreed they are covered with a cloth and sent off.

Filippo Sassetti, a Florentine merchant and writer who lived in Lisbon from 1578 to 1582, expressed disgust at what he witnessed. "It is sad to see how they bring [the slaves] in on the decks of ships, 25 or 30 or 40 at a time, naked, poorly fed, tied together back-to-back," he wrote in a letter.

I can't resist telling you about an episode that made my jaw drop, revealing as it did [the slaves'] misery and the inhumanity of their masters. I saw in a city square, arranged on the ground, about 50 of these beings forming a circle in which their feet were the outer ring and their heads in the middle. They were all tied together, struggling to reach a big wooden barrel that had water in it. I stood watching what they were doing. All the effort of those wretched beings was so that they could lick the sides of the barrel, where water was oozing out.

Though records are far from complete, a census in 1551–52 suggested Lisbon had just shy of 10,000 slaves. That was equivalent to roughly 10 per cent of the city's population. In 1620 there were just over 10,000 slaves in a city population of some 143,000. In the first half of the eighteenth century, the proportion was 22,500 in 150,000 residents. Professor Didier Lahon, an anthropologist, reckons that from the second half of the fifteenth century up to 1761, when new slave arrivals were banned, around 400,000 slaves were brought to Portugal. Almost all were Africans, though some came from kingdoms around the Indian Ocean and Arabian Sea.

"Do you know what the difference was between the king and a prostitute?" asked French writer and anthropologist Jean-Yves Loude, who has explored Lisbon's African legacy. "None. They both kept slaves. It was said that the only ones who didn't have slaves at that time [in the sixteenth century] in Lisbon were the beggars."

Black slaves were a common sight in Lisbon homes, workplaces and streets. Even the clergy and convents bought and kept slaves. Inevitably, the slaves were trusted with the most physically demanding and unpleasant jobs. Women slaves in domestic service had the unpleasant task of disposing of the contents of chamber pots. Every morning and evening, hundreds of them made their way down to the river, balancing pots called *calhandras* on their head or shoulder, and dumped the contents in the Tagus. These women called *calhandeiras* performed, indeed, an important public health function.

Slaves had a broad range of work. The women frequently worked in houses as cleaners, maids and cooks, and in the streets as sellers of snacks: mussels, whelks, boiled prunes, cakes and lupin beans. The men were blacksmiths, water-sellers, tailors, fishermen, cobblers, carpenters and stonemasons. They later won fame as *caiadores*, who whitewashed Lisbon buildings. Some slave owners rented out their men to various professions and made a comfortable living by doing nothing themselves. The owner would receive the pay for work done by his slave as, for example, a cobbler or carpenter.

Men slaves also worked as personal guards in what could be a dangerous and violent city, and went on the voyages of discovery. More than 2,000 black soldiers were in the army that fought Filipe II of Spain's invading force in 1580. Slaves who had learned Portuguese were rented out to ships heading to Africa so they could barter with tribal leaders and bring other slaves back to Lisbon. After bringing a certain number, they might win their freedom.

Some slaves could marry and live away from their master's house, and all moved unmolested around the city. They might be freed by their owner after long and loyal service or when they were old, though this brought new problems for slaves who lost a roof over their head and their guaranteed food. Many found solace in alcohol. Before that happened, some tried to break free. The Lisbon newspaper *Hebdomadário Lisbonense* of 8 November 1766 reported that Manoel Rodrigues da Silva Pereira, who lived in Rua da Atalaya in the Bairro Alto, was "missing a black man" called Francisco José, approximately twenty-two years old with the following distinguishing characteristics: well-built, tall, bulky, good eyes, a cheerful air, an ear pierced with a yellow topaz gemstone, and a round head of hair.

From Africa, the slaves brought their own cultures. That included black magic and witchcraft, and the Inquisition was coiled to pounce. In 1738 a slave called Afonso de Melo who worked for the Duke of Cadaval appeared before the Holy Office in Lisbon and made a confession. He said that a year earlier his master had started treating him badly and beating him. At a loss, he had asked for help from fellow slave José Francisco. Melo said he wanted his master to go back to treating him like before. He had no intention of harming his master, Melo said. José Francisco concocted a remedy. He brewed a potion containing the blood of a black chicken, pieces of cotton and brandy and then burned the chicken's heart on a cloth with shavings from the sole of the master's shoe. Melo said he was also told that another solution would be to chew a piece of wood before breakfast and then spit on the floor where his master would be sure to place his left foot.

It is still possible to get a whiff of what might be West African sorcery in Lisbon. At subway station exits, ebony-skinned men hand out slips of paper advertising the services of what appear to be witchdoctors. One of them, called Mestre Mafudji, says he is a "great scientist" and "a descendant of an old family with powers". He handles cases involving love and loss, business failures, impotence, and drug and tobacco addictions. One of his rivals, Mestre Sila, claims he is "a descendant of an old and wealthy family with knowledge of black and white magic". As well as voodoo spells, both of them provide their address and phone number.

African slaves in Portuguese society during the sixteenth and seventeenth centuries are depicted in several artistic renderings of the capital. The *Chafariz d'el Rey* oil painting, an anonymous Flemish work from 1570–80 in the Berardo Collection in Lisbon, illustrates how deeply black and white lives were entwined. In the busy scene at this important public fountain there are numerous black figures. Some carry water, others accompany their masters. In a small boat on the Tagus, one black person rows while another plays a tambourine for a white man and woman. There are even a black man and white woman dancing together. Another black man is apparently drunk and being hauled away; another is on horseback in a cape bearing the sign of the Order of Santiago. This figure was probably the court jester João de Sá, better known as Panasco. He was a slave who had been born in Portugal and was regarded not just as a funnyman with biting wit but also as a deeply spiritual person, according to the historian Maria do Rosário Pimentel, and King

João III rewarded him with the conspicuous cloak. It is safe to say that a black man on a mule wearing a cape of the Order of Santiago would have turned heads in Lisbon streets and would be talked about in the capital. That would explain his inclusion in this depiction of this exceptional city.

Black people are working as stevedores, sailors and rowers along the Lisbon quayside in Theodor de Bry's 1592 engraving of the port of Lisbon. The two paintings of Rua Nova dos Mercadores from around the same time held by the Society of Antiquaries of London show black people carrying baskets on their head, a *calhandreira* carrying the contents of chamber pots, and one riding a mule. The 1657 *View of Jerónimos Monastery and Belém Riverbank* by Filipe Lobo has white men on horses accompanied by black men on foot as well as black women street-sellers. Dirk Stoop's painting of the Terreiro do Paço in 1662 also renders black members of society.

Emancipation, which would happen piecemeal, began in 1761. A royal charter signed by Sebastião José de Carvalho e Melo, King José I's chief minister and a prominent figure of the Enlightenment in Portugal, outlawed the transportation of slaves to Portugal on religious and moral grounds. That is often regarded as a pioneering decision in the context of the history of European slavery. It was not as benevolent or high-minded as might be imagined, however. It also took its cue from practical requirements. One of its principal aims was to re-route slaves to Brazil, where the Portuguese needed them to work on labour-intensive plantations and in gold mines. Portugal desperately needed the money from those enter-prises. Furthermore, the charter explained, bringing "such an extraordinary number of black slaves" to work in the king-dom had the unwelcome consequence of "young men who, left without any occupation, give themselves over to idleness and surrender to vices."

Slave numbers in Lisbon, and Portugal generally, began to decline, but it would take more than 100 years before the Portuguese slave trade was completely abolished. There was no groundswell abolition movement to drive it forward. Opponents of slavery were lonely voices. Some influential people made fortunes from the slave trade. For others, it afforded a comfortable life that otherwise would have been out of reach.

The chains started coming off in 1773, with what was called the *lei do ventre livre* (literally, free womb law). It handed freedom to all those born after 16 January of that year, as well as to anyone whose family had been slaves since their great-grandmother's generation. It was a beginning, and emancipation continued in fits and starts. It gathered pace in the nineteenth century when a committed Portuguese abolitionist—a rare bird—came to power. Viscount Sá da Bandeira, a leading Liberal, introduced a law in 1856 granting freedom to children whose mothers were slaves. In a sop to his opponents, however, those children had to work for their mother's master for free until they were twenty.

Two years later, another decree chipped away more of the status quo. It stated that within twenty years, slavery would be abolished in Portuguese territories. An 1869 decree extended that deadline, however, as competing interests elbowed each other. It was a lengthy game of political chess, with feints and parries, between abolitionists and businessmen. The new decree abolished slavery and freed slaves, on the one hand, but on the other hand classified them as *libertos* (freed men and women) who had to continue toiling for their masters until 1878. In the end, three years before that dead-line, the *liberto* classification was scrapped and those freed were allowed to work in any Portuguese land.

Sá da Bandeira, by now a marquis, earned a bronze statue for his endeavours. The sculpture, cast in Rome and inaugurated in July 1884 by King Luís I, is by Italian Giovanni Ciniselli and was paid for by a public fundraising campaign. It stands in gardens close to Lisbon's Cais do Sodré suburban train station, next to the Tagus. On the steps up to the plinth sits a figure of a bare-breasted African woman with broken chains on her ankles and a child in her lap. She looks at the child and points up to Sá da Bandeira, as if she is telling the story of their champion; the awed infant, symbolizing the future, offers up a laurel wreath to him.

The model for the female figure was Fernanda do Valle, a mixed-race woman known as Preta Fernanda (Black Fernanda). She was one of the few non-white Lisbon residents who left a mark on the city's history. Some others were known by word of mouth, such as Violante Fernandes from West Africa, a sixteenth-century brothel-keeper in the Bairro Alto district, or Bárbara Fernandes, a black woman who rented out rooms in the same *bairro* for the same ends. Both had been freed from slavery.

Fernanda do Valle was a *fin-de-siècle* celebrity, as infamous as she was famous. She was a renowned courtesan with enough pluck to try her hand at bullfighting on horseback, too. She also published a ghost-written autobiography. She was born Andreza de Pina in Cape Verde in the second half of the nineteenth century. Her birthdate is uncertain—her 1912 memoirs, entitled *Recordações d'uma Colonial* (Recollections of a Colonial Subject) tell her extraordinary story but don't always tally with other sources. She moved to Lisbon with a wealthy German who turned out to love beer more than he loved her, so she walked out on him.

The statue modelling job helped her make ends meet, though she got into a row with the artist who reportedly was displeased by the unsightly bunions on her feet. She then found work in domestic service at the Lisbon house of the distinguished Cavalcanti family. She got to know the cream of the capital's society and started having with some of its members what she termed "lewd" relationships. Her calculatingly candid autobiography contained a long list of lovers. With her savings, she opened one of Lisbon's most popular brothels. It had a select clientele and became a meeting place for the city's bohemians. The great Portuguese novelist Eça de Queirós invited Fernanda to his box at the Teatro da Trindade. She was provocative and sensual, exotic and passionate. She was a lightning rod for scandal.

Fernanda do Valle shocked polite Lisbon society. The city newspaper *A Capital*, in its 15 April 1917 edition, reported in a tone of outrage the First Futurist Conference, organized by the nascent Portuguese Futurism movement and held the previous day at the Teatro da República. The occasion witnessed the presentation of the *Futurist Manifesto of Lust*, a work by French writer and artist Valentine de Saint-Point, who insisted on equality between men and women and sexual freedom. One of the Portuguese intellectuals behind the event was José de Almada Negreiros, himself of mixed race.

The newspaper article was headlined "The eulogy of madness" in that day's edition, where the front-page lead story was about Portuguese soldiers arriving in France as the country joined World War I. The journalist reported that "a well-known Cape Verdean woman", who had once dressed up "like a transvestite" as a male bullfighter on horseback and performed at a Lisbon bullfight (getting her trousers torn in the process, the paper takes relish in noting), followed "with tireless attention" from a box close to the stage everything that Almada Negreiros said. She reportedly was accompanied by other members of the Lisbon *demi-monde*. Almada Negreiros was heckled and left the stage, and many people walked out, the paper reported, but the "celebrated horse-rider" was one of those who stayed. She reportedly blushed "only a couple of times" at what was said.

Almada Negreiros also ruffled feathers. Born in the twin-island archipelago of São Tomé and Príncipe in 1893 to a Portuguese cavalry lieutenant and a moneyed local woman, he became for many people the father of Portuguese modernism. Bourgeois Lisbon society found his irreverent, unconventional and sometimes caustic attitudes distasteful—especially coming from the son of an African woman who, in their view, ought to have known his place. Almada Negreiros refused to bend. "Anyone who thinks for himself just wants to get at the truth; justifications are for others," he wrote. At the First Futurist Conference he came on stage wearing a full-body flight suit of the kind used by pilots in the war, and the black-and-white photograph depicting him in that garb is perhaps the most recognizable picture of the artist. He cuts a gaunt figure, with his trousers billowing at the thighs like jodhpurs and tight at the ankles, the high collar buttoned up. His right hand rests on his hip and his chest is pushed out, unrepentant.

Almada Negreiros was a poet, novelist, essayist, designer and painter. He was a close friend of the poet Fernando

Pessoa, with whom he contributed to the famous Lisbon literary magazine *Orpheu*. His reputation is assured by his outstanding body of avant-garde work, plenty of which can still be seen in Lisbon, especially at the Gulbenkian Foundation Center for Modern Art. He also produced two of the decorative panels on a wall of A Brasileira café in the Chiado district, where a bronze statue of Pessoa sits at an outside table. The works are *Banhistas* (Bathers) and *Auto-Retrato em Grupo* (Self-Portrait in a Group), which features the artist on the far left.

A forgotten mixed-race contemporary of Almada Negreiros is Mário Domingues. Born in 1899 on the island of Príncipe, he moved to Lisbon as an infant. His appetite for writing was voracious, and was a respected journalist, historian, novelist and essayist. He published more than 200 works of fiction and non-fiction, making him one of the most prolific Portuguese writers ever. His works included the popular twenty-three-book *Série Lusíada* on Portuguese history and translations of Charles Dickens and Walter Scott, as well as crime thrillers. His 1960 novel *O Menino entre os Gigantes* (The Boy among Giants) tells of the racism endured by a mixed-race boy among the petite bourgeoisie of early twentieth-century Lisbon. Like the author, the boy is taken from his African mother and sent to live with his white father's family in the imperial capital. Domingues said the novel was "an appeal for fraternity between men of all colours and rank".

Another formerly well-known figure who has been relegated to a historical footnote is Pai Paulino. He was a black entertainer at nineteenth-century bullfights staged in the Campo de Santana, now called Campo dos Mártires da Pátria, which drew large crowds. His charisma opened other doors for him. He belonged to several religious brotherhoods which sought to stand up for the rights of Africans. Paulino fought on the side of the Liberals against the absolutists in Portugal's 1828–34 civil war. He was also a *caiador* (whitewasher) and a piper in Corpus Christi street processions. He did not merit a statue but, just as flatteringly, the prominent illustrator and caricaturist Rafael Bordalo Pinheiro made a china bust of him in 1894. Like others of his official status, however, Paulino was destined to be buried in an unmarked ditch, in his case at the Alto de São João cemetery.

There would be no such neglect for the memory of nineteenth-century mixed-race doctor José Tomás de Sousa Martins. Astonishingly, more than a century after his death, bouquets of fresh flowers are still placed daily at the foot of his statue in Campo dos Mártires da Pátria, across the road from Lisbon's Faculty of Medical Sciences. Around the white stone pedestal, behind a waist-high wrought-iron fence, scores of engraved stone and marble plaques offer him thanks. People can frequently be seen at the monument with their hands clasped, in silent prayer. In a blackened and warm metal box on legs, candles burn, sending whiffs of melting wax across the square. It is an unofficial shrine.

A cult grew up around Dr Sousa Martins, who was regarded by some as a miracle-worker and a saint. It is not hard to see why he inspires people. He cared for people of all colours and creeds without discrimination in a life of selfless dedication. He treated the Portuguese royal family and aristocrats at their palaces and he treated poor black people in the Lisbon slums. Indeed, he charged the wealthy a lot so that he could charge the poor nothing. Some called him the Father of the Poor. He was a prestigious university professor and scientist. He was a pioneer in tuberculosis research, for which he became known internationally, and specialized in treating the infectious disease, which was one of the city's scourges.

What also set him apart were his human touch and his bedside manner. He told his students: "When you go into a hospital at night and you hear a patient moan, go to their bed, see what that poor sick person needs and, if you have nothing else to give, give them a smile." When Dr Sousa Martins died in 1897 aged fifty-four—inevitably, perhaps, of tuberculosis—King Carlos I said of him, "On his departure from this world, all the lands that knew him wept. It was an irreparable loss, a national loss, extinguishing the greatest light in my kingdom." A first sculpture of Dr Sousa Martins had to be scrapped after it sparked a scandal. Created by Aleixo Queirós Ribeiro and inaugurated in 1904, it portrayed the doctor in a sitting position, and the people of Lisbon didn't like it at all. It was replaced by the current statue of him standing in his professor's toga and gesturing to an imagined audience, by the sculptor Costa Mota, which became a site of pilgrimage.

Two twentieth-century additions to this Afro-Portuguese hall of fame both grew up in Mafalala, one of the biggest neighbourhoods of the colonial Mozambican capital Lourenço Marques, now Maputo. They were childhood friends and they both made a splash in their separate fields when they moved to Lisbon as young men.

Ricardo Chibanga, whose mix of Portuguese Christian name and African surname perfectly captures the blend of cultures, is believed to have been the first black matador. The Spanish painters Pablo Picasso and Salvador Dalí reportedly feted him, and he earned standing ovations at bullrings around the world.

Chibanga was born in 1942. He was brought to Lisbon on a Portuguese Air Force flight in 1962 to develop his promising bullfighting skills. He later recalled his first impressions of the Portuguese capital: "It was all so beautiful," he said. "I came from an African village, and those good houses, all pretty, the paved roads ... I was amazed that there weren't any black people!" The times when 10 per cent of Lisbon's population was black were long gone.

Chibanga made his debut in 1968 at Lisbon's prestigious Campo Pequeno bullring, a red-brick neo-Islamic building from the end of the nineteenth century which now has a shopping mall beneath it. When he was twenty-eight he lost sight in one eye during a bullfight when he was clipped by one of the barbed sticks called *bandarilhas* that are used to spear the animal. He gave an acclaimed performance in Seville in 1971, then went to Madrid, Barcelona, France and Latin America, where he was known as *El Africano*. He said he never felt racist discrimination: "On the contrary, I always felt that people appreciated me."

The other son of Mafalala who found stardom is by far Lisbon's most famous African. His fame and prestige were such that he was known globally by just one name: Eusébio. This football player's explosive power and feline agility, developed on dirt-hard fields in southern Africa, won him the nickname *Pantera Negra* (Black Panther).

His journey from Lourenço Marques to the empire's capital was a cloak-and-dagger operation. Scouts from Lisbon's two biggest football clubs, Benfica and Sporting, had both identified Eusébio da Silva Ferreira as a hot prospect, and both courted him. Benfica seized the initiative, persuading his mother to sign him up for the club. But it feared that Sporting had not capitulated and would still attempt to lure Eusébio away with a better offer. The only way to prevent that was for Benfica to keep up its guard and keep the prodigy away from the crosstown rivals. Despite Eusébio's lifelong fear of flying, Benfica's representatives in Lourenço Marques hustled him onto one of national airline TAP's Lockheed Super Constellation flights to Lisbon, in December 1960, when he was eighteen. To throw Sporting officials off the scent, they registered Eusébio as a woman—"Ruth Malosso"—on the passenger manifest.

During a career that brought many accomplishments with the Portuguese national team, Eusébio shone at Benfica, whose fans worshipped him. One of his unforgettable games was an epic European champions final against Real Madrid in 1962. A first-half hat-trick by the legendary Ferenc Puskas looked like it would be enough to secure the trophy for the Spanish club. But in a thrilling comeback Eusébio scored the last two goals to give his team a 5–3 triumph and clinch Benfica's second straight continental champion's title. Some called him *A Pérola Negra* (The Black Pearl).

Known for his humble and gentle manner, as well as his sincerity and frankness, Eusébio's popularity was such that in 1964, when Italian clubs offered to buy him for sums that were astronomical at the time, Portugal's then-dictator António Salazar decreed him to be a "national treasure"—meaning that he could not be sold abroad. In 1998, a panel of 100 experts gathered by football's world governing body FIFA inducted Eusébio into its International Football Hall of Fame as one of the sport's top ten all-time greats. "Look, there are only two black people on the list: me and Pelé," Eusébio commented on the honour, referring to the Brazilian great who was a friend. "I regard that as a great responsibility because I am representing Africa and Portugal, my second homeland."

Eusebio's superstar status ensured special treatment. His remains were moved in 2015, the year after he died, to the National Pantheon. He was only the twelfth person to be granted such an honour and the first athlete. A statue of Eusébio, poised in mid-kick, stands outside Benfica's Stadium of Light. Jean-Yves Loude, the French writer, wryly noted that Eusébio was "the only African worker immortalized during his lifetime for services to the nation".

Lisbon has, on the whole, provided unpromising soil for the ambitions of most black or mixed-race people. Like other Europeans, many white Portuguese held negative attitudes toward them based on prejudices and stereotypes. Mixed-race people were long considered more black than white. Still, they largely lived among the Portuguese rather than apart from them. As the historian Francisco Bethencourt has remarked, Portuguese racism manifests itself through discrimination, not segregation.

The Africans, brought in massive numbers to work as slaves, were sometimes the targets of mockery. They were forced to learn Portuguese, and the results were seen as comical. Their way of speaking was called *língua de preto*, a term still used for the pronunciation of speakers from Portugal's former African colonies. Some of the earliest examples of this derision were in royal playwright Gil Vicente's 1524 tragicomedy *Frágua de Amor* (Forge of Love), performed at the marriage of King João III and Catarina, sister of the Holy Roman Emperor Charles V. In it, the black characters are objects of satire for their grammatical *faux pas*.

Once they were baptized, black slaves were allowed to take part in some religious celebrations. In doing so, they could also

1. A view of Lisbon's Alfama district, showing the São Vicente de Fora Church and Monastery (top centre) and the dome of the National Pantheon (right). (Wikimedia Commons)

2. Lisbon Cathedral (Sé de Lisboa) pictured in the nineteenth century. (Public domain image, Tumblr)

LISBONA.

OLISIPO, SIVE VT PERVE
TVSTÆ LAPIDVM INSCRIP
TIONES HABENT, VLYSIPPO,
VVLGO LISBONA FLORENTIS
SIMVM PORTVGALLIÆ EMPORIV.

3. A sixteenth-century view over Lisbon from the south bank of the River Tagus, showing the royal palace's broad courtyard (Terreiro do Paço) in the foreground, with the royal shipyards on one side and Rossio Square behind, as well as St George's Castle and its palace on the hilltop. (Wikimedia Commons)

4. An aerial view of the São Vicente de Fora Church and Monastery, with the National Pantheon behind and the Sea of Straw beyond. (Wikimedia Commons)

5. The Belém Tower (Torre de Belém), with the 25 de Abril Bridge in the background. (TTstudio/Shutterstock.com)

6. The *Chafariz d'el Rey oil* painting, an anonymous Flemish work from 1570–80 in the Berardo Collection in Lisbon, shows the King's Fountain on the riverfront below Alfama in the sixteenth century. It illustrates how deeply the lives of black and white people were entwined in the Portuguese capital. (Wikimedia Commons)

7. A view of the riverside Jerónimos Church and Monastery in a 1657 painting by Filipe Lobo, held at Lisbon's Museum of Ancient Art (Museu Nacional de Arte Antiga), also showing white men on horses accompanied by black men on foot as well as black women street-sellers. (Wikimedia Commons)

8. A famous photograph of the early twentieth-century African-born artist and bohemian Almada Negreiros, wearing a full-body flight suit of the kind used by pilots in the First World War. (Wikimedia Commons)

9. An old, hand-painted Portuguese ceramic tile, held at Lisbon's Tile Museum (Museu do Azulejo), depicting the Terreiro do Paço, now known as the Praça do Comércio. (Vlada Photo/Shutterstock.com)

10. The enchanting cloisters of the Jerónimos Monastery are richly sculptured, like stone filigree. (Benny Marty/Shutterstock.com)

11. An 1813 engraving called *Sopa dos Pobres em Arroios* (Soup Kitchen in Arroios, a district of Lisbon), one of Portuguese artist Domingos Sequeira's most celebrated works. It depicts soup being distributed to the poor from rural areas who sought shelter in the capital, their crops having been destroyed by advancing French troops during an 1810 invasion. (Wikimedia Commons)

12. Sunrise over Vasco da Gama Bridge, completed in 1998 and Europe's longest. (Lance Sagar/Shutterstock.com)

13. The 25 de Abril Bridge, Lisbon's first over the River Tagus. Completed in 1966, it was originally named Salazar Bridge after the country's dictator at the time. (Wikimedia Commons)

express some of their own culture and, perhaps, let their hair down. A wide-eyed friar described in 1633 how black people on one such occasion wore colourful clothes and danced down the street, "some of them like they do in Africa, to the sound of castanets, guitars and drums, flutes and African instruments. Some men carried bows and arrows, the women had baskets on their head given to them by their master."

The eighteenth-century Italian writer Guiseppe Baretti offered a glimpse of how bigotry and racism stalked Lisbon. Not only was he disgusted by the awful smells and ravenous dogs he encountered as he walked around the city, but he was also taken aback by how blacks and whites had produced children together. That gave rise to an informal caste system. "To such a degree has the original race of the Portuguese been depraved, that, to be a Blanco, that is, a perfect white, is become a title of honor," Baretti wrote, "so that, when a Portuguese says he is a Blanco, it is not to be understood that he is a white, but that he is a man of honor, a person of family and consequence."

Black people were perceived as being inherently unequal to whites and barely possible to educate. The historian Oliveira Martins attempted to prove scientifically, no less, in the 1880s that Africans were "congenitally inferior". However, they were believed, as in the 1766 description of the escaped slave, to have sunny dispositions despite their misfortune. They were also regarded as being musically gifted, and their playing was especially popular in the famous Corpus Christi procession, where Pai Paulino performed. The pageant had been a major Lisbon tradition since the Middle Ages, centred on the downtown church called Igreja dos Mártires. A José Malhoa oil painting from 1886 shows the group known as Os

Pretos de São Jorge (The St George Blacks), which for years played in the procession. Two of them beat drums, two played trumpets and one was on a flute. All five of them wore red and orange striped capes. This is how the writer José Fialho de Almeida described the splash they made: "Lisbon was theirs, and there was nobody watching the procession, with its innumerable crosses and thick with priests ... who didn't cry out impatiently to those around them, How dull! Bring on the blacks now!"

Later, for twentieth-century dictator Salazar, such musical merriment had to have useful political ends, or it was unwanted. A *fado* song called "Mãe Preta" (Black Mother), a version of a Brazilian song, gained popularity in 1950s Portugal but as it spread beyond the capital it was abruptly banned by Salazar. The touching song told of the hardships endured by a slave wet-nurse, nurturing her white master's child while her own child goes without.

More palatable entertainment for Salazar was a showcase of the Portuguese Empire and its singular deeds. The 1940 Portuguese World Exhibition was a mammoth propaganda stunt. The four-month event was intended to demonstrate the country's greatness, as well as take Portuguese minds off World War II, which Portugal stayed out of but still felt acutely through food and fuel shortages. Staged in Belém, the huge exhibition sought to recapture the spirit of the Age of Discovery and, with a swagger, flaunt its conquests. It featured areas where African life was recreated in technicolour cliché: thatched huts, cooking over wooden fires and bare-chested men and women who were brought especially from Angola and Mozambique. They sang and danced to their traditional music. There were lions, zebras and monkeys, too. And the inevitable elephant.

The people of Lisbon were both shocked and thrilled by it all. Lisbon newspapers carried articles describing how black people lived in Africa. As Ricardo Chibanga remarked, there were few black people in Lisbon under the dictatorship, and the Portuguese were unfamiliar with African cultures beyond school textbooks and news bulletins. The curiosity was reciprocal: one black man brought to the capital from the African empire told a Lisbon journalist he usually only saw one white man a year, at the time of tax collection in his village. Once the dictatorship was gone, after a 1974 coup, the exhibition was criticized as creating a "human zoo".

That coup, known as the Carnation Revolution, brought independence for the African colonies and generated a new surge of Africans heading to Lisbon. In their minds' eye, the former imperial capital was a land of milk and honey. The city's African bonds, which had slackened since the nineteenth century, drew tighter again a century later.

The first big wave of African immigrants had come from Cape Verde in the years leading up to the revolution. In the 1960s, thousands of creole-speaking Cape Verdean men arrived in Lisbon. They were needed as labourers to make up for Portuguese men who went the other way, to fight African independence movements, or who left for better-paying jobs elsewhere in Europe. These Cape Verdeans settled in what became known as the "creole triangle"—an area of Lisbon around São Bento, the site of the parliament building, Rua do Poço dos Negros and the Santa Catarina neighbourhood. In this part of the city, stores opened selling imported Cape Verdean food, restaurants sold Cape Verdean fare, nightclubs played Cape Verdean music, and travel companies offered air passage and freight to and from Cape Verde.

After independence, these immigrants' families and friends came to join them. Cape Verdeans began to refer to Lisbon as their nine-island archipelago's tenth island. West African creole grew into Lisbon's second-most-spoken language at the time, some claimed, though the evidence to support that was anecdotal rather than empirical. These immigrants worked in low-paid blue-collar jobs. The men went onto construction sites; the women often took cleaning jobs. They found places to live that were on the fringes, physically and metaphorically. With the Portuguese capital short of housing, they gathered scraps of corrugated iron and scavenged wood and bricks to create *bairros de lata* (shantytowns) on the edges of the city. Women carried water to their homes in buckets on their head while their children skipped around on the bare dirt. To many these seemed like scenes from Africa, and they were viewed as a disagreeable feature of Lisbon until European Union development funds allowed the government and City Council to clear them away by the early twenty-first century. The cramped, high-rise housing projects thrown up to replace the shantytowns did little to rid these communities of stigma, however. They bred the same social problems witnessed in other European cities.

The Portuguese who returned home from the colonial outposts after independence also came with African culture in their heart. These people were called *retornados*. They made a similar journey to the French *pieds noirs*, but two decades later as Portugal became the last European country to surrender its African colonies. The Portuguese had been the first to settle in sub-Saharan Africa, and they were the last to leave. Half a million Portuguese came home in the space of about a year. Despite difficulties, Lisbon made room for these new arrivals. There was a crush that forced the government to requisition all available Lisbon hotel rooms, and the city's quayside was for weeks piled high with wooden crates containing belongings shipped from Africa. Many *retornados* still nurse a deep fondness for Africa.

The immigrants have endowed Lisbon with something of an African feel. It is not hard to find a restaurant offering *muamba*, a stewed chicken dish from Angola, or Cape Verde's very substantial *cachupa*, which as well as corn and beans contains boiled bananas and potatoes, or *calulu* from São Tomé with banana, cassava and ground corn, or a Mozambican curry that is just as authentic as Indian equivalents. All these recipes pack a spicy punch and are not for the faint-hearted. At the Restaurante Tambarina in Rua do Poço dos Negros, most of those dishes are on the menu. The low-ceilinged establishment hard against the pavement belongs to Senhor Domingos de Brito, a slightly-built Cape Verdean who came to Lisbon in the 1970s. He blends his own home-made chilli sauce, using fresh tomato and onion, which adds an aftertaste to dishes that might be described as lively. At the end of the meal he offers a shot of Cape Verde's *ponche*, a throat-pinching firewater, to help digest the load.

Like African food, that continent's music and nightlife have also seeped into Lisbon culture and put down roots in a European home. The music has brought new words into Portuguese vocabulary and new choreography into the capital's night clubs. There is the *kizomba*, an Angolan style of electronic music accompanied by a slow, belly-to-belly dance which the British tabloid *The Daily Express* once described as "incredibly sexual". Cape Verde brought the *morna*, a romantic, smouldering, mostly acoustic style of composition made internationally famous by Cesária Évora, the Barefoot Diva. A livelier Cape Verdean style is *funaná*, with accordion accompaniment. Then there is *kuduro*, made famous by Buraka Som Sistema.

This band drew on their experiences of Africa and their experiences of Africans in Lisbon's blue-collar commuter belt. Two of its members grew up in Angola and two in Amadora, on Lisbon's rim. The group married influences from Brazil, Africa and Europe, and achieved acclaim over ten years before splitting up in 2016. They produced a powerful alloy of house music, funk, grime and dubstep, with unvarnished and occasionally playful lyrics, mostly in Portuguese but also drawing on Angolan expressions. "We managed to ... create something specific, made to fit the city of Lisbon," said João Barbosa, a white member of the band who is known as Branko. The group's hits helped stir Lisbon's cultural mix. Many young Portuguese, who normally were pushed by marketing campaigns toward Western cultural commodities, metaphorically crossed the frontier to Africa and liked what they found.

Kalaf Ângelo, another member of the band who is also a writer and designer, said after living in Lisbon for some twenty years that his 2014 book, *O Angolano Que Comprou Lisboa (por Metade do Preço)* (The Angolan who Bought Lisbon (for Half the Price)), was a "love letter" to the city he had chosen to stay in. "History has connected us," he said, "and there is no way of avoiding that."

José Eduardo Agualusa, the Angolan writer, and Mozambican novelist Mia Couto are admired by Portuguese readers, but Africans and people of African heritage are on the whole conspicuous by their absence from the cultural, political and professional elites. They are unlikely to be seen teaching in a Lisbon classroom, treating the sick or speaking in Parliament, though the justice minister who took office in 2015, Francisca Van Dunem, was born in Angola and is the exception that proves the rule. As the Brazilian writer José Ramos Tinhorão noted in his 1988 book on black people in Portugal, they are a "silent presence".

Even so, evidence of their long Lisbon history is within easy reach. Dozens of Africans still gather every day in São Domingos Square, next to Rossio. They meet to chat, some in traditional, colourful dress, some standing and others lounging. There are men and women, Christians and Muslims among them. Some set out baskets and sell those eye-watering African chillies. A passer-by would not imagine that Africans have been assembling on this very spot for about 500 years.

The São Domingos Church, part of its namesake monastery, was home to the first black brotherhood. The Brotherhood of Our Lady of the Rosary of Black Men was founded here in the early sixteenth century. It was the first of its kind in the capital and was helped financially by King Manuel I, who in 1508 granted it an allowance for each caravel that arrived from West Africa. The brotherhood was already accepting white men, and from the mid-sixteenth century it was divided into two: "one for honourable people, and the other for the freed blacks and slaves of Lisbon". The reasoning of the Catholic clergy could at times be tortuous. While it segregated those of African blood to avoid conflicts with white people, it gave its blessing to the worship of black saints. The Graça Church, for example, possesses an altar with the figure of Our Lady of the Rosary and the figures of St Ephigenia and St Elesbaan, both from Ethiopia, and St Benedict the Moor. São Domingos

Square was where freed African men gathered to offer themselves for work as whitewashers.

The quarters where Africans settled in the late twentieth century—São Bento and Santa Catarina, and around Rua do Poço dos Negros—feature heavily in Lisbon's African past. Near to Santa Catarina Church in the sixteenth century was the Cruz de Pau (Wooden Cross), where slaves were tied up and punished. Rua do Poço dos Negros (literally, Black Pit Street) is named after the deep hole where King Manuel decreed in 1515 that dead slaves be thrown. They had previously been discarded in the streets where they gave off a stench and were eaten by dogs. Lime was tossed into the pit to quicken the decomposition of bodies.

Such macabre medieval details contrast sharply with this part of the city nowadays. These neighbourhoods feel like *echt* Lisbon and constitute some of the nicest parts of town. The steep streets are lined with slender, four- and five-storey apartment buildings, many of which are painted in pastel colours—pale yellow or faded pink or light blue. The scene feels straight out of one of Manuel Cargaleiro's geometric, colour-splashed paintings. The buildings have wrought-iron balconies painted dark green. Steel tram lines glint in the slanting sun. Washing hangs over quiet, cobbled streets that are narrow, just wide enough for one car, creating that village feeling so often encountered in Lisbon. Hills promise the reward of a spectacular vista at their brow but more houses and streets stretch out, in straight lines and soft curves, often leading to a small square with plane trees and a fountain. Suddenly, unexpectedly, the arresting panorama anticipated earlier springs into view. In the distance is the smooth, seductive blue line of the river or the ocean. Only the names of some streets, such as Beco do Carrasco (Executioner's Alley), hint at the district's macabre past.

Just to the west of this area is a place once known as Lisbon's most African neighbourhood. It even had an African name: Mocambo, meaning "hamlet" or "place of shelter" in Kimbundu, the principal African language spoken in Angola and its capital Luanda. Located on the edge of the city when it was created by royal decree in 1593, this *bairro* was where freed slaves and nuns lived. The Convento das Trinas do Mocambo was the biggest of several convents in the area and needed cheap labour. Nearby brickyards and blacksmiths also provided work. From the seventeenth century, the neighbourhood was gradually taken over by fishermen, mostly from northern Portugal. The name was changed to Madragoa, its current designation, perhaps taken from Casa das Madres de Goa, a religious house for ladies from India. The Convento das Trinas is now the headquarters of the Hydrographic Institute.

Some busts of African figures that were made by sculptor Manuel de Oliveira for the 1940 Portuguese World Exhibition can be found at the Tropical Botanical Gardens in Belém. Scattered around the grounds, the black busts about three times bigger than real life stand on white cement pedestals with no indication of what they are. The major public works projects that transformed Lisbon in the 1990s, such as the 12-kilometre-long Vasco da Gama Bridge over the Tagus, bear no mention of the vital and abundant African labour that helped build them.

The inattentiveness toward black history suggests a case of cultural amnesia. Local ears are not attuned to the silence of the African presence. While the capital's Jewish history has captured attention in recent times, Lisbon's African legacy is not something the city tries to market to the millions of tourists it attracts every year. Perhaps the Portuguese need to acknowledge their rich African heritage themselves, before they can tell others about it.

FIVE—CATASTROPHE

All Saints' Day in 1755 fell on a Saturday. It began with what was, by all accounts, a beautiful November morning, crisp, with a blue sky and bright sunshine as a spell of fine weather from the previous month lingered in the fashion of those agreeable Indian summers that still bless Lisbon. Shortly after church bells tolled for 9:30 a.m., people would later recall, there was a deep rumbling sound, like faraway thunder. Others likened it to heavy carriages hurrying through the city's streets. It was, in fact, the drum-roll for the biggest earthquake to strike Western Europe in modern history.

Three violent jolts, with brief intervals between them, immediately shattered about two-thirds of Lisbon's buildings, which came down with a terrifying crash. A 6-metre-high tsunami sped up the Tagus, capsizing ships and dragging survivors on land to their death. A massive fire broke out that burned unchecked for six days and made it bright enough to read at night. Earth, water, fire: it felt like the wrath of God, Old Testament-style. The disaster clipped Lisbon's wings after a half-century of lofty ambition financed by Brazilian gold, and the lengthy reconstruction would change forever the tenor and the tone of the city's downtown district. Those seven deadly minutes shook Europe, too, bringing urgent questions about God's intentions and the value of science.

The people of Lisbon were no strangers to earthquakes. In the previous 400 years or so they had endured fifteen of them, with substantial damage recorded in 1356, 1531 and 1597. The 1755 quake, however, was the Big One. Its epicentre was 250 kilometres to the south-west, beneath the sea. Tectonic plates stirred and the sandy, gravelly earth under some of the oldest parts of Lisbon twitched. The city's stone and timber buildings crumbled. The narrow streets of Lisbon, which over the centuries had grown haphazardly, according to necessity and opportunity rather than grand design, were death traps.

The destruction was epic in scale. Thousands of people were killed, in varied and horrible manners: either crushed or suffocated or burned or drowned. The survivors had traumatic tales to tell. Their chilling accounts are the stuff of modern disaster movies.

Father Manoel Portal was buried in the rubble of a monastery called Convento da Congregação do Oratório, his leg trapped beneath fallen masonry. Two men pulled him free and he limped into the street, "my eyes covered in blood". The scene outside was horrifying. "As soon as I had left by the carriage gate, I was treading on the dead," he recounted in his book the following year entitled *Story of the ruin of the city of Lisbon caused by the fearsome earthquake and fire that reduced to dust and ashes the best and biggest part of this unhappy city*.

Thomas Chase was on the top floor of a building that collapsed beneath his feet, plunging him down four storeys. This Englishman living in Lisbon was badly injured, with broken bones, sprains, cuts and bruises, but he managed to drag himself out of the debris. On the street, survivors were gripped by dread and terror as the air turned grey. "The people were all at prayers, covered over with dust, and the light appeared just as if it had been a very dark day," Chase wrote in a letter home the month after the earthquake.

The Reverend Charles Davy, a visiting Anglican priest, also mentioned the "prodigious clouds of dust and lime", probably a consequence of weeks without rain. The dust darkening the sun left him gasping for breath for ten minutes and added to the feeling of apocalypse. Survivors, wandering around in shock, were coated in the pale dust, like those near to the 11 September 2001 terror attacks in New York. Bloodied people staggered through the rubble, searching for loved ones. Children screamed. Dogs and mules were left to die in noisy agony.

The superstitious people of Lisbon were spooked, according to the Reverend Richard Goddard, the vicar of Lacock Abbey in south-west England, who stumbled in a daze through the city streets amid the aftershocks. All Saints' Day was one of the biggest Catholic occasions, when saints are celebrated. He wrote:

> No Words can express the Horror of my Situation at that Instant, involved in almost total Darkness, surrounded with a City falling into Ruins, and Crowds of People screaming, and calling out for Mercy, while from the violent and convulsive Motions of the Earth, we expected every Moment to be swallowed up.

The calamity whipped people into a religious frenzy. They fell to their knees in the street and prayed; they kissed and brandished crucifixes. The Reverend Goddard said that when he came upon one group they forcibly converted him on the spot. He feared the "mob" of more than 100 people would kill him as a heretic if he objected. Afterwards, they smothered him, "almost killing me with their Embraces; several Priests falling down before me, embracing the Knees and kissing the Feet of their New Convert." Apparently, he reported, they believed that converting someone would help atone for their sins and spare them further suffering.

But their ordeal was far from over. Some, fleeing falling masonry and blocked streets, ran in desperation to the nearest wide-open space they knew: Terreiro do Paço, the broad square next to the king's palace overlooking the Tagus. It was a fatal choice. Shortly, the waters of the river and the Sea of Straw began to buck and churn, tearing ships from their anchors like toys. Davy recorded this "heaving and swelling" of the water and continued: "In an instant there appeared, at some small distance, a large body of water, rising as it were like a mountain. It came on foaming and roaring, and rushed toward the shore with such impetuosity, that we all immediately ran for our lives as fast as possible." Ships were "tumbling and tossing about as in a violent storm", while others "were whirled around with incredible swiftness; several large boats were turned keel upwards." The formidable Stone Quay, weighing many tonnes, and the people who sought safety on it "were all swallowed up, as in a whirlpool, and nevermore appeared."

José Moreira de Mendonça, another earthquake survivor, said the bed of the Tagus was laid bare and that the retreating tsunami sucked people back into the river. Outside the city, Davy reported, as some people "were riding on horseback in the great road leading to Belem, one side of which lies open to the river, the waves rushed in with so much rapidity that they were obliged to gallop as fast as possible to the upper grounds, for fear of being carried away."

The tsunami, which swept up into the city almost as far as Rossio Square, was so powerful it was felt on three continents, as North Africa also suffered damage. About ten hours later it washed up in the Caribbean, too.

Chase observed that the survivors gathered in the Terreiro do Paço Square thought it was Judgement Day. They prayed and clutched crucifixes, and each time an aftershock hit they cried out "Mercy! … in the most doleful accents imaginable". Davy noted how social status was rendered meaningless as "people of both sexes, and of all ranks and conditions, among whom I observed some of the principal canons of the patriarchal church, in their purple robes and rochets" were praying on their knees, "every one striking his breast and crying out incessantly, *Miserecordia meu Dios!* (sic)" ("Have mercy, my Lord"). There were also "ladies half dressed, and some without shoes".

At 2:00 p.m. the dust began to settle and the sun reappeared, Chase said. As the air cleared he noticed that the royal palace was burning. Candles, lamps and hearths in homes and churches across Lisbon set in motion the third calamity of the day. A stiff north-east breeze in this windy Atlantic city whipped up firestorms, stoked by the timber of houses. Most survivors had fled, to the river or the countryside, leaving few people able or willing to fight the flames.

Davy recalled that the city "was on fire at least in a hundred different places at once, and thus continued burning for six days together, without intermission, or the least attempt being made to stop its progress." The fire spread from the Ribeira area on the riverbank to Rossio and Bairro Alto and then up to Alfama, according to Mendonça. He reckoned that one-third of the city—including its wealthiest and most populous areas—was engulfed by the flames. By nightfall, Davy said, "the whole city appeared in a blaze, which was so bright that I could easily see to read by it." The fire spread with "irrepressible swiftness," Chase reported. Both sides of the opulent Rua Nova were in flames. A few breaths of the toxic smoke were enough to kill. That night, there were still bodies lying in street, and Chase could hear people crying out for help.

The flames consumed much of what was left standing in the heart of one of Europe's greatest cities. The fire sealed the fate of Lisbon's riches. If buildings had simply fallen, it would have been possible to salvage something. But the flames obliterated so much more.

Mendonça, in his 1758 book *História Universal dos Terremotos* (Universal History of Earthquakes), lists three dozen churches and about sixty convents and monasteries that were lost that day. Still nowadays, when referring to grave events, the Portuguese say *Cai o Carmo e a Trindade* (The Carmo and the Trindade come crashing down), in reference to the two prominent Lisbon convents of those names which fell during the earthquake. There were thousands of rare books in them all. Also gone were six hospitals, including the formidable Todos os Santos; the royal palace; the royal opera house; the royal archive; the royal arsenal; the archbishop's palace; the India House; and the Customs House. The royal palace's library, reduced to ashes, housed tens of thousands of books. The palace itself had tapestries on the walls and Persian carpets on the floor that were of incalculable worth. Gone, too, were royal documents that held invaluable records from the Age of Expansion.

The British historian T.D. Kendrick provided an illustration of the priceless property and possessions that were lost by considering the Lisbon palace of the Marques of Louriçal, which was destroyed. The riches included, among other things, some 200 pictures, including works by Titian, Correggio and Rubens, 18,000 printed books, 1,000 manuscripts, including a history written by the Emperor Charles V in his own hand, and a vast collection of maps and charts relating to the Portuguese voyages of discovery.

Once it was all over, Lisbon looked like a bombed-out city. Davy wrote:

> I assure you that this extensive and opulent city is now nothing but a vast heap of ruins; that the rich and the poor are at present upon a level; some thousands of families which but the day before had been easy in their circumstances, being now scattered about in the fields, wanting every conveniency of life, and finding none able to relieve them.

Estimates of the death toll vary wildly. Some reckon it was as high as 60,000, but a more modest—and broadly accepted—assessment is that between 10,000 and 20,000 people perished. That was in a city of more than 200,000. Two-thirds of Lisbon's homes were rendered uninhabitable.

The royal family was at its country house in Belém when the quake struck and was unharmed. But, the papal nuncio in Lisbon, Filippo Acciaiuoli, wrote in a letter to a brother, the king fled his palace in his nightshirt. For several days he and the rest of the royal family slept outdoors in the back of a wagon until a tent was found. King José was so shaken by the event that from then on he lived in wood and canvas tents for fear of falling masonry and did not return to the city centre for six years. Lisbon's nobles also had to live rough.

Some three dozen palaces were destroyed, forcing the aristocrats to scavenge timber and canvas from the riverside shipyards to erect makeshift huts.

Acciaiuoli noted that survivors walked around in a daze. He said that "in summary, everything is horror and misery, and Lisbon is a pile of rubble." Davy similarly remarked that the earthquake "has made this once flourishing, opulent, and populous city, a scene of the utmost horror and desolation." The most conspicuous Lisbon scar of that week, when the achievements of six centuries were undone and the city's treasures stripped away, is the Carmo Convent.

The disaster resonated across Europe. It inspired poems and novels; philosophical, theological and scientific treatises; and artistic representations. Eminent voices of the Enlightenment, such as the German philosopher Immanuel Kant and the French philosopher Jean-Jacques Rousseau and writer Voltaire, joined in the debate about what the earthquake meant. The English Methodist John Wesley felt compelled to speak out, too. Was the hand of God at work, or could the phenomenon be explained by science? Why did God choose Lisbon, where the Inquisition flourished and from where the Portuguese had taken the word of God across the globe? And why did it happen on that holy day?

The sensational news of Lisbon's misfortune sent a chill across the continent. Was anywhere safe from such a fate? The German writer Johann Wolfgang von Goethe described the disaster as "an extraordinary world event". In his memoirs he commented: "Perhaps the demon of terror had never so speedily and powerfully diffused his terrors over the earth." In January 1756, the *Gazette de Cologne* in Germany remarked that "the earthquake is still on people's lips."

Lisbon was no longer best known for its elephants and rhinos.

* * *

Born nearly fifty-five years after the earthquake, Diogo Alves was an oxherd by day and by night, a serial killer. The scene of many of his nineteenth-century murders was the spectacular Lisbon aqueduct, a city landmark that remains iconic. This architectural gem withstood the 1755 earthquake and serves today as an emphatic reminder of an electrifying period in the first half of the eighteenth century that furnished the city with memorable monuments.

The Aqueduto das Águas Livres (Free Waters Aqueduct) approaches Lisbon from countryside on the west and enters the city across the deep Alcântara Valley, where Filipe II of Spain's forces had routed the local defenders in 1580. Alves used to lie in wait for women on the pathway that runs along the top of the aqueduct's striking Alcântara span. The pathway was commonly used by washerwomen who tended the laundry of wealthy families in the city. After robbing them of their meagre earnings, Alves flung the women over the wall and to their death dozens of metres below. Officials and locals initially presumed the deaths were suicides. As the numbers of dead grew, that explanation grew increasingly unlikely. The mounting deaths, reported in Lisbon newspapers, began to spread terror in the city.

The authorities closed the pathway, called Passeio dos Arcos (Walkway of the Arches). But Alves wasn't stopped until he and his gang were caught red-handed at a burglary in Rua das Flores, in downtown Lisbon, where they murdered a doctor's family. The proceedings of the trial that sentenced him to death are held at the Torre do Tombo national archive in Lisbon. Alves was hanged in 1841, placing him among the last people to be executed for their crimes before Portugal fully outlawed capital punishment in 1867.

The memory of his wicked deeds lived on, however. Alves was originally from Galicia, in north-west Spain, and his crimes inspired a backlash against other Galician immigrants in Lisbon. They were numerous and commonly made a living as water-sellers, gradually replacing the slaves who had traditionally done that job. Galicians also made up the city's first fire brigade. Alves' infamy extended to the following century, when his crimes were the subject of Portuguese cinema's second feature film. *Os Crimes de Diogo Alves* (The Crimes of Diogo Alves), a silent black-and-white film by João Tavares, had its first showing in April 1911 at the Salão da Trindade and later had regular showings at O Paraíso de Lisboa cinema. On a more macabre note, after he was hanged curious scientists had Alves' head cut off and set aside for research. It is still kept, in formaldehyde, in a glass jar at Lisbon University's Faculty of Medicine. He has thin, russet-coloured hair down to his ear lobes and a wispy beard. And his eyes are wide open.

Traffic nowadays snakes around the mighty legs of the aqueduct as it crosses the Alcântara Valley in still spectacular fashion. This section is the most striking feature of the Aqueducto das Águas Livres national monument and is an outstanding accomplishment. It features the biggest stone arch of its kind in the world. The *arco grande*, marked with a stone plaque, stands more than 65 metres high and more than 28 metres wide. Legend has it that this arch has three keystones and that only a special sound can sunder them. Nobody knows what the sound is, but it certainly wasn't the sound of an earthquake.

The aqueduct is plain and to the point, free of decorative flourishes. Its splendour comes from its size. "In solidity and grandeur, it is a work worthy of ancient Rome," Sir Nathaniel Wraxall, a British traveller, wrote in his eighteenth-century memoirs. Samuel Broughton, a British officer who passed through Lisbon during the nineteenth-century Peninsular War, remarked that the aqueduct was "a sublime monument of human ingenuity, taste, and industry: certainly, since the time of the ancients, no European production has equalled it in usefulness and grandeur."

This Alcântara section is the trunk of the entire water collection network. It contains thirty-five arches over 941 metres. The footpath, which can be visited, runs for about 1.5 kilometres along each side of the central gallery where water flowed. The hard, weathered stone speaks eloquently of the structure's continuing sturdiness. Its clean straight lines and symmetry prefigure what the medieval centre of the city would, within decades, look like.

The network that harnessed and channelled water initially ran 14 kilometres, stretching from the Sintra hills north-west of Lisbon, where water is abundant and where a generous spring has been known since the twelfth century, to the Amoreiras neighbourhood of the capital. It follows a route first traced by an old Roman aqueduct. Like the Roman version, it used gravity to deliver the water. In Amoreiras, the Mãe d'Água water deposit, with 5-metre-thick walls, stored the water that was distributed mostly through underground galleries to two dozen city fountains. These often majestic fountains, mostly designed by architects, became a city hallmark.

Additional water sources repeatedly had to be found to keep pace with demand. Built up over decades and finally completed on the cusp of the nineteenth century, the network eventually extended 58 kilometres. It was made up of pipes and conduits above and below ground that conveyed water into Lisbon from about sixty springs. It was a feat of Baroque engineering that remained in use until 1968.

King João V had signed the order for building work to begin in 1731. It allowed the enterprise to cross any and all private property without exception. Illustrious architects, engineers and stonemasons were assembled, including architects António Canevari, an Italian, Carlos Mardel, a Hungarian, and Johann Friedrich Ludwig, a German; and Portuguese army engineer Colonel Manuel da Maia. Other specialists would come to replace them over the years, until the first water reached Amoreiras in 1748, as the project made a stuttering start amid bickering over such things as whether to use iron or stone pipes (stone won).

Five years after construction began, Sergeant-Major Custódio Vieira da Silva replaced Maia, who himself had replaced Canevari, and became a central figure in the aqueduct's history. He had previously come up with an ingenious method for lifting 120 bronze bells into the bell towers of the Mafra convent north of Lisbon. He is believed to have used the same technique to build the Alcântara aqueduct's arches, but inventories and logs recording the construction were other casualties of the earthquake. Vieira da Silva oversaw the completion of the *arco grande* in 1744 before dying the same year.

The Aqueducto das Águas Livres was one of the biggest civil engineering works ever undertaken in Portugal and one that had an enormous impact on people's lives in the capital. Lisbon had long endured chronic water problems. Francisco de Holanda, in his 1571 book *Da Fábrica que Falece à Cidade de Lisboa*, had rhetorically asked: "If Lisbon wants to be the biggest and noblest city of the world ... how come it doesn't have enough water to give the people of the world?"

There was plenty of water in the Tagus, but it was salty. By the early eighteenth century, with the population reaching some 250,000, the problem was acute. Public fountains sometimes ran dry in the summer. The scarcer the supply, the higher water-sellers pitched their prices, stoking resentment against them. Fights broke out at fountains. Something had to be done.

The municipal authorities called on the Senate, pleading poverty. But the monarch compelled the city's officials to act. Finally, the Senate gave its blessing to a new tax on certain common goods such as meat, wine and olive oil. The revenue would go to pay for a clean, reliable water supply for the capital. The project changed Lisbon for the better and reflected glory on King João V, who during his reign earned the epithet the Magnanimous One.

The monarch, in recognition of the outlay shouldered by the people of Lisbon, ordered a commemorative plaque placed on the aqueduct in the Amoreiras neighbourhood. It read:

> In the year 1748, in the reign of the pious, joyful and magnanimous King João V, the Senate and the people of Lisbon, at the expense of these people and to their great satisfaction, brought into the city the Free Waters that had been craved for two centuries, and this was done over twenty years of hard work, levelling and cutting through hills over a distance of 9,000 paces.

Years after the earthquake, authorities took that plaque down and replaced it with one that made no mention of the cost being met by the people. The new one read:

> With King João V, the greatest of monarchs, overseeing Portugal's well-being, very salubrious water was brought into the city, through extremely solid aqueducts that will last forever, and which form an extension 9,000 paces long, this construction having been achieved with an acceptable level of public expenditure and with the earnest approval of all.

The empire's bounty afforded the king an opportunity to hatch ambitious plans. After a listless seventeenth century, Lisbon's dreams of grandeur returned on the back of Brazil's blessings. The first shipment of Brazilian gold—500 kilograms of it—arrived in Lisbon in 1699, eight years before João V came to the throne. From then, driven by a gold rush, the cargoes grew and reached their peak in 1720, with 25 tonnes offloaded at the Lisbon quayside. On top of the 20 per cent tax it took on that, the Crown's income included revenue from taxes on Brazilian diamonds, sugar, tobacco and timber, as well as the trade in African slaves sent to harvest it all. The Crown had never been so rich, even during the golden days of the sixteenth century.

Plentiful cash invites extravagance, and João V was not squeamish about splurging the Crown's wealth. His reign became a byword for lavish spending. Comparisons were drawn with the French King Louis XIV. Wraxall, the British traveller, described the massive convent and palace at Mafra as "the Versailles of Portugal". It has more than 4,700 doors and windows and 156 staircases, and in the busiest phase of its construction employed some 52,000 workers. It also came close to breaking the back of the Portuguese economy.

While the aqueduct brought practical improvements, other projects such as the king's keen patronage of the arts and sciences aimed to confer international prestige on his reign. The bibliophile monarch instructed Portugal's diplomatic corps across Europe to purchase books with which he stocked the *biblioteca real* (royal library) in the Paço da Ribeira. A committee of wise men was placed in charge of acquisitions and cataloguing. The library also housed novel objects for study. The writer and cleric António Caetano de Sousa reported that, apart from the "many thousands of books", the library held modern mathematical instruments and clocks.

The court in Lisbon was once again talked about for its opulence and consumption. The royal household bore the cost of up to 400 courtiers. Fabulous wealth was flaunted at home and abroad. In foreign policy, it was employed to secure influence. The most flamboyant example of this approach, and an embodiment of Portugal's early eighteenth-century splendour, is still on show at a museum in Belém.

The king sent an embassy to Pope Clement XI in Rome in July 1716, and this time there were no elephants. The mission's centrepiece was a golden carriage that, three centuries later, remains stunning. It is kept at Lisbon's National Carriage Museum, and it is easy to see why the sumptuous Portuguese procession along the streets of Rome turned heads and set tongues wagging. Its pageant-like progress to the Quirinale Palace, now the official home of the Italian president, took hours. It set out in the early morning and returned after midnight.

Five large carriages and ten smaller ones took the king's ambassador in Rome, the Marquis of Fontes, and his retinue to meet the pontiff. They included the *Coche do Embaixador*

(Ambassador's Coach), the *Coche dos Oceanos* (Coach of the Oceans) and the *Coche da Coroação de Lisboa* (Coach of the Coronation of Lisbon). It had all taken years to prepare.

The Coach of the Oceans stole the show. Around 8 metres long and close to 3 metres high, it has Baroque wooden carvings of human figures and cherubs, all burnished with gold leaf. It is upholstered with red velvet and golden silk. On the back, as the figure of Apollo looks on, two bearded elderly men, representing the Atlantic and Indian oceans, shake hands, with a globe in the background. The scene symbolizes the link between two worlds which the Portuguese achieved by rounding the Cape of Good Hope.

The embassy was a shrewd calculation by King João V, who was intelligent as well as learned and pious. He found other ways to impress the pope. With the Ottoman Empire encroaching through the Mediterranean, the pontiff asked for help in beating the Ottomans back. Portugal jumped at the opportunity, while Spain held back, and the Portuguese fought alongside men from Venice and the Papal States. Another diplomatic trump card for the Portuguese envoy in Rome was the proselytizing Portugal had conducted during the Age of Expansion.

What Lisbon wanted now in return was the elevation, in the ranks of the Catholic Church, of Lisbon. The investments paid dividends. Three months after the Marquis of Fonte's visit, the pope issued a bull granting the Portuguese capital the status of patriarchate—a garland previously bestowed only on Venice. The royal chapel in the Paço da Ribeira became the seat of the Patriarch of Lisbon—a bishop one notch down in ecclesiastical rank from the pope. It deeply enhanced Lisbon's international prestige.

The royal chapel, located next to the palace, roughly where Lisbon City Hall stands today, was already known for its splendour. The French encyclopaedist Louis Moréri's *Great Historical Dictionary* of 1674 had described it as one of Europe's greatest churches at the time. Now, as the city's Igreja Patriarcal, it acquired even greater riches. They were swept away in 1755, but a glimpse of what it was like can be gleaned from the São Roque Church, which was largely spared by the earthquake.

The Igreja de São Roque, next to the Bairro Alto, was where the Jesuits established themselves in Portugal in the sixteenth century. Its Capela de São João Batista (St John the Baptist Chapel) is a breathtaking piece of religious art and is regarded as a miniature version of the one-time Patriarchal Church. It is also a masterpiece of European eighteenth-century art. King João V ordered the chapel in 1740 from the Roman architects Luigi Vanvitelli and Nicola Salvi, who built it in Rome between 1742 and 1747. Blessed by Pope Benedict XIV—an act for which the Portuguese king paid handsomely—the chapel was dismantled and shipped on three carracks to Lisbon, where it was reassembled at the São Roque Church. It is exceptional and extravagant. Beyond the plentiful gilt bronze, it presents a kaleidoscope of colour: maroon Carrara marble, lapis lazuli, creamy alabaster, rich ruby agate, purple amethyst, yellow marble and jade. The mosaic work, by Mattia Moretti and Enrico Enuo, is delicately hued and exquisite. It is, perhaps, a little inappropriate for a saint remembered for his austere lifestyle.

Some say the monarch's extravagant purchase was an attempt to quash gossip, at home and abroad, that his kingdom was not as financially well-endowed as it appeared.

Certainly, the Crown's coffers were depleted when the Magnanimous One died in 1750. Brazil's bountifulness had ebbed as gold mines were exhausted, and Portugal's trade in the East was being squeezed by its bigger European rivals. João V's forty-three-year reign took up most of the first half of the eighteenth century, bequeathing to Lisbon a Baroque extravaganza and lean finances. For a monarch's pet project, however, money could always be found.

King José I played the violin and his passion for music matched his father João V's love of books. Father and son also shared a taste for grandeur. When José came to the throne in 1750, he too set about putting his stamp on Lisbon and making an emphatic statement to Europe. No expense was spared to build a glittering, grandiose opera house that would create a sensation and win fame as one of the continent's grandest theatres. It opened on Queen Mariana Vitória's thirty-eighth birthday, on 31 March 1755. It was the jewel in Lisbon's crown, and it lasted 215 days.

The king, again, like his father, turned to Italian specialists to give shape to his dream. He brought in Giovanni Bibiena, from a prestigious family of theatre designers who for generations had a reputation for producing dazzling sets. Bibiena arrived in Lisbon with his team in 1752. The Teatro Real da Ópera (Royal Opera Theatre), known popularly as the Ópera do Tejo (Tagus Opera), was a bulky, eye-catching building, about six storeys tall, adjacent to the riverside palace. The papal nuncio, Acciauoli, wrote that workers laboured day and night for months in their haste to get the theatre ready in time for the queen's birthday and that the king paid frequent visits to check on progress. Indeed, José I reportedly kept a close eye on everything, from the decor to the costumes.

For the venue's spectacular inauguration, the production was *Alessandro nell'Indie*, about Alexander the Great's campaign in India. The librettos were by Pietro Metastasio, an Italian poet who was the most celebrated librettist in Europe at the time, and the music by Davide Perez, a Neapolitan who was the resident composer and maestro of the royal chapel. The international cast featured two stars of the stage. The tenor Anton Raaff played the title role. His on-stage rival Poro was played by his off-stage rival, the celebrated and temperamental Caffarelli (Gaetano Majorana). The performances, in three acts over five hours, usually took place on Sundays and Wednesdays.

The sumptuous opera house could hold around 600 people. Of those, 350 were seated in the stalls and the rest in thirty-eight boxes spread over four levels. Admittance was by royal invitation only. This was a private entertainment of the king's, and the Crown financed the whole costly business—from cast and orchestra to set designers, wardrobe supervisors and carpenters. On entering the theatre, and before taking their seat, guests had to bow or curtsey toward the royal box. Between acts, each time they stood up, they were required to bow or curtsey again.

Inside, the theatre was stunning. The main colours were gold and white, with gilt bronze decorations and marble pillars. "One cannot deny that one is struck, when entering this room, by the gold and magnificence which bursts forth and shines on all sides," wrote French visitor Charles-Christian des Courtils.

One of the most talked-about features of this opera house was the vast size of the stage. It covered more than twice the area of the stalls. That meant that in *Alessandro nell'Indie*, twenty-five horses were able to come on stage at the same time. One of the king's riding-masters rode the horse playing Alexander's famed Bucephalus. Gerard de Visme, an Englishman resident in Lisbon, recounted in astonishment that it outshone the production efforts of the celebrated castrato Farinelli in Madrid. In Lisbon, Visme wrote, the new opera house "surpassed, in magnitude and decorations, all the modern times can boast".

The second opera to be produced was *La Clemenza di Tito*, also with music by Perez. Opening night was on 6 June, King José I's birthday. An engraving at the National Library in Lisbon of a set used in the production demonstrates how the deep stage, elaborate stage machinery and *trompe l'oeil* effects allowed Bibiena to juggle perspectives. He pulled off a huge, statue-lined gallery with a hilltop palatial backdrop that dwarfed the players. Royal Navy captain Augustus John Hervey, sent a ticket by the king's secretary, described the opera house as "the most magnificente (sic) theatre I ever saw" and remarked of the *La Clemenza di Tito* production: "The scenary (sic) of this opera surpasses anything I had ever seen of the kind."

Without doubt, Lisbon on the night of 31 October 1755 was a splendid city.

* * *

The royal family slept in a garden on the Saturday night of the earthquake. Most other survivors, too, slept outdoors. By the light of the fires consuming Lisbon, criminals who walked out of the collapsed Limoeiro prison in Alfama marauded rubble-strewn streets. Looters plundered collapsed buildings.

Nuns, scattered across the devastated city, were molested. The dead and the dying were largely unattended. Food and water were scarce. But by nightfall on Lisbon's darkest day, authorities had begun work on a disaster response that was remarkable for its swiftness and efficiency, even by twenty-first-century standards. Some regard it as the first modern, centralized state response to catastrophe. Certainly, the prompt action saved lives.

Within seventy-two hours, detailed written orders and instructions went out. They were later documented, in 1758, in the book *Memorias das principaes providencias, que se deraõ no terremoto, que padeceo a Corte de Lisboa no anno de 1755* (Memories of the Main Directives Issued in the Earthquake which Hit the Lisbon Court in 1755). It contains more than 350 pages of official edicts, orders and decrees produced over three days. It is fulsome in its praise of King José I, though the mastermind was his cool-headed first minister, Sebastião José de Carvalho e Melo. The instructions marshalled the Crown's resources and focused minds. The effort also helped restore morale and encourage public faith in state institutions, despite the sense of dread and paralyzing fear brought on by scores of aftershocks. The instructions were numbered:

1. Faced with the pressing concern that the thousands of putrefying bodies might spread disease, magistrates, priests and soldiers were required to expedite burials, which the 1758 book reported were "as merciful for the dead as useful for the living". The Patriarch of Lisbon gave his blessing to Carvalho e Melo's recommendation that, to hasten the undertaking, bodies be piled onto ships, weighted down and dumped in the sea beyond Bugio lighthouse;

2. Stocks of food were commandeered in Lisbon and outlying areas and distributed around the city from designated depots. To prevent profiteering, food prices were not permitted to rise above those practised the previous month. Millers and bakers were drafted into the capital;

3. Buildings that were still habitable were listed so that the injured and the sick could be sent there for treatment;

4. Lisbon residents who had fled to the countryside were obliged to return to the capital to help with restoring life in the city to normal;

5. To stop looting and to punish offenders, magistrates were requisitioned and brought into the city. They held dozens of verbal trials, with summary executions carried out on the same day. The guilty were sent to six gallows built across Lisbon. Their bodies were left hanging for days, as a message. The pillaging soon stopped;

6. Lisbon port was shut and ships searched, to stop looters and their booty getting away (some foreign sailors had run amok);

7. Aid was sent to southern parts of Portugal, which also were hard hit;

8. Regiments of artillery, infantry and dragoons were deployed across the city;

9. The costs of house rents were frozen and temporary wooden huts were built, and timber arriving in the city was exempt from duties;

10. Religious services were to resume in the few churches still standing and repairs begun;

11. Nuns were to be gathered up and provided for;

12. To help meet the various needs of the people, soldiers had to help put out fires, clear the streets of rubble and salvage belongings;

13. There were to be "Religious acts by His Majesty to placate Divine wrath and thank the Lord for so many blessings";
14. Means for the rebuilding of the city were to be prepared.

Those measures were speedily put into action. There were no epidemics, and nobody starved. Despite the limitations of eighteenth-century tools and imperfect scientific knowledge, the disaster management worked. "The response was exemplary," says João Duarte Fonseca, a lecturer at Lisbon's Instituto Superior Técnico and an author on the Lisbon earthquake.

A discovery 250 years later helped reconstitute events in Lisbon during that terrible first week of November. The revelations were like a ghoulish postcard from the past. When construction workers restoring a seventeenth-century Lisbon convent started burrowing beneath its cloisters in 2004, they made a chilling find: countless human bones, many showing signs of butchery, heaped together in a mass grave.

Archeologists took over and unearthed skulls smashed by blunt objects and scorched by fire, and a skull with an apparent bullet hole in the forehead. There was also a child's thigh bone with signs of dog bites, and a bone with knife marks that raised suspicions of cannibalism. Forensic experts and historians who studied the find beneath what is nowadays the Lisbon Academy of Sciences eventually solved the mystery of the bones. This was, they said, the first mass grave ever encountered of victims of the 1755 earthquake. "This could only have been some singular, calamitous event," said Miguel Telles Antunes, curator of the Lisbon Academy of Sciences who coordinated the investigation.

The jumble of skeletons lying silently for centuries beneath the thick-walled Franciscan convent had a story to tell. Forensic scientists acted as sleuths and, using the latest technology in a kind of "CSI: Lisbon", gradually reconstructed events. The mass grave did not contain only human bones. Amid the clutter were also animal and fish bones, bits of pottery and ceramics and personal items such as clay pipes, buttons, medallions, rosaries and even a thimble. All pre-dated the earthquake.

Historians knew that the authorities had hastily buried the dead to prevent an epidemic, but they didn't know where. The grave shows just how much of a hurry they were in. "When they gathered up the bodies to cart them away, they also scooped up bits of whatever else was lying around," said João Luís Cardoso, a professor of archaeology at the Open University in Lisbon who oversaw the dig.

Cristiana Pereira, a forensic dentist at Lisbon University, was given more than 1,000 teeth from the grave for analysis. Using the same procedures employed to identify victims in mass graves in the former Yugoslavia or from the 2004 Asian tsunami, she classified seventy-nine victims, including months-old babies. The largest age group was those between seventeen and thirty-five, leading her to conclude that Lisbon had a young population. Evidence of Portugal's slave-trading were bones from a monkey—presumably a pet—and small sea shells, called cowry shells, that constituted currency in Africa and Brazil and were commonly used by European traders to buy slaves.

Many skulls had been crushed, probably in the earthquake's first jolt which brought down masonry and beams. A small, sharp stone still jutted out of the skull of a child aged about three. Scientists also analyzed charcoal, partly melted medallions and sand that had turned into glass. They deduced that temperatures in the post-quake fire reached a staggering 1000°C (1800°F). Lisbon must have experienced horrific firestorms similar to those witnessed during the World War II fire-bombings of German cities such as Hamburg and Dresden. Two round bullets made of lead were found in the grave, and one skull had a roundish hole. That led historians to suspect that some of those buried here had been victims of soldiers sent to crack down on looting. "You can begin to imagine what a hellish time it must have been," Antunes said. Experts believe that the remains of some 3,000 quake victims lie under the Academy of Sciences. Some say that Lisbon was built on its dead.

Despite the calamity, anarchy in the city was short-lived. The kingdom did not unravel. King José I, on the other hand, was a nervous wreck. His dreams of Lisbon's greatness were shattered. His cherished opera house was in ruins. He was haunted by the earthquake. The Belém district where he stayed was largely spared, but José I was as bewildered as anyone. The nuncio reported that "in summary, everything is horror and misery, and Lisbon is a pile of rubble."

The royal family moved into makeshift wooden lodgings which became known as the *barraca real* (royal hut). When the British traveller Wraxall arrived, in 1772, the monarch was still there. He had never again been able to live under a proper roof. Wraxall recounted:

> The King, Queen, his brother Don Pedro, his three daughters, and the young Prince of Beira lived all under the same roof, and inhabited a long wooden range of apartments at Belem, lower down the bank of the Tagus than Lisbon. The

terrors and recollections of the earthquake of 1755 were so deeply impressed on their minds, that they preferred residing in a wooden building, however mean in its fabrication or inconvenient, rather than encounter the perils annexed to a stone edifice. Joseph [King José] had never slept under a house properly so denominated during near seventeen years.

Around 250 aftershocks in the six months after 1 November were a constant and traumatic reminder of that wretched day, and the king reportedly turned to drink to calm his nerves. Wraxall explained:

> Previous to the memorable earthquake of 1755, he was considered as temperate, drinking usually water at his meals; but such was the effect produced on his mind, and so severe the dejection of spirits which he experienced after that awful convulsion of the planet, that it seriously affected his health. His physicians prescribed the use of wine as necessary to restore his constitution; a prescription which proved so agreeable to the patient, that it was believed his Majesty indulged himself too freely in its use.

The sense of disorientation was understandable. Mendonça, the earthquake survivor, commented, "You search for Lisbon in Lisbon, and it's not there." Some, however, maintained their *sang-froid*. And one of them, consequently, became a towering figure in Lisbon and Portugal's history. Because of his achievements after the earthquake, Carvalho e Melo shot to national and international prominence—in 1769 he received from King José the title of Marquês de Pombal (Marquis of Pombal), by which he is best known.

With the king paralyzed by shock and anxiety, Pombal stepped into the leadership vacuum. His influence is to be found everywhere in the emergency response and the Lisbon rebuilding programme. He was an outstanding administrator.

He had an astonishing work rate and possessed admirable decision-making power, as he had demonstrated when a fire broke out at the Todos os Santos hospital three months before the earthquake. His iron hand was just what was needed to restore order after a calamity. "The Marquis de Pombal exercised, in fact, all the functions of the monarchy," Wraxall observed.

But Pombal was also a cold fish and his heavy-handed, autocratic style did not make him very endearing in more settled times. The son of a cavalry captain who was a *fidalgo* in the royal household, Pombal ruthlessly cemented the monarch's absolute power by cracking down on political schemers and factions—occasionally by recruiting the help of the Inquisition. Some people, consequently, have regarded him as a Portuguese version of France's Cardinal Richelieu. At the same time, Pombal was an enlightened despot who introduced key reforms in education, the state administration and the economy, modernizing and secularizing each of them.

Abílio Guerra Junqueiro, the Portuguese writer and politician, wrote of Pombal in 1915: "He made himself feared, not loved. Head of bronze, heart of stone." Over an almost three-decade career in Lisbon, Pombal went from saviour to dictator, from glory to disgrace. Love him or hate him, Pombal is a titan in Lisbon and Portugal's history. José Hermano Saraiva's bestselling twentieth-century *History of Portugal*, which was made into a popular television series, carries a portrait of Pombal on its cover.

Born in 1699, Pombal was sent in 1738 as an envoy to the Court of St James and spent seven years in London. Then, from 1745, he served for four years as an envoy in Vienna. In London he would have become familiar with the story of the rebuilding of the city after the Great Fire of 1666. In both of those cities, he was exposed to Enlightenment ideas. It is tempting to see Pombal's stays in those cooler climates as informing the reconstruction and redesign of downtown Lisbon, which he oversaw. This architectural style became known as *pombalino*. The gridiron street pattern and low, squat buildings are sober, symmetrical and harmonious but also cold and impassive. It is a million miles from the animated and exuberant Manueline style. When the Marquis of Pombal dreamed, he no doubt dreamed of straight lines and 90-degree turns. The *Baixa pombalina*, as Lisbon's rebuilt downtown is described, has none of the passionate, anarchical impulses so characteristic of the Portuguese. Indeed, its unrelentingly rigid features can be found in only one other town in Portugal: Vila Real de Santo António, in the Algarve, where Pombal's hand was also at work.

King João V was not fond of Pombal, but King José I was. After the earthquake José granted Pombal unprecedented free rein and the official title of secretary of state for the kingdom's affairs. Pombal assembled a team of leading architects and engineers, almost all of them from a military background, who were to come up with proposals for the rebuilding of Lisbon. The team's leader was Manuel da Maia and it also included Carlos Mardel and Eugénio dos Santos. Their offices were known as the Casa do Risco das Obras Públicas (Office of Public Works Planning). Pombal and his team had, to a large degree, a blank canvas to work with. The most affluent people had abandoned the ruined downtown and moved to a safer area further west that became called Lapa. It earned a reputation as an aristocratic area, and nowadays its large houses are home to most of the city's embassies.

For the downtown makeover he was looking for, Pombal picked a project by Eugénio dos Santos, one of five that were put forward. It involved razing what was left of the city centre, squashing it flat, laying wide new streets and erecting buildings that would not exceed the streets' width. Work began in 1758, using gunpowder to bring down the ruins that still littered the area. Legal wrangling with proprietors held up the work, just as it had in London after 1666. Indeed, even fifty years later, foreign visitors to Lisbon would still comment on seeing earthquake rubble lying around.

The 1755 earthquake redrew the shape of Lisbon. King José I had hankered after a modern, European city, but that was finally achieved neither through his own will nor through the gold from Brazil. Nature started the job, and Pombal and the Age of Reason did the rest. "Out of the ruins of a city that was still medieval, with narrow, dirty and disagreeable streets, a city rose up that rendered a new urban concept, drawn on a new scale, in completely innovative fashion—a rational and functional city from the realm of the Enlightenment," wrote the historian Maria João Campos in 2005.

The Baixa's neat-as-a-pin, patrician dimensions stand as a stark contrast to Alfama's cluttered and sinewy seediness. The two neighbourhoods feel like they belong in different places—the Baixa in northern or central Europe and the Alfama in North Africa. It is the Baixa that seems grafted on. Its main streets run north to south, arrow-straight. They link Rossio Square—once the scene of burnings at the stake, beheadings, a lively Tuesday market, bullfights, military parades and popular uprisings, as well as the site of the Inquisitors' palace and the Todos os Santos hospital—with the broad square by the river. This square was the Terreiro do Paço, the palace courtyard, but King José I had no intention of rebuilding the palace there. Instead, merchants' taxes paid in part for the new square, and so it was named Praça do Comércio. Graceful arches soften the severe symmetry of the low buildings that line three sides of the square.

Safety, standardization and prefabrication were watchwords in the building of the new downtown district. Some of the methods were either invented at the Casa do Risco or were state-of-the-art solutions. To help buildings withstand future earthquakes, a wooden trellis termed a *gaiola* (cage) was incorporated into walls to provide elasticity. Carpenters put together the timber frame, then stonemasons filled it in. At one point, a military detachment was ordered to march over a *gaiola* placed on the ground to test its sturdiness.

This structure was only used from the first floors upward, however, due to a traumatic earthquake memory: fire. Hearths were on the ground floor, and the team of experts worried that the trellis would help fuel any outbreak. To contain fires, the new buildings had thick masonry walls that rose above the roofs to act as firebreaks. Workshops were set up to prefabricate pieces of the new buildings, both structural and for interiors, and to accelerate the work. Carpenters dressed timber and masons worked stone off-site. Parts of stairways and panels of tiles were transported through the streets.

Codices in Lisbon City Council's archive show that 848 properties in 171 streets were rebuilt between 1755 and 1778. Notably, and contrary to the wishes of the eminent men of the Casa do Risco, none of them had plumbing and the streets were given no drains or sewers, so Lisbon's famous reek continued. As part of the broader reshaping of city, the celebrated shipyards were moved from close to where the palace once stood to the south bank of the Tagus, where modern shipyards can still be seen.

The crowning moment of the reconstruction project came in 1775, twenty years after the earthquake. Portugal's first bronze statue was erected in the middle of Praça do Comércio, even though the square was not yet finished. It shows King José I astride a prancing stallion, holding the royal sceptre and wearing armour he never pulled on. Often regarded as Lisbon's most beautiful statue, it returned a regal touch to a square that had lost its royal connotation. The official inauguration in June 1775 was the cue for a grand three-day party that was talked and written about for years afterwards. It included fireworks, parades, floats and banquets. The holes of unfinished buildings around the square, like missing teeth, were plugged with wood and canvas.

An elephant, inevitably, is on the large pedestal below the statue. There are also figures representing Triumph and Fame. It is the creation of the famous Portuguese sculptor Joaquim Machado de Castro, whose work can also been seen at the Estrela Basilica and at the Ajuda Palace, which was built on the hill where the royal family's wooden lodgings were erected after the earthquake. Machado de Castro was self-taught. He studied widely and eventually published half-a-dozen books. He never travelled abroad, however, and always regretted it. Machado de Castro was the victim of a great historical wrongdoing: when the statue was being lifted into place, he was shooed away by a policeman and missed the event. There are two footnotes to that episode: firstly, it was Pombal who established the first Portuguese police force worthy of the name; secondly, the statue is said to be slightly lopsided because its creator was not there to oversee its positioning.

The statue had been cast the previous October at the Arsenal do Exército (the Army Arsenal, which now houses the Military Museum), about 1,000 metres to the east along the river. The bronze took twenty-eight hours to melt, and the cast was filled in eight minutes. The statue weighs almost 30 tonnes. The following May around 1,000 men pulled it, over three and a half days and with much pomp, by cart from the foundry to its current location. The carts they used are kept today at the Military Museum.

When Pombal, accompanied by his twenty-seven-year-old son Henrique, unveiled the statue there was a portrait of him on a large, round bronze medallion, the size of a small table, on the front of the pedestal. Two years later a mob threw stones at the medallion before tearing it off. Pombal's time in the sun ended abruptly with the death of King José I in February 1777. The monarch's successor Queen Maria I, like João V previously, disliked Pombal. He was stripped of his powers and banished from Lisbon.

Pombal possessed an uncompromising nature and unshakable beliefs. He won admirers and made enemies. Wraxall's account in 1772, when Pombal was still in favour, is revealing:

> At the time that I saw him he had attained his seventy-third year; but age appeared neither to have diminished the vigour, freshness, or activity of his faculties. In his person he was very tall and slender; his face long, pale, meagre, and full of intelligence. He was so unpopular, and so many attempts had been made to assassinate him, that he never went out without guards. Even in the streets of Lisbon his carriage was always accompanied or surrounded by a detachment of cavalry with their swords drawn for his protection.

Pombal was not a man to be crossed, as the Jesuit priest Father Gabriel Malagrida could testify. After the earthquake, when many people were speaking of divine wrath and paying penance, Pombal was behind the publication of a pamphlet that attributed the disaster to natural causes and explained it through science. Father Malagrida disagreed, producing his own pamphlet explaining the disaster as God's punishment and urging people to repent their sins. Pombal was incensed. He had Father Malagrida's pamphlet burned in public and had the priest sent away from Lisbon. But Father Malagrida refused to back down and sent a letter to the capital reaffirming his beliefs. That was the final straw. He was thrown into a Lisbon jail before being handed over to the Inquisition, which garroted him and burnt him at the stake in 1761.

Pombal targeted the Jesuits generally, along with sections of the Portuguese nobility, after a failed attempt on King José I's life in 1758. The monarch was hit by gunshots fired by three men on horseback as he travelled in his carriage in the Ajuda neighbourhood, where now the Largo da Memória (Memory Square) is located. Pombal's investigations concluded that the influential Távora family was behind the assassination attempt. The Marquis and Marchioness of Távora, their children and some others in their household were sentenced to death in a summary trial. At 8:00 a.m. on Saturday, 13 January 1759 they were led onto a scaffold erected in Belém where they were executed with extraordinary cruelty: their bodies broken on wheels and beheaded before the scaffold was set alight. The ashes were cast into the Tagus, and use of the surname Távora was from then on prohibited. The attempt to strike the Távora name from Portuguese history books was indeed so comprehensive that orders were received at the Cardaes Convent in the Bairro Alto, which was established in the seventeenth century by

Luísa de Távora, for the founder's tomb to be built over, blotting out the local memory of her.

Pombal also judged that the Jesuits had conspired with the Távoras against the king. Jesuit assets were seized by the Crown. In September 1759, a year to the day after the assassination attempt in Ajuda, the Society of Jesus was outlawed in Portuguese territories. Jesuits were either jailed or expelled. Their libraries were destroyed and their books burned. Some scholars regard it as a cultural massacre.

The nineteenth-century writer and historian Camilo Castelo Branco, in his 1882 book *Perfil do Marquês de Pombal* (Profile of the Marquis of Pombal), depicted his subject as a bloodthirsty tyrant. Pombal's champions, however, pointed to a host of laudable reforms he introduced. He adopted a rational and scientific approach in a country that in many ways seemed preserved in amber. In 1746, for example, the dean of the College of Arts in Coimbra had published a decree outlawing "new opinions, rarely accepted or useless for the study of the major sciences, such as those of René Descartes ... Newton and others". Portugal was a fortress of the Counter-Reformation, and its burning of supposed heretics at the stake was viewed as barbaric by the northern European countries that traded with Portugal.

Pombal is credited with marking the beginning of the end of Portuguese slavery. He created the first lay teachers in Lisbon and opened elementary schools to teach reading, writing and arithmetic. Instead of frittering away the contents of the Treasury, he steered money toward investments in industry and agriculture, including the establishment of the world's first demarcated wine region along the River Douro where port wine grapes are grown. He was behind a national scientific survey of the earthquake, now held at the Torre do Tombo national archive in Lisbon, which asked thirteen questions of all the country's parishes, including how long the quake lasted and what its local consequences were.

Queen Maria I was a determined adversary of Pombal, but showed him more mercy than he had shown his own enemies. Though he was arrested, tried and found guilty, he escaped punishment and was sent into exile in Pombal, the rural town 170 kilometres north of the capital that had provided him with his title. He died poor, five days before his eighty-third birthday, in 1782. The Crown would not allow him to be laid to rest in his family vault at the Igreja das Mercês in Lisbon so he was buried at the Igreja do Cardal in Pombal.

There would be no place in the National Pantheon for this historical heavyweight. But Pombal would, in some respects, get the last laugh. The medallion of him on the pedestal of King José I's statue was returned to its place in 1833 by the Liberal government of the time. The Liberals rehabilitated Pombal, who was a hero for them for having brought down a powerful family of privilege and quashed a religious order. Also, Pombal was the grandfather of the Duke of Saldanha, a leading Liberal statesman of the nineteenth century. Consequently, in the middle of that century, Pombal's remains were brought to Lisbon and placed in the Mercês Church where he was baptized, not far from his birthplace in the Rua do Século in the Chiado district. That house, a plain, three-storey palace in white stone, is a neglected building today with weeds growing out of the roof tiles. A plaque from 1923 indicates that Pombal was born there.

That was the same year that Pombal's remains were moved to where they are kept today: the Igreja da Memória, in Ajuda's Largo da Memória, built to commemorate King José I's escape from the nearby assassination attempt. The church is seldom open nowadays. Behind a brown door, in a bare, modest side chapel which also serves as an unofficial store room, a dark wood and iron urn about the size of a large suitcase sits on a marble pedestal. Inside it lie Pombal's remains.

Pombal would probably have enjoyed another tribute, from the twentieth century: his own bronze statue, on top of a 40-metre-high pedestal. After a public fundraising campaign, a competition for designs was held and won by Francisco Santos. The clay mould of Pombal's head, 1.8 metres high, fell apart when it was in the artist's studio—on the very day of Santos' death—and it was completed by Simões de Almeida. For the pedestal, huge blocks of stone were brought from near Sintra, taking five days on ox-drawn carts to arrive in the capital. On the column holding up the statue, Pombal's wide accomplishments in the fields of education, administration and economy are listed. The statue was inaugurated on 13 May 1934, 235 years to the day after Pombal's birth. Today it stands at the centre of a major roundabout and gives its name to an underground station, ensuring that Pombal keeps his place in Lisbon's memory.

SIX—FOREIGN RULE, TURMOIL AND TEMPTATION

For three straight days as winter approached in 1807, a constant flow of horse-drawn carriages hurried through the streets of Lisbon to the quays and jetties that punctuated the Belém riverbank. There, they hastily unloaded passengers, trunks and boxes, turned round and went to fetch some more. The carriages drove through pelting rain that drenched clothes and turned the city's unpaved roads into treacherous seas of mud. Storm winds tore at clothes and canvas on the exposed riverbank. Small boats ferried people and cargo out to three dozen ships that were riding at anchor in the Tagus, waiting on the choppy water with their sails folded. Around 15,000 people squeezed onto those ships. They included the royal family and members of the royal household, noble families and their retinues, including ladies-in-waiting, cooks and servants. Members of the clergy, ministers of state, magistrates and lawyers, military officers and soldiers, civil servants, diplomats, doctors and advisers boarded the ships, too, as did their wives and children. The normal hubbub of departure was amplified by fear. All along the riverbank, there was feverish haste. Panic was not far from the surface. The pressure-cooker atmosphere was understandable: Napoleon's army was bearing down, unopposed, on the Portuguese capital.

During those hectic seventy-two hours, Portugal's destiny once more converged on Belém. It was the epicentre of frantic efforts to save the Portuguese regime and its riches—the movable ones, anyway. Royal palaces were stripped. Paintings were taken down from the walls; carpets and tapestries were rolled up. Gold, silver and porcelain ornaments were wrapped. A legendary gold nugget mined in Brazil in 1732 and weighing more than 20 kilograms merited special care. The famous silver dinner service of the Ajuda Palace, made up of more than 1,000 pieces, was crated up and placed in the carriages heading to the port. Some 60,000 books from the Ajuda Royal Library were taken down to the river in more than 300 boxes. About half the coins in circulation departed, after the Treasury was emptied. It was as if the Portuguese were ransacking their own city before the French could.

Tents and awnings were erected along the riverbank to shelter the distinguished waiting passengers from the rain. Officials handed out the chits and waybills that people needed to get themselves and their possessions on board. Not everything went according to plan. The royal master of the horse, Bernardo Pacheco, though permitted to leave, had failed to pick up his authorization, and the frigate captain refused to let him climb aboard: no chit, no voyage. He was left on the riverbank.

Along the waterfront, luggage trunks, storage chests and lockers were piled up in the rain. They contained clothes and jewels and everyday objects that would be needed in a future home. The clergy gathered what they could of the Church's wealth. Documents from the royal archive and clerks were added to the enormous cargo. Food and barrels of drinking water were stacked on board. On the shore there were cursory but emotional farewells. There was weeping and fainting. The royal guard, meanwhile, held back the rank-and-file Portuguese who were going to be left behind.

The historical enormity of the occasion was not to be underestimated. The enterprise was dizzying and unprecedented in its scale. In essence, the idea was to uproot Portugal and replant it 8,000 kilometres to the south, in Brazil. Desperate times demanded desperate measures. The plan's architects certainly did not lack ambition. It was an exceptional moment in European history. The historian Rui Ramos remarked in the 2011 book *História de Portugal* that "many people had sought in the Americas the freedom and opportunities they lacked on the Old Continent. This was the first time that a state, in the shape of its highest representatives and officials, did the same."

The purpose of moving the royal family to Brazil was to deny the French invader legitimacy. Many crowned heads of Europe would use the same ploy during World War II invasions. Confronted with the inevitable, the Portuguese royal family cut its losses. After all, better to rule unfettered from Brazil than be a prisoner at home, and they would live to fight another day. In essence, the Crown could not afford to lose Brazil as it was what made Portugal economically viable. And Brazil offered a comforting continuity. The Portuguese had dwelt there since 1500, and by the early nineteenth century it was home to hundreds of thousands of them.

The clock began ticking for Lisbon's elite on 25 November. Four days earlier, the British frigate HMS *Confiance* had docked in Lisbon and handed to the authorities a copy of the French newspaper *Le Moniteur* of 11 November. That day's edition contained an item about plans to dethrone Portugal's royal family. Napoleon had ordered French allies and neutral countries, including Portugal, to shut their ports to British ships as part of his campaign against Britain. Ostensibly, the French army was coming to Portugal to ensure that the decree was enforced. But the Portuguese suspected less innocent French motives, and *Le Moniteur* confirmed their suspicions.

Portugal was to be the next victim of Napoleon's imperial ambitions. The emperor had already co-opted Spain into his Portuguese adventure through secret clauses in the Treaty of Fontainebleau, signed on 27 October 1807. The treaty's ultimate and confidential goal was the conquest of Portugal. It contained covert plans for the dismemberment of the Portuguese kingdom, parcelling it out between France and Spain. Historians have noted that Napoleon was keen to get his hands on the Portuguese fleet to compensate for his naval losses at the Battle of Trafalgar. The port of Lisbon would be an additional trophy. The Portuguese were no less scheming, however. On 22 October, they had signed their own secret bilateral agreement, with Britain. In an emergency, the Royal Navy would ensure the Portuguese royal family's escape to Brazil. In return, London would earn trade concessions.

With the French army closing in, Portugal's rulers had run out of options. The Council of State met on the morning of 25 November at the Ajuda Palace. It decided to set in motion a contingency plan that had been kept in a drawer since the seventeenth-century wars with Spain: move the Portuguese state, lock, stock and barrel, to South America. Sensing trouble on the horizon, Prince Regent Dom João—who, owing to his mother Queen Maria I's infirmity, had become *de facto* ruler—had been preparing a possible getaway for several months. As a precaution, ships were being fitted out in the Lisbon arsenal's shipyards from August onward.

The Council of State's decision was the starting gun for three frenzied days of preparations for the lengthy voyage. It was a race against the clock as General Jean-Andoche Junot led a column with thousands of French troops overland from Spain toward their target: Lisbon. Portuguese officials and servants worked themselves into a lather. On 27 November the queen and the men and boys of the royal family boarded the *Príncipe Real*, the Portuguese fleet's flagship and one of its biggest warships, with 110 cannon. The royal women and girls went separately on the *Afonso de Albuquerque*. About 1,000 people crammed onto the *Príncipe Real* alone. (If the *Príncipe Real* had sunk at sea, three generations of the royal House of Braganza would have perished without heirs.) Other *naus*, or galleon-like carracks, in the flotilla—which constituted the core of the Portuguese fleet—were the *Conde D. Henrique*, the *Medusa*, the *D. João de Castro* and the *Martim de Freitas*. As well as those massive ships, there were four frigates, three brigs, a schooner and more than two dozen merchant vessels. They were the only way out of Portugal and Napoleon's clutches.

Dom João, the prince regent, was distraught as he waited to set off into the unknown and fought hard to maintain his composure. José Acúrsio das Neves, an eyewitness, described him as being "in a daze and haggard". He staggered on the quay and wept as he took his leave. Queen Maria I, who by 1807 had already been unsuccessfully treated for what was popularly believed to be dementia or senility, was in no better shape. She had come to the throne in 1777, aged forty-three.

She is regarded as Portugal's first female monarch, though some historians dispute that owing to a twelfth-century claim by Teresa of León. Queen Maria I's son, Dom João, took over her duties in 1792 after her emotional state worsened. Deaths of people close to her had taken their toll. In the space of two years she had lost her beloved husband, her first-born son and heir to the throne, her daughter and Spanish son-in-law and her confessor. As with other European sovereigns, the French Revolution had also been a severe strain on her nerves.

Searching for a cure for her ailments, the Crown hired Dr Francis Willis, an English priest who had a keen interest in medicine and was known for treating the insane at his own home. He was credited with successfully treating King George III. Willis, in his seventies, was persuaded to travel to Portugal at the end of the eighteenth century. He was paid, according to historian Luís de Oliveira Ramos, £1,000 up front, plus the same amount for each month he spent in Lisbon, as well as his travel expenses. But his treatments came to naught. Nowadays, Queen Maria I is believed to have suffered from major depressive disorder.

In the rush to get out of Lisbon, however, Queen Maria is credited with making one of the most clear-headed remarks of the time. As her carriage sped through the city streets toward Belém, she shouted to the driver, "Don't go so fast! They'll think we're running away!" Nevertheless, as her biographer Jenifer Roberts has described, the tension began to affect the queen. When her carriage arrived at the quay, where the prince regent was waiting for her, she became hysterical and refused to step out into the mud. "I don't want to! I don't want to!" she shouted, perhaps unintentionally capturing the mood of others. Eventually, a naval officer was ordered to pick her up and put her into the royal cutter.

Considering that the evacuation plan existed only on paper and had never been rehearsed, the departure went reasonably well, though it was far from perfect. Euzébio Gomes, another eyewitness, noted in his diary that there was "a lot of clutter and commotion" on the quay where "30,000 things" were stacked. Many of the belongings were left behind on the riverbank after their owners boarded. Among them were the 60,000 books from the royal palace. The 317 boxes of books were forwarded later in three shipments, between 1810 and 1811, once the French had gone. At the same time, other belongings were taken aboard but their owners left on the riverbank. Also, Acúrsio das Neves reported that when the evacuation ships were being readied, some of their water barrels were stolen and there was a scramble to find new ones. He said that "everything was confusion and chaos to prepare within a few days only that which was absolutely indispensable for such a long voyage."

After the sleepless days of hurry and bustle this Noah's Ark, as the essayist Eduardo Lourenço has described it, was finally ready to take the Old World to the New. But the ships had to wait where they were in the Tagus for an agonizing thirty-six hours. A heavy storm prevented the flotilla from going out beyond Bugio. The nerve-wracking interlude afforded passengers the opportunity to gaze at the Jerónimos Monastery on the bank, where it stood as a silent reminder of kinder times.

The ships finally sailed away on Sunday, 29 November. The following day at 8:00 a.m. the French army arrived at the gates of Lisbon. As Junot barged in the front door, the royal family slipped out from the back. Throughout its history Portugal has tried to run between the legs of bigger powers, outwitting them and darting just beyond their reach. But it could not dodge them forever, and in the nineteenth century, as in the sixteenth, it was caught.

Some people later chided the royal family for a departure they saw as ignominious. Later in the nineteenth century, the historian Oliveira Martins described the flight as an "embarrassing episode" whose consequences bore comparison with the 1755 earthquake. He wrote: "Three centuries earlier Portugal had embarked, full of hope and avidity, for India; in 1807, it embarked on a funeral procession to Brazil." Others defended the departure as the wisest course of action in the circumstances.

In the mouth of the Tagus, as planned, a squadron of Royal Navy ships under the command of Sir Sidney Smith was waiting. Smith, a national hero in Britain for his feats in the struggle against Napoleon, detached four vessels to escort the Portuguese across the Atlantic. On 10 January, at around 11:00 a.m., the flotilla crossed the equator and Queen Maria I became the first European sovereign to enter the southern hemisphere. On-board conditions were far from regal, however. The long voyage, as well as inflicting a painful political and emotional state of limbo, was deeply uncomfortable. The ships were cramped and lacked dignified toilet facilities, food and water were strictly rationed, and lice compelled the members of Portuguese high society to cast their wigs overboard, with the women on one ship forced to shave their heads. The flotilla arrived in San Salvador on 22 January and in Rio de Janeiro, where the royal family would take up residence, on 7 March.

The French invasion set the tone for what would, on the whole, be a wretched century. Over the course of the 1800s,

Lisbon not only witnessed the flight of the royal family and ruling class, the loss of its status as capital city, and occupation by a foreign army, but it would also be tormented by five coups, two revolutions, two military rebellions, a civil war, and national bankruptcy. The nineteenth century's identifying feature was turmoil. Portugal was often, in those years, like a kite in a hurricane.

The prince regent left behind, as well as anxiety, a royal decree that placed six of his most trusted men in charge. They would form a Council of Governors, or Regency Council, to run the country during his absence. In the decree, dated 26 November, Dom João explained his reasoning to his people:

> Seeking to avoid the possible deadly consequences of a defence, which would be more harmful than beneficial, bringing only bloodshed, and which might aggrieve the troops who are crossing this Kingdom with the promise to commit no hostilities; being also aware that they are coming very specifically for my royal personage, and that my loyal subjects will be less alarmed if I take leave of the Kingdom: I have decided, for the benefit of those very same subjects, to proceed with Her Majesty the Queen, My Lady and Mother, and all the royal family, to the states of America, and take up residence in the city of Rio de Janeiro until peace returns.

Furthermore, the prince regent insisted, the French army was to be afforded a cordial welcome, "well accommodated and aided in all they need for as long as they remain in this Kingdom, avoiding any and all kinds of insult and severely punishing any that does occur." Surely knowing his decree would be found by the formidable invaders, the prince regent was apparently seeking to win favour for those he had left behind.

Napoleon's army had a reputation for invincibility. It dominated continental Europe, and for the Portuguese army—in a neglected state at the time—making a stand would have been honourable but doomed. The prince regent wanted the French to be welcomed as the ostensible allies they were, and Junot met no resistance when he arrived at the capital. Representatives of the Council of Governors and Lisbon freemasons—Junot, too, was a freemason—went to meet the invader. Junot was at the head of an advance detachment of 2,000 men who had endured a forced march through pouring rain as the invaders raced to catch the royals before they left. In all, 6,000 troops under French command would be billeted in Lisbon. Many were put up in monasteries, compelling the priests and monks to move out and into the countryside. Others demanded room and board, for free, at the homes of Portuguese nobles and the middle class.

Junot offered the people of Lisbon a somewhat different point of view from the prince regent's. On 30 November, an announcement in Junot's name was posted around the capital, addressed to its inhabitants. In French and Portuguese, it declared, "My army is going to enter your city." Junot stated that his intention was to save Lisbon and the prince regent from the "malign influence" of England. But the prince regent, he said, had been misled by his advisers, who had delivered him into the hands of his enemy. Junot went on: the prince regent's "subjects were not taken into account at all, and your interests were sacrificed to the cowardliness of a few courtiers." He concluded: "THE GREAT NAPOLEON, my master, has sent me to protect you, and protect you I shall!"

That prediction, it turned out, was wildly off the mark. The following nine months in Lisbon were often nasty and bloody as Junot's men struggled to take control of one of Europe's biggest cities and one of the continent's most instinctively subversive people. The French occupation left scars so deep that they entered the Portuguese language as figures of speech that are still widely used.

Junot's kind words for the people of Lisbon were a lie, and his promise of protection was a fig leaf for sinister ambitions. His wife Laure wrote, in her extensive memoirs, that Napoleon's orders to his general were succinct: "Concede nothing to the Prince of Brazil, even if he promises to declare war on England. Go into Lisbon, seize the ships and occupy the ports." Subjugation was the goal. Junot swiftly usurped power. He stacked the Council of Governors with his own men and effectively took over the public administration. He also took possession of the wealth the prince regent was unable to take with him—his palaces, his furniture, his carriages. Junot kept the best for himself and let his senior officers share out the rest among themselves. Uncounted treasures were spirited out of Portugal to France. They were, in a way, the spoils of war, and France's explanation for its presence in Portugal was a sham.

The French, like other European foreigners before and after them, were taken aback by the insalubrity they encountered in Lisbon. There were menacing packs of stray dogs that barked all night. There were dark and muddy streets where danger lurked in the shadows. The contents of chamber pots still flew unpredictably from windows, even though an 1803 decree limited the activity to a specific time of day. Only the rebuilt part of the Baixa was airy and well-paved. A decree by the French-run city police in April 1808 announced that stray dogs would be killed. It also prohibited cows and goats on the city streets after 11:00 a.m. Acúrsio das Neves acknowledged that the French occupation improved some city features: the streets were cleaner, better-lit and safer at night. Those aspects were, of course, in the French interest.

Lisbon's social life certainly improved. The Portuguese phrase *viver à grande e à francesa* ("living it up, French-style") describes an extravagant and flamboyant lifestyle and is believed to stem from this period. Junot selected as his Lisbon residence and headquarters the Quintela family's palace in the Chiado's Rua do Alecrim, where it still stands. The Quintelas were one of the capital's wealthiest merchant families, and their home was close to the heart of the city. Their reputation for grand parties may also have informed Junot's choice. Balls and banquets were held at the capital's grand palaces for Junot and his officers, whose presence in Lisbon had the blessing of the city's Cardinal Patriarch José Francisco Miguel António de Mendonça and Chief Inquisitor José Maria de Melo. Portuguese nobles and prominent businessmen attended. Laure Junot, especially, had a reputation for lavish spending and dug her husband into debt. When Junot learned, less than two weeks after he took Lisbon, of the birth in France of his first son he threw a glamorous party to which he invited the cream of local society.

Bullfights provided the most popular entertainment at the time. They mostly catered for working-class tastes, though aristocrats and foreigners also went out of curiosity. Having no fixed venues in Lisbon, the bullfights took place in makeshift wooden rings erected in open spaces, including the Praça do Comércio. For more polished tastes, the Teatro de São Carlos was the preferred destination. As the middle class had gradually recomposed itself after the 1755 earthquake, the theatre's construction was paid for by a group of Lisbon merchants whose wealth had surged during the city's rebuilding. It had been inaugurated in 1793, with the royal family as patrons.

Junot was said to be fond of going to the São Carlos, where he flirted with high-society ladies and his officers' wives. This opera house, called then the Real Teatro de São Carlos, staged Italian works that were often performed by Italian artists, including famous castrati. It replaced the Royal Opera that was lost in 1755. This national monument in the Chiado district has a straightforward neoclassical style. Designed by José da Costa e Silva, it bears a strong resemblance to La Scala in Milan, right down to the three entrance arches. It was known to have perfect acoustics, though some other aspects were less successful. Its first seats had to be changed because they were uncomfortable, and tallow candles that lit the entire opera house gave off a foul smell. The São Carlos was purchased by the state in 1854, becoming the Teatro Nacional de São Carlos, and modifications later that century altered the acoustics. There was another major renovation in the 1930s. Nowadays, apart from its usual programme, the opera house in summer provides free outdoor concerts at night beneath the trees in its enchanting courtyard.

Junot and his officers were cocky and ambitious. Junot was thirty-six and, after a meteoric rise through the ranks, eager to make the most of the Lisbon enterprise. In eight years from 1793 he had risen from sergeant to Napoleon's *aide-de-camp*, brigadier general and general of a division. Appointed governor of Paris in 1800, he was sent as ambassador to Lisbon in 1804. Junot was nicknamed *la Tempête* for his brash and sometimes injudicious conduct and earned a reputation as a Don Juan. After five months as envoy to the Portuguese capital, he went off to fight at the Battle of Austerlitz. Next, at the Battle of Loubino in France's war against Russia, his misjudgements led him to be relieved of command. Later in his career, after leaving Lisbon, Junot showed symptoms of madness, including turning up at a ball naked, and committed suicide in 1813. His name is listed on the Arc de Triomphe in Paris.

Junot stationed around 6,000 troops in Lisbon. But that was not enough to stamp out dissent and insurrection. The first sign of trouble came on Sunday, 13 December. A French military parade was held in Rossio Square, with Junot and his senior officers appearing in full dress uniform in front of the assembled troops. Thousands of local people came out to watch. Up on the walls of St George's Castle, French cannon fired a salute as the Portuguese flag was taken down and the Tricolour raised in full view of those down in the square. French soldiers shouted, *Vive l'Empereur!*

It was a spectacle, a piece of theatre to show who was in charge now. But it backfired. The ceremony gave physical and symbolic shape to Portugal's humiliation. It was, as it turned out, a crass miscalculation by Junot. Rumblings of discontent ran through the crowd. Some began to shout curses at the French troops, who were probably unable to understand the words but were probably left in no doubt about the meaning. Unnerved by the increasingly ugly mood, French soldiers opened fire on the crowd. The people fled into side streets but the bloodshed did not stop there. For hours afterwards, the people of Lisbon hurled insults and stones at the French patrols. Some small French detachments were beaten and stabbed. The French brought up cannon to quell the mobs, while the Portuguese fought back with sticks. It was mayhem, and it was just the start.

The lesson was not lost on Junot. He set about disarming and demobilizing the Portuguese army and militias. Christmas Mass was prohibited to prevent gatherings. Junot banned fishermen from going out to sea in case they passed information to the Royal Navy ships lurking at the entrance to the Tagus. But, once again, the strategy proved to be a blunder. Trade by sea dried up, and the maritime city felt the crunch. People began losing their jobs and economic ruin beckoned. The mood was increasingly hostile.

On 23 December Napoleon, from Milan, dropped a bombshell. He signed a decree demanding from Portugal a payment of 100 million francs. It was an eye-watering amount and a round number that was apparently—and arrogantly—plucked out of the air. Essentially, Napoleon was demanding tribute. The decree also ordered the confiscation of the assets of the royal family and of all those who went to Brazil with it, including the contents of places of worship. These announcements were published in the *Gazeta de Lisboa*, the capital's newspaper which had become the occupiers' mouthpiece. Police chief Pierre Lagarde ran the paper, taking the Portuguese royal coat of arms off the masthead and replacing it with the French imperial eagle.

On 1 February, in a ceremony at the Palace of the Inquisition in Rossio Square, Junot read out a proclamation. It stated that, by leaving, the royal house had forfeited its right to govern Portugal and that Napoleon wanted it to be governed in his name by the head of his army, Junot himself. Acúrsio das Neves described it as "Portugal's death sentence". Outside the palace were twelve cannon and Junot was kept under heavy guard, with French troops lining the route from his HQ to Rossio.

The new council assembled by Junot to run the country was a travesty, according to Acúrsio das Neves, the French martinets governing with the aid of local stooges:

> The new government, which is truly military, presided over by the general-in-chief, was divided into departments where each one had at its head French secretaries of state and Portuguese advisers. These advisers were automatons, wholly subject to the general's will, and they came into this organization for two very clear motives: to dupe the people into thinking that the Portuguese had a hand in government, and to make use of them, for whatever end; because as Portuguese they would make the riskiest operations easier, and because neither Junot nor any of his minions possessed the knowledge required to run the kingdom.

The rebellion against French rule began in earnest in the spring. News of the Dos de Mayo revolt against the French in Madrid spread across the border. Insurrections blew up in Portuguese cities and towns where the high-handed manner of the occupiers had bred resentment. Junot had disbanded Portuguese regiments in an attempt to defang Portuguese resistance. But those demobilized men, like the former Iraqi troops who fought the United States after its 2003 invasion, would form the backbone of the irregular units' resistance. Junot sent his cruel, brutal and loathed General Louis Henri Loison to crush the uprisings. Loison had only one arm, due to a hunting accident. People summoned to appear before him had a tendency never to be seen again, hence the colloquial expression *ir ao maneta* (literally, "go to see the one-armed man") used today when someone or something isn't expected to return. Rebels were executed by firing squad, and Junot looked increasingly like a tyrant. Events span out of his control.

Junot's time in Portugal ended after British troops under Sir Arthur Wellesley, later the 1st Duke of Wellington, defeated his French army at the Battle of Vimeiro, about 70 kilometres north of Lisbon, in August. Under the Convention of Sintra—which was signed in Lisbon, not the eponymous town west of the capital from where news of its signing was sent by letter—Junot and his army were allowed to go home. They began to board ships to France on 15 September. Along with Junot went Aires José Maria de Saldanha, the Count of Ega, who was a fervent supporter of the French and threw magnificent parties for the occupiers at his Lisbon palace, and his wife the Countess of Ega, who was having an affair with Junot.

The French occupation had lasted roughly nine months. There would be two more invasions over the next two years, but neither of them reached Lisbon. At Entrecampos Square in the capital, a dramatic statue is dedicated to the Portuguese heroes of the Peninsular War. It was an animated start to a century which would only get worse.

The last French soldiers departed in December, leaving behind rancour and scores to settle with those deemed to have been collaborators. One evening that same month, three soldiers arrested Domingos Sequeira in the street as he was leaving a dinner at the home of the Marquis of Marialva, a distinguished diplomat who had served under the prince regent. Regarded as a pioneer of Romantic painting in Portugal, Sequeira was director of painting at the Ajuda Palace when the French invaded. He stood accused of defaming the prince regent in a Lisbon café.

Sequeira was born in Belém in 1768. He won financial support from Queen Maria I to go and study in Rome and he became a success in Italy. He returned home in 1796 but nobody could afford his prices and he was deeply disappointed. In 1800 he became a monk in the Carthusian Order at a monastery in Laveiras, just west of Belém. While there for two years, he painted large-scale religious works. In 1802 the prince regent, Dom João, appointed him the royal court's first official painter.

During the French occupation Sequeira became friendly with Louis Nicolas Philippe Auguste, the Comte de Forbin, an art lover who would later become curator of the Louvre. Sequeira was hired to paint a portrait of Junot, showing the French general allegorically "protecting Lisbon". Junot didn't like it and it was never finished. Still, it was enough for charges of collaborationism to be brought against Sequeira.

Sequeira was accused of glorifying Junot, who was pictured in his hussar's uniform in the portrait, and of diminishing Portugal. He protested that he had not acted voluntarily, that he had to either obey Junot or flee the country. Even so, he said, he outwitted Junot in the allegorical work by portraying the seated figure of Lisbon as sad, protected by the genius of the Portuguese nation. Sequeira added that he had refused to paint other works requested by Junot. Nevertheless, he spent the following nine months in Limoeiro prison in Alfama.

One of Sequeira's most celebrated works hangs at Lisbon's Museu Nacional de Arte Antiga. It is an 1813 engraving called *Sopa dos Pobres em Arroios* (Soup Kitchen in Arroios, a district of Lisbon) and is considered one of the most important Portuguese works of art. It depicts soup being distributed to the poor from rural areas who, with their crops destroyed by advancing French troops in the third invasion in 1810, sought shelter in the capital. Other important works by Sequeira, such as the famous *A Morte de Camões* (The Death of Camões) are known only from their preparatory drawings. Others still were taken on the ships to Brazil.

* * *

When he was twenty-three, and still to become one of the most famous writers of Portugal's Romantic movement as well as a leading light of the *Geração de 30* (1830s Generation) of intellectuals, João Almeida Garrett took a stroll through the bucolic Odivelas district on Lisbon's outskirts. There, he took a detour into the Gothic church of the Mosteiro de São Dinis e São Bernardo to visit the monastery's fourteenth-century tomb of King Dinis. What he encountered angered him and marked him. The tomb containing the remains of one of the country's most admired monarchs was in a shocking state of neglect and disrepair. The experience of that afternoon stayed with Almeida Garrett. In a collection of early work he published in London during his self-imposed exile seven years later, in 1829, he wrote of the experience with aggrieved disillusionment. He identified in the monument a symbol of the rot that was eating away at nineteenth-century Portugal.

"I have never felt such deep and sad disappointment," he wrote in *Lyrica, de João Mínimo* (Lyrics, by João Mínimo), at seeing the tomb of the "great king ... abandoned, covered in spiders' webs, unseemly". He reflected: "So, rich sepulchral monuments inside and outside churches, which in England or any other Christian country would be conserved with respect and the veneration reserved for relics, there they stand, ruined, the inscriptions illegible, some patched up with modern plaster … What a disgrace, what a national dishonour!"

There was plenty to be shocked about in Almeida Garrett's time. The temptations of power and sex seduced crowned heads and their rivals. Idealists inspired by the French Revolution stood Portugal on its head, and royalists fought to set it right again. Broad dissatisfaction provided fertile ground for revolt and bloodshed on the capital's streets.

The 700-year-old Odivelas monastery is a treasure chest of tales that illustrate their time. Philippa of Lancaster, the daughter of John of Gaunt whose marriage to King João I in 1387 sealed the Anglo-Portuguese alliance, died at the monastery in 1415 after taking refuge there from the plague gripping Lisbon. She was the mother of what Camões in *Os Lusíadas* called the Illustrious Generation: seven of the nine children who reached adulthood left their mark on Portuguese history during the Age of Expansion. Before they departed for Ceuta, her eldest sons Duarte, Pedro and Henrique (later Henry the Navigator) visited her at the monastery where she blessed them and gave them swords. The plague took her life, however, before her sons famously claimed their North African prize.

The monastery's history is also rich in scandal. In the seventeenth century, King Afonso VI still kept alive a royal court tradition that dated back to King Dinis: cavorting with Odivelas nuns. In the eighteenth century, almost two dozen nuns were convicted of "amorous misdeeds" with *fidalgos*. Two nuns swooned over the ribald Afonso VI, who promised to make one of them—Ana de Moura—his queen. King João V outdid all his predecessors, however.

João V was an incorrigible womanizer with an irrepressible sweet tooth. Irresistible, then, were the monastery's ladies and their famous white marmalade. The sovereign fathered children by various women at the Odivelas monastery. The whispered joke at court was that the monarch was so religious that even his lovers were nuns. The children born out of wedlock were given a home at a mansion in the capital called Palácio da Azambuja, which today serves as the Spanish ambassador's residence. They became known as the *Meninos de Palhavã* (Children of Palhavã) after the district of Lisbon where the manor house is located.

João V's favourite mistress of all was the monastery's mother superior, Madre Paula. She was thirty years younger than the king and bore him a son called José. Madre Paula's quarters at the convent were said to be princely. She occupied fifteen rooms over two floors. They were decorated with gold and silver, thick carpets and chandeliers. There was also a monastic cell at the mother superior's disposal, should she prefer it.

Another activity that earned the monastery notoriety were open-air poetry competitions called *outeiros*. Nuns threw down notes from their windows and poets waiting in the patio sought to outdo each other by improvising spoken verses from them. Some were said to be rather risqué. The tradition lasted until the mid-nineteenth century, and one of the participants was Almeida Garrett. Nowadays, Odivelas is a city in its own right, though just 10 kilometres from downtown Lisbon as the crow flies and enmeshed in the capital's fabric. The monastery itself appears to be under siege by low apartment blocks and parked cars.

King Dinis laid the foundation stone for this women's monastery, belonging to the Order of Cistercians, in 1295. It took ten years to complete and is one of Portugal's largest monasteries. It was later remodelled, with the church being built in the 1600s and the cloisters in the 1700s. King Dinis was laid to rest in the first royal tomb in Portugal to be topped with a recumbent statue, which was executed in a Gothic style. He was also the first lay figure in Portuguese history permitted by the clergy to be interred inside a church.

In the 1755 earthquake, the dome above the hefty tomb collapsed and badly damaged the carvings. Parts of the monastery were rebuilt, in neoclassical style, but it was only around a century later that restoration of the tomb was attempted, by the wife of King Pedro V. Queen Estefânia's effort was, no doubt, well-intentioned, but it made a mess by employing nineteenth-century techniques and styles. The king's appearance on the statue was ruined. His clothes, hair and beard were made over in a style that came into fashion centuries after his death. Symbols such as the sword he was holding, and his spurs, vanished. The hand that held his sword looks like it is holding the hem of his clothes. Even his crown was remade in a nineteenth-century style. No original documentation about the tomb has been found, but when it was opened in the 1940s by the Lisbon Geographical Society the skeleton was intact. King Dinis also died with all his own teeth, at what was then the ripe age of sixty-three. Governments were still grumbling in the twenty-first century that they had no money to restore the tomb, though it was at least cleaned, in 2017.

King Dinis is one of Portugal's most esteemed monarchs. He reigned for forty-six years—an astonishing length of time for that period, when governing stability was rare in Europe. He racked up a series of firsts: he is believed to have been Portugal's first fully literate monarch; he founded Portugal's first university, in Lisbon near the Chiado district's Largo do Carmo, though it later moved to Coimbra; he adopted

Portuguese as the country's official language; signed the Treaty of Alcanices with Castile in 1297 to define Portugal's modern borders; and in 1308 signed Portugal's first trade agreement, with England. He also re-established relations with the Holy See and developed seafaring and farming. Indeed, he was known as the "Farmer King". On top of all that, he wrote troubadour poetry and music.

Dinis' long reign had an unhappy end, however, when his son went to war against him. Afonso feared that his father was preparing to pass the crown to his illegitimate half-brother Afonso Sanches, who was widely regarded as the monarch's favourite and who, like his father, impressed the court with his troubadour flair. During the 1320–24 civil war, Lisbon was struck by a strong earthquake, which people interpreted as a sign of God's anger over the bloodshed between father and son. The country's fate was decided in 1325 when Dinis died and Afonso IV acceded to the throne.

Looking back in time through Almeida Garrett's disenchanted nineteenth-century eyes, Dinis' reign was easy to idealize. It was part of the glorious past, in comparison with Almeida Garrett's mad present of the 1820s. Portugal seemed to be losing its sense of self in that unruly decade. Political, social and economic havoc reigned. The Liberal Revolution of 1820, which started in Porto, was when the French Revolution finally caught up with Portugal. The Portuguese revolt was inspired by the principles of equality, democracy, the separation of powers and respect for people's rights. More broadly, it aimed to restore the country's honour and dignity. It sought to rid Portugal of the British, who had stayed on after defeating the French and were squeezing Portuguese trade, and to bring the monarch home from

Brazil, despite his apparent reluctance. Almeida Garrett was caught up in the early flush of excitement with liberalism. He would end up disaffected with both politics and patriotism.

Almeida Garrett was known as something of a dandy but he was also a gallant figure who was unafraid to take sides. He backed the 1820 Revolution while still a law student at Coimbra University. As the revolution's fortunes see-sawed—and eventually ignited a civil war between Liberals and royalists—Almeida Garrett twice had to flee the country for three-year periods. Going into exile was the preferred option because the alternative was the fearsome Limoeiro prison in Alfama, where he spent several months in 1827. He and other journalists on the Lisbon daily *O Portuguez* were charged with incitement to rebellion for their writings.

Almeida Garrett's spell in Limoeiro prison placed him in distinguished company. Apart from Domingos Sequeira, the celebrated poet Barbosa du Bocage was also locked up there. Limoeiro, lying below St George's Castle, was a mint in the early fourteenth century and later that century became a medieval royal palace, where the future King João I killed the Count of Andeiro in 1383. At the end of the fifteenth century Limoeiro became a courthouse and jail, being rebuilt in more or less its current shape as Lisbon's main prison after the 1755 earthquake. It was infamous for its foul conditions and contagious diseases that could kill. Oliveira Martins described it during Almeida Garrett's period thus: "Men were heaped up, prodded with wooden staffs into the company of murderers, into those vile rooms where informal miseries dwelt. They were beaten with clubs and each day provided with a lump of bread and a clear broth in which, rarely, a bit of green floated." Limoeiro is now a training centre for magistrates.

Almeida Garrett produced poems and plays and in 1846 published *Viagens na Minha Terra* (Travels through My Land), a narrative snapshot of his times with a heavy dose of irony. It blends various styles of writing—journalism, political analysis, travel writing of a journey from Lisbon to Santarém, all in a novelistic setting. It is, above all, a reflection on society.

The 1820 Liberal Revolution accomplished its aims: General Beresford and his British officers departed, the country's first elections were held, a Constitution promising equality and freedom was adopted, and on 3 July 1821 the king and his court arrived back in Lisbon. Before that, when the members of the Provisional Junta and the so-called revolutionary army arrived in Lisbon from Porto on 1 October 1820, there were jubilant scenes in Rossio Square. José Hermano Saraiva, in his *História de Portugal*, quotes an eyewitness:

> Rossio was so packed with people that it looked like no more would fit. All you could see were thousands of heads and faces. The windows of the buildings along the sides of the square were the same. The cries of "Viva!", echoing all around, were accompanied by hats being waved and innumerable white handkerchiefs that, because of the huge throng and the movements, made for a beautiful sight.

King João VI had stayed away for almost fourteen years, even though Junot had been gone for about thirteen years. The sovereign, who had taken the crown since leaving his homeland following the death of his mother Queen Maria I in Brazil, arrived in Lisbon after a string of postponements. The monarch came on a *nau* bearing his name that anchored off the Cordoaria Nacional, the low, elongated rope factory that still occupies a spot on the Belém riverside and serves as a venue for exhibitions. Some 4,000 people sailed with the king from Brazil on board two frigates and nine merchant ships. Cannon were fired in celebration from St George's Castle and the riverside forts as the sovereign formally disembarked at Praça do Comércio on 4 July, after receiving delegations from the Lisbon authorities on board his ship. The king proceeded to the Ajuda Palace where he gave his blessing to Portugal's first Constitution, which turned his subjects into citizens. There was none of the riverside drama witnessed when João, as prince regent, had left Lisbon. The drama was not long in coming, however, both in Portugal and in Brazil.

Prince Pedro, in his father's absence from the territory, declared Brazil independent on 7 September 1822 and took the Brazilian throne as Emperor Pedro I. Three weeks later, in Lisbon, João VI signed the Portuguese Constitution, which stripped him of absolute power and installed a parliament but allowed him generous privileges. The signing ceremony on 1 October was in the presence of the elected members of the new Congress at the Palácio das Necessidades. The king entered with his retinue at 12:24 p.m., more than two hours after the session had opened, and sat on the tribune set aside for the royal family. Prince Miguel—who was five when his family fled Lisbon—was there with him, but not the king's scheming Spanish wife, Carlota Joaquina. Her absence was noted and correctly interpreted as an ominous sign. On a throne on the dais, João VI announced in a speech that he endorsed the new constitutional monarchy as "an expression of the general will". After his signature, there were shouts from the elected members of *Viva a Constituição! Viva o melhor dos reis!* ("Long live the Constitution! Long live the greatest of kings!")—to which the king replied, *Viva o soberano Congresso!* ("Long live the sovereign Congress!")

Others were deeply unhappy, and they hatched a plot to kill the Liberal dream. Adding insult to injury, the revolt would once again come from within the king's own family. As if the start of the century had not been tumultuous enough, Lisbon would now live through another spasm of chaos and bloodshed.

The following May, after conspiring with his mother Carlota Joaquina, Prince Miguel—Prince Pedro's younger brother—led a counter-revolution. Its aim was to bring down the Liberal regime, restore an absolute monarchy and tear up the 1822 Constitution. João VI, seeing his own fate hanging in the balance, supported his son. The coup won enough popular support for the king to dissolve the Congress.

But it wasn't over yet. Behind the scenes Carlota Joaquina was pulling the strings. When she had refused to attend what she regarded as her husband's capitulation by signing the Constitution, the authorities removed her from Lisbon's Bemposta Palace. That palace was where Catherine of Braganza had lived after the death of her husband, King Charles II of England, and since 1837 it has been the home of the Portuguese Military Academy. Carlota Joaquina was taken from the Bemposta Palace to the Ramalhão *quinta* (estate) in Sintra, about 30 kilometres away, in the hope of isolating her from the skullduggery in the capital. In fact, the seclusion gave her intrigues room to breathe and grow. The Liberal government got wind of one of her plots when pamphlets calling for the return of absolute rule were found at a printer's shop in Lisbon's Rua Formosa, now called Rua do Século, in the Bairro Alto district. The so-called "Rua Formosa Conspiracy" may, however, have been contrived to provide a pretext for the arrest of some of Carlota Joaquina's alleged sympathizers.

Prince Miguel's relationship with his father was uneasy, and the temptation of the throne was too great to resist. With his pushy mother whispering in his ear, telling him to grab the prize and save the royal house, Miguel raised the Lisbon garrison in April 1824 and had his father moved to the Bemposta Palace. That was said to be for the monarch's own protection, but it was just a ruse to pressure João VI into surrendering the throne. The king, however, with English and French help, outsmarted his presumptuous son. Under the pretence of going out for a ride, João VI, escorted by the British and French ambassadors, made a beeline for the Royal Navy's HMS *Windsor Castle* anchored in the Tagus. The king summoned his son to the impressively powerful ship and, with British might at his back, told Miguel he was being relieved of his of the army and sent into exile in Austria. João VI later gave the ship's crew medals for their support.

In March 1826, João VI died at the Bemposta Palace. His eldest son, Emperor Pedro I of Brazil, who had refused to return to the land he left when he was nine, was declared King Pedro IV of Portugal. Pedro placed conditions on giving up the Brazilian throne and returning to Lisbon: Portugal must accept a Constitutional Charter he would author, adapted from the one he gave to Brazil, and his daughter Maria would marry his brother Prince Miguel when she came of age. Sympathetic to the Liberals, Pedro drew up a new Constitution granting the people rights but also ensuring that the monarch had veto power over the decisions of elected officials. In Lisbon's Rossio Square, whose official name is Praça de D. Pedro IV, a bronze statue of the king erected in 1870 stands on top of a 27-metre-tall column. Wearing a general's uniform, he holds in his right hand his

Constitution of 1826. This same downtown square would be a battleground over the Constitution, in 1831, when the 4th Infantry Battalion, in defence of Pedro IV's document, faced down forces loyal to Miguel. More than 300 people died in that bloody city-centre confrontation.

Several years after acceding to the throne of Portugal, Pedro IV abjured the Brazilian crown. But then came the knife in his back: his brother Miguel returned to Lisbon from exile and claimed the Portuguese throne, taking absolute power with the backing of nobles and clergy who wanted their old privileges back. It was a declaration of war.

On top of his brother's treachery, Pedro was deserted by four sisters who took Miguel's side. Pedro arrived in Portugal at the head of an army of Liberal supporters and the War of the Two Brothers began in 1832. (Almeida Garrett threw himself back into the fray, joining Pedro's Academic Battalion.) The following year the Duke of Terceira, the chief of Pedro's army, took Lisbon after fighting his way up from the south. His battle-ready forces crossed the Tagus from Almada on the south bank on the morning of 24 July, landing at Cais do Sodré. They moved into the city but found nobody to fight because Miguel's troops had fled the capital before dawn. A statue of the duke, from 1870, stands in Praça Duque da Terceira, the square outside Cais do Sodré train station, and Avenida 24 de Julho leads off it.

Defeat of the royalists in two more battles in 1834 brought the civil war to a close, and Miguel went into exile once more. He died in Germany in 1866 but in 1967 his remains were flown to Lisbon for burial at the São Vicente de Fora Church.

The first half of the century still had some nasty surprises in store. In 1836–37 there was a revolution, a coup and a rebellion in the space of ten months. Six years later there was another coup, followed in 1851 by an uprising led by Field Marshal João Carlos Saldanha Oliveira e Daun, the first Duke of Saldanha, which largely placed a lid on the turmoil. In the meantime, the economy had stalled. While elsewhere in Europe the Industrial Revolution was in full swing Portugal languished, bound up in its unending crises. A financial crisis in 1846 forced the Banco de Lisboa—the country's first bank, established in 1821, whose seal was designed by the artist Domingos Sequeira—to merge with the Companhia Confiança Nacional, a company specializing in government debt. The result was the Banco de Portugal, now the country's central bank.

The Liberal triumph in 1834 was a milestone. The centuries-old order of things was upended. Oliveira Martins described it as "the greatest and most brusque social and political change" in Portuguese history. The monarch no longer had a free hand. The legal system, taxation and the relationships between different areas of power were radically reshaped. The Catholic Church, which for so long had been wed to the Crown, was subjected to one of the period's hallmark measures: the dissolution of religious orders and the confiscation of their convents and monasteries for secular uses. The government intended to weaken the Church's influence.

A law of 30 May 1834 ordered the immediate dissolution of the religious houses of the male orders and nationalized their assets. A quarter of a century later, on 4 April 1861—when the last cloistered nun passed away—female convents met the same fate. In Lisbon, that meant that the Church had to surrender dozens of monasteries and convents and church-run colleges, hospitals, hospices and other properties. These former religious buildings were drafted into public service, becoming schools, courthouses, hospitals, military barracks, post offices and other institutions. Those measures did not on the whole change the face of Lisbon, because their architecture mostly remained, but they changed the character of a city that from the thirteenth century had piled up religious buildings.

The 1834 law explains why the Carmo Convent in the Chiado, founded in the fourteenth century by national hero Nuno Álvares Pereira, became a police barracks; why the São Bento da Saúde Monastery, built in 1570, became the parliament building; and why the Boa Hora building, which when it opened in 1633 was a theatre and in 1677 became a convent, was turned into a courthouse. The Academy of Fine Arts and the National Library moved into the São Francisco da Cidade Monastery, which they shared with the Lisbon Civil Government. The National Conservatory took over the Caetanos Monastery, while the Academy of Sciences was awarded the Franciscans' Convent of Jesus. The seventeenth-century Santa Joana Convent, on Rua de Santa Marta near the Marquês de Pombal roundabout, became famous in the twentieth century as the police station where Lisbon people went to pay their traffic fines and the following century was purchased to create a luxury hotel.

Other buildings met more radical and sometimes brutal ends, being in part or wholly demolished and sold off in plots. One of them was the huge Santíssima Trindade Monastery in the Chiado. The government had planned to turn it into a courthouse in 1834 but then divided up the land and sold it to private investors. It was also partly demolished to make way for the Rua Nova da Trindade, as the authorities redrew the city's street plan. Some regretted the passing of the buildings that were roughly treated. Almeida Garrett wrote in 1837 that "we destroyed, because destruction was a caprice of the time."

One notable institution that escaped such a sad fate, and which had also emerged largely unscathed from the 1755 earthquake, is the Cardaes Convent, whose founder's name the Marquis of Pombal had tried to obliterate. It is a small religious house, which was home to fewer than two dozen nuns. It is a discreet presence on the Rua do Século, like a little secret amid the hubbub, and inside it is intimate and well-preserved. The pretty interior contains some exceptional seventeenth-century art, though its blend of Baroque and Rococo is as rich as a fruit cake. The convent was not plundered, it is said, because the tax inspector sent to assess it wrote a note to his superior along the bottom of his report that guards should be posted outside to protect its contents. It has enchanting cloisters and one of the most remarkable wardrobes you will ever come across. Another point of interest is that here lies one of the few remaining examples of the coat of arms of the Távora family. Pombal's instructions for it to be built over as part of his *damnatio memoriae* had the unintended consequence of preserving it for posterity. The Cardaes Convent is one of those small city museums that fully reward a visit.

* * *

The flight of the royal family, the French invasions and the chaotic political times that followed put a brake on Lisbon's development. Perhaps the best symbol of that hiatus is the Ajuda Palace, arguably the nineteenth century's most eminent construction project.

The makeshift wooden apartments known as the *barraca real*, on the Ajuda hill where the unnerved royal family made its home after the 1755 earthquake, burned down in 1794. King João VI considered the bucolic area, with its magnificent views over the Tagus and out to sea, a fine spot to build a palace. Construction work began in 1796 but stopped shortly afterward due to a lack of funds. Building resumed in 1802, only to be cut short when Junot invaded in 1807. It started again in 1813, though little progress had been made by the time the royal family returned from Brazil in 1821. The Liberal victory in 1834 halted the work one more time. The palace was occasionally used as a royal residence or for royal events, even though it was unfinished, from 1826 onward.

Its long gestation meant that Ajuda started out as a Baroque palace and ended as a neoclassical one. It is the home of the bulging Royal Library, of the legendary eighteenth-century dinner service made by Paris silversmith François-Thomas Germain (most of which King João VI brought back from Brazil with him in 1821) and wall paintings by Domingos Sequeira. Dom Miguel swore to uphold the 1826 Constitutional Charter in the palace's magnificent Throne Room, where in the twentieth century Queen Elizabeth II, the president of China and US President Bill Clinton were received on separate occasions. In 1968, the palace became a museum. There was still one thing missing, though: the palace's rear wall. Ajuda was—and is—a thing of beauty, as long as you didn't poke your head around the back. Its rear was naked and ugly and was destined to remain that way until at least December 2018. Governments had pleaded poverty or deliberately neglected the palace for more than 200 years. In September 2016, the authorities decided it was finally time to finish what had been begun in 1796.

As the climate of civil war subsided after 1834, a drive to make up for lost time gradually gained traction. Perhaps the greatest cultural symbol of this effort at revival is the Teatro Nacional D. Maria II (Queen Maria II National Theatre), which stands on the north side of the Rossio Square and opened in 1846. Almeida Garrett led the ideological project to create a national theatre. It would have a civic function to educate citizens. Its location, on the site of the former Palace of the Inquisition, was not intended as a political statement (the palace had burned down in 1836) but a page was conspicuously turned. The Inquisition's power had waned in the second half of the eighteenth century, and the last burning at the stake was that of Father Malagrida in 1761, but it was formally extinguished only in 1821 with the Liberal movement.

The ruins of the austere palace were demolished and the theatre, the most significant public building of the Liberal period, was built by Italian architect Fortunato Lodi in neoclassical style. The elegant façade includes six columns that were taken from the extinguished São Francisco da Cidade Monastery. On top there is a statue of the dramatist Gil Vicente, flanked by figures representing tragedy and comedy. The theatre's early days did not go smoothly, as the aftermath of the revolutionary period still fuelled rivalries between prominent figures involved in running the theatre. Water seepage in the building was another problem but, more damningly, the acoustics were so poor that the audience found it difficult to hear the actors on stage.

The opening work was a historical drama in five acts by Jacinto Loureiro called *Álvaro Gonçalves, o Magriço, ou os Doze de Inglaterra* (Álvaro Gonçalves, Defender of Ladies, or the England Dozen) based on a chivalrous story told in *Os*

Lusíadas about twelve Portuguese knights who went to England. The theatre's darkest hour came when it fell victim to a long-standing theatrical curse. The National Theatre was gutted by fire on the night of 2 December 1964, when it was staging Shakespeare's *Macbeth*. The play is cursed, according to superstition, which is why people in the theatre refer to it obliquely as "the Scottish play", lest they bring the hex down on their heads. The cause of the blaze was believed to have been a short circuit. The following day's edition of the *Diário de Notícias* newspaper tried hard to convey the drama of the loss, dedicating its entire front page to the calamity and publishing a photograph that occupied most of it. "Macbeth's Curse", the paper announced in its bold-type headline. The caption of the photo, which was taken from the Bairro Alto looking down on the Baixa, with a huge smoke plume rising up from the inferno, read: "In the centre of the capital, which was sleeping soundly, a volcano's crater opened up, implacable, phantasmagorical, hypnotic, and blew embers across the city."

The National Theatre, which was rebuilt, was not the only nineteenth-century hallmark building to suffer bad luck. Lisbon's Paços do Concelho (City Hall) has appeared jinxed, too. The city authorities were left homeless after the 1755 earthquake and in 1774 moved into a new, purpose-built building close to Praça do Comércio designed by the post-quake architect Eugénio dos Santos. It was almost completely destroyed by a fire in 1863. It was rebuilt over fifteen years, with its frontage by French sculptor Anatole Calmels adopting a neoclassical style. Calmels, however, went a little too far with his modernism in conservative Lisbon. The *bas-relief* on the façade's triangular pediment features the first completely naked male statue in public in the Portuguese capital. To make matters worse, it was positioned so as to be full-frontal. It caused a city scandal, with loud voices denouncing it as immoral, and also spawned some jokes. In one of them, the newspaper *Diário Ilustrado* recounted how a man walked through the square outside city hall with his two nieces and told them, "Don't look, girls, it's indecent." To which one of them replied: "You're right, uncle, we'd noticed."

City Hall re-opened in 1880. But another fire in 1996 wrecked the upper floors. The reconstruction sought to restore some of the building's original features. It is noted today for its balcony and its memorable staircase with a dome above it.

The tide turned for Portuguese fortunes when the government headed by the Duke of Saldanha, one of the great statesmen of the nineteenth century, came to power in 1851. After being deeply entangled in the decades of political wrangling that marked the first half of the century, in April 1851 Saldanha attempted to incite a military insurrection that would take power. He thought he had failed and, crestfallen, took refuge in north-west Spain, only to be informed soon afterward that his power grab had earned broad military and popular support. That persuaded the reluctant Queen Maria II—as head of the constitutional monarchy—to give her blessing to Saldanha's leadership of the country. The queen had dismissed a previous Saldanha government two years earlier, prompting the military veteran to publish a caustic and confrontational objection to Her Majesty's decision. He got his revenge when he returned in triumph to Lisbon amid popular acclaim and marched his troops past the Palácio das Necessidades where the queen, with false bonhomie, had to take his salute.

The new political stability provided the starting gun for a period that would become known as the *Regeneração* (Regeneration). After a half-century of mayhem, there would now come a half-century of progress to turn Lisbon into a modern European capital.

The architect and driving force behind many of the city's social and technological enhancements was a politician who, when he joined Saldanha's government aged thirty-one, was known only for a handful of speeches in Parliament. But he proved himself to be energetic, resolute and diligent. António Maria Fontes Pereira de Melo, head of the newly created Ministry of Public Works, Trade and Industry, stamped his mark on Portuguese history. He burned with enthusiasm for his work, political intrigue left him cold, and he wasn't in it for the money. He was not a typical member of the Lisbon political class. "Rather than spend his evenings reading French novels, playing whist [and] paying attention to rumours, he occupied himself with writing articles for the *Military Magazine*, writing preambles, studying inventions," writes historian Maria Filomena Mónica, his biographer.

Fontes Pereira de Melo oversaw the construction across the country of hundreds of kilometres of new roads and more than a dozen bridges, as well as Portugal's first train line and telegraph network. He also introduced the metric system. In the capital, Fontes Pereira de Melo's legacy abides. He gave the city the port of Lisbon, the Santa Apolónia train station and the Lisbon-Sintra railway. Later, he masterminded the restoration of the Jerónimos Monastery and created the Hospital Dona Estefânia. He also subsidized the introduction of steam ships on the Tagus and founded Lisbon's Industrial and Trade Institute and its Agricultural Institute, which sought to introduce modern European approaches and skills.

The dream of a better life in the increasingly sophisticated capital drew more and more people from the impoverished countryside. Lisbon's population swelled from around 200,000 people in the middle of the nineteenth century to some 300,000 by its close. The mass migration squashed people into the city. Extra floors were built onto houses, and Alfama and Mouraria were like ants' nests, with overcrowded streets. Beggars and thugs were commonplace.

Lisbon's urban development gathered pace over the second half of the century. Arguably the most important public works project in Lisbon—and one of the biggest in Portugal during that period—was the *aterro da Boavista*, a huge mid-century earthwork that reclaimed land from the river and created an embankment where the Avenida 24 de Julho was built. The project was executed by Vitorino Damásio, head of the Industrial Institute. The road leading west out of the city helped Lisbon stretch out and gave it some room to breathe. It linked Cais do Sodré to Santos and Alcântara. The tree-lined path along the riverside embankment was hugely popular. It was a breezy place to escape the cramped and fetid older parts of the city. In 1873 the capital's first horse-drawn trams, known as *caminhos de ferro Americanos* (American railways), ran along here, from Rossio Square to Belém. They were replaced by electric trams in 1900.

The embankment also helped clean up an insalubrious sliver of beach where sludge and waste accumulated. The Tagus was still acting as Lisbon's cesspit. Between 1855 and 1857 there were outbreaks of cholera (more than 3,000 deaths) and yellow fever (more than 5,600 deaths). The new buildings and streets created after the 1755 earthquake had drains and sewers, but owners of pre-quake properties balked at the expense of installing the pipes. The centuries-old problem of Lisbon's lack of hygiene had not gone away.

Samuel Broughton, the British officer who visited Lisbon during the Peninsular War, had the same reaction as the French he was fighting. In his collection of letters from Iberia, published in London in 1809, he recalls approaching Lisbon from the sea. It was, he reports, "a commanding city [that] rose in white majesty to the view of the admiring traveler." But on closer inspection he found "a chaos of nastiness, poverty and wretchedness ... on every side". He turned his nose up at the "squalid misery", not least because of the blight that was *água vai*, potty-tossing, which had also nauseated the French.

Lisbon, however, lacked the money required for the major sanitation project that everyone recognized it needed, especially in Alfama and Mouraria. The order to build a city-wide sewer network came only with a municipal decree of 24 May 1858, though it would take decades for it to extend across the city. The push for cleanliness was helped by the government which, at the request of the City Council, decided in 1864 to create a committee that would draw up "a comprehensive plan for improvements in the capital". It operated within the framework of Fontes Pereira de Melo's broader national ambitions.

Lisbon fattened out. The opening of the Hospital de D. Estefânia gave birth to the Bairro da Estefânia in the 1880s, and early the next century the city's eastward expansion would continue to what today is called Avenida Almirante Reis, a main thoroughfare. The city was growing away from the Tagus, its cradle.

Frederico Ressano Garcia, who took over as Lisbon City Council's chief engineer in 1874, became a central figure in the capital's growth. Trained at the École des Ponts et Chaussées in Paris, he imported the latest engineering techniques and fashions. Ressano Garcia helped make Lisbon a modern city. He expanded infrastructure such as public transport (including Lisbon's famous funiculars), a water supply network and sewers to most neighbourhoods, and he spread Lisbon to the north. He took his cue from Baron Haussmann's ambitions in Paris and Ildefons Cerdà's work in Barcelona. Ressano Garcia would bring far-reaching changes to Lisbon's physiognomy.

Under his guidance, public parks and gardens and woodland gained new weight in the city's urban planning. They were viewed as wholesome places for leisure and socializing. It was about quality of life. The gardens at São Pedro de Alcântara, on the edge of Bairro Alto, from where the photograph of the burning National Theatre was taken in 1964 and which is a popular tourist spot today for its unobstructed view of St George's Castle, were created as part of this policy. Already open was the Jardim da Estrela, across from the basilica, which still offers leafy walkways, ponds with water lilies and lawns. This garden was the home of the famous caged *Leão da Estrela* (Estrela Lion), donated in 1871 by colonial administrator Paiva Raposo, which gave its name to a popular twentieth-century play and film.

Broad boulevards sprouted and became the arteries that gave life to new *bairros*. The central Avenida da Liberdade, a kind of mini-Champs-Elysées, is the best-known fruit of this policy. It provided the backbone, or substructure, for Ressano Garcia's push northward with the building of the so-called Avenidas Novas (New Avenues). There were two dozen of these, including Avenida Fontes Pereira de Melo and what is now called Avenida da República.

The Avenida da Liberdade, a boulevard with plane trees overhanging the busy road and lush lateral gardens featuring palm trees and fishponds, links the Restauradores Square with the Marquês de Pombal roundabout. The *Guia de Portugal* says it is "one of Europe's prettiest avenues", though it rubbishes the buildings along it as being "generally in poor taste and with little architectural dignity". It continues: "When [the buildings] avoid banality they are cold or pretentious, sometimes showing on their unkind façades doors and windows in an Arab style"—an apparent reference to the house of local biscuit baron Conceição e Silva at 226–228 Avenida da Liberdade. This Moorish revival style was popular in Lisbon at the time. The Praça de Touros bullring at Campo Pequeno, on Avenida da República, is a prominent example of this fashion. It was modelled on the Fuente del Berro bullring, now gone, in Madrid. Portuguese architect António Dias de Silva added three towers topped with domes. Some people referred to it as "Lisbon's Kremlin" because of its onion-shaped domes. The first bullfight was staged there in 1892. Three bullfighters have died in the arena. Two *forcados*—the young men who grab the charging bull around the neck and hang on for dear life—have also been killed there.

Rosa Araújo, Lisbon mayor in the 1870s, is regarded as the father of the Avenida da Liberdade, a city emblem. By the late twentieth century it had become run-down and seedy, though. Its revival in the early twenty-first century was largely due to rising property prices and the arrival of luxury brand shops. It has remained the city's most polluted street.

The Avenida da Liberdade grew out of the Passeio Público (Public Promenade), a gated garden close to Rossio which was begun in 1764. It was built over kitchen gardens that were on damp earth, and earthquake rubble was put down to help stabilize the ground. It was Portugal's first French-style public garden and a product of Enlightenment thinking about the benefits of contact with nature.

In the first decades after its opening, the Passeio Público was regarded as a less than thrilling place to visit. It was small, symmetrical and unchanging. Even so, as João Paulo Freire in his 1932 book *Lisboa do meu tempo e do meu passado* (Lisbon of My Time and My Past) noted, it did offer some relief from the entertainment-starved lives of city-dwellers who otherwise gathered "only for religious processions or burnings at the stake".

It was enlarged in the 1830s with a small lake, a wider variety of trees and a bandstand. It became known as the Municipal Garden and grew more popular. Concerts and firework displays drew crowds, but only for the *beau monde*. To keep out beggars and undesirables, men had to wear a tie to get in. Even the royal family went there for a stroll. When gas lights were installed in 1851, changing Lisbon's routines and opening up new possibilities, night-time strolls in the park attracted thousands of people in just a few days.

Portugal's great nineteenth-century novelist José Maria Eça de Queirós, an astute recorder of social habits and mores, described the Passeio Público as "a dismal pleasure". It was more a place for people to be seen than to see. It was fashionable among the Lisbon bourgeoisie, especially on Sundays. In Queirós' novel *O Primo Basílio* (Cousin Basílio), it serves as a symbol of unwholesome social aspirations: a Lisbon housemaid blackmails her mistress over an affair and parades her new clothes, purchased with her ill-gotten gains, at the Passeio Público. On the other hand, in Queirós' novel *Os Maias* (The Maias), one of the characters damningly says, "Lisbon is Portugal. There's nothing outside Lisbon."

Eça de Queirós, a statue of whom is on Rua do Alecrim, across the road from the palace that Junot commandeered in 1807, was a leading light of the so-called *Geração de 70* (1870s Generation). Whereas the *Geração de 30* of Almeida Garrett and Alexandre Herculano found its inspiration in Romanticism, this new group was inspired by realism and science. It was a young and gifted group of intellectuals, fired up by the new ideas and possibilities bubbling in Europe. Others in the group included Camilo Castelo Branco, who wrote his best-known novel *Amor de Perdição* (Doomed Love) in two weeks. After a life of pushing at the frontiers of acceptable behavior with his scandalous love life, Castelo Branco went blind due to syphilis and shot himself in his right temple. He wrote more than 100 books over some forty-five years. Another prominent member was Antero de Quental, a philosopher-historian with a keen intellect who was a passionate orator. He fought relentlessly for social justice and freedom of thought. He had pedigree as a Liberal: his grandfather André da Ponte de Quental was a signatory of the 1822 Constitution.

Many of the *Geração de 70* had travelled widely and saw themselves as the embryo of a new Portugal—because when they looked out of the window, they perceived a broken and dispirited land, scarred by years of tumult. In March 1871 they rented a first-floor room with tall windows and a high ceiling at the Casino Lisbonense in the Chiado district, on a sloping street in the Largo da Abegoaria. There, they planned to hold ten of what they termed *Conferências Democráticas*

(Democratic Symposia). Eça de Queirós later described these as "the first time a revolution grounded in science had a stage" in Portugal. They would hold only five of the intended events, however, because the authorities stepped in and shut them down.

Eça de Queirós gave the fourth lecture, entitled "The New Literature, or Realism as an Expression of Art". Quental chose a broader, and more controversial, topic. His lecture was called *Causas da Decadência dos Povos Peninsulares* (On the Causes of the Decadence of the Iberian People), and he pulled no punches. In a brilliant, 12,000-word speech, he sought to solve the conundrum of why Portugal was a European straggler. One of the causes he identified was religious conservatism (the other causes were political centralization and the invitation to indolence that was spawned by the Age of Expansion). He pointed his accusing finger straight at the Catholic Church. Seldom had the Church been the target of such unvarnished, uncompromising criticism as that meted out by Quental. The authorities were already jumpy due to the 1868 revolt in Spain which deposed Queen Isabel II, and in France the Paris Commune was ruling. A royal decree halted the lectures.

That Portugal had fallen behind Europe was indisputable. Lisbon, Eça de Queirós said, was still like a big village. The streets were reminiscent of Africa, with few stores and most shopping done from street hawkers who went door-to-door—the *aguadeiros* selling water from barrels, *leiteiros* selling milk, the *lavadeiras* with their bundles of laundry, the *padeiros* selling bread from baskets. Lisbon's first department store, the Grandes Armazéns do Chiado, opened in 1894—about a century after the first such stores in Paris and London. The first car on Portuguese roads was delivered by ship from France to the Lisbon quayside in October 1895. It was a Panhard et Levassor and was purchased by Jorge d'Avillez, a young aristocrat who lived in Santiago do Cacém, a town 150 kilometres south of the capital. It took him three days to drive home.

* * *

Sunday, 12 January 1890 was a busy day for the police in Lisbon. Several thousand protesters shouting patriotic slogans roamed through the city's downtown. Mobs threw stones at the British Consulate and the Portuguese Foreign Ministry, breaking windows. Students gathered outside the Café Martinho in the Praça do Comércio and, chanting, marched up to the Chiado. Police and cavalry were deployed to quell the disturbances that extended from the afternoon into the night. More than fifty people were arrested.

The enraged fist-waving erupted in the hours after what is still felt as a national humiliation: Portugal's capitulation to Britain in a standoff over their possessions in Africa. The episode was felt particularly keenly because Britain was the country's oldest and, ostensibly, closest ally. It was, in retrospect, a Rosebud moment. Marcello Caetano, a university professor and later national leader, explained this loss of innocence in terms of *realpolitik*, remarking that "no matter how close and old alliances are, there is no pact of friendship that can make powerful nations give up their interests or moderate their covetousness for a small nation if the latter doesn't first have the awareness, the intelligence and the enthusiasm for its own affairs."

The source of the trouble was the Berlin Conference five years earlier, which unleashed the so-called "Scramble for Africa". European powers, meeting more than 2,000 kilometres away from Lisbon, introduced the rule of effective colonial occupation: you could say a territory was yours only if you were there and ran it. Portugal, since the Age of Expansion, never had enough people to settle far beyond the coast of the vast lands where it planted the flag.

There was another problem. The Portuguese wanted possession of a coast-to-coast swathe of Africa, stretching from Angola in the west to Mozambique in the east. This ambition was known by shorthand as the *Mapa Côr-de-Rosa* (Pink-coloured Map) and was dear to Portugal. It was a Romantic idea given form by army captain Alexandre de Serpa Pinto. He was an explorer and a national icon in the mould of Britain's Henry Stanley and Dr David Livingstone. Serpa Pinto was a leader of Portugal's first official scientific expedition, between 1877 and 1879, into the heart of the Dark Continent. His two-volume book about his adventures, called *Como eu atravessei a África* (How I Crossed Africa), caught the popular imagination. The Lisbon Geographical Society, founded in 1875, was behind the prestigious expedition.

But Britain had its own Cairo-to-Cape Town imperial ambitions, and on 11 January 1890 London bluntly told the Portuguese to get out of Britain's way. At 9:00 a.m. that day the British envoy to Lisbon, George Glynn Petre, informed the Portuguese minister for the navy and overseas territories, Henrique de Barros Gomes, that the Portuguese troops stationed in African areas coveted by Britain must leave. The unspoken words were: "or else". A memorandum containing that message became known as the British Ultimatum. On that

Saturday evening, King Carlos I—who had ascended to the throne about two weeks earlier—summoned his Council of State to an emergency meeting. It went on until after 1:00 a.m.

The Portuguese had little choice but to comply with London's demands. They were trapped, as with Junot's invasion, between the devil and the deep blue sea. Portugal could not hope to match the military might of Britain, which had deployed warships to Gibraltar—including HMS *Colossus*, one of the first of a new generation of modern battleships—and Vigo in north-west Spain, as well as to Zanzibar off the eastern coast of Africa near Mozambique, in a pointed show of force. Oldest ally or not, Portugal would not be spared Albion's perfidy. A cartoon from the time by Bordalo Pinheiro, a celebrated caricaturist, shows John Bull standing in Africa and firing the Ultimatum from a blunderbuss at Lisbon, represented by the Belém Tower.

Many Portuguese were incensed. A tide of patriotic fervour and anti-British sentiment rose up. Republicans derided the monarchy as spineless and treasonous for caving in. Groups shouting the name of Serpa Pinto and patriotic slogans went through the city. They banged on the door of the Sociedade Geographica de Lisboa whose secretary-general lowered the Portuguese flag to half-mast. A mob barged into the Teatro Nacional de São Carlos, regarded by republicans as a nest of royalists, between the first and second acts of the evening performance and yelled, "Today there's no show, today is a day of mourning!" The 12 January edition of *O Século* asked: "Will Lisbon be bombarded?" The next day, the front-page headline of republican newspaper *Os Debates* was simply "Treason".

A stirring piece of new music that came out later that January captured the public mood. Later, in 1911, it would

be chosen as Portugal's national anthem. It was composed by
Alfredo Keil, who asked Henrique Lopes de Mendonça, a
navy officer and poet, to set words to it. *A Portuguesa* is a rousing, and flattering, call to arms:

> Heroes of the sea, noble people,
> Brave, immortal nation,
> Exalt today once more
> The splendour of Portugal!
>
> ...
>
> To arms, to arms!
> On land and over the sea,
> To arms, to arms!
> Fight for our homeland,
> And against the cannon march on, march on!

Some of the protesters in Lisbon's streets changed the
word "cannon" (*canhões*) to "British" (*Bretões*). Before it was
adopted as the national anthem, the music was so popular
that it was played at Lisbon theatres and printed on cans of
sardines and packets of biscuits.

Particularly vexing was that the British and Portuguese had
always appeared to get on so well since their fourteenth-
century alliance. They were—are—very different but seemed
to complement each other, to be a good fit. British phlegm, a
down-to-earth approach and careful planning provided a
counterpoint to the passionate, inspired and adaptable
Portuguese. But British self-interest always spoke louder, and
Britain took what advantage it could of the Portuguese kingdom. As the French clergyman and diplomat Abbé de Pradt
remarked: "Portugal existed only for England. It was, so to
speak, entirely devoured by her." The Marquis of Pombal
saw through the British, whom he held in low regard, and

viewed Portugal's dependence on them as one of the main reasons for his country's backwardness.

In the early nineteenth century, Portugal had been a battlefield in a proxy war between Britain and France. Once the British had helped dislodge Junot from Lisbon, they settled in. Initially, the British were highly popular. Broughton said Lisbon welcomed British troops with "public rejoicing". British Lieutenant Wright Knox wrote in a letter home in October 1809 that Sir Arthur Wellesley, later the Duke of Wellington:

> made a pompous entry into Lisbon a few days ago, he was received by the Militia and Volunteers of the place under arms, with Minute Guns firing from the Castle for half an hour, the populace seemed to pay him a kind or adoration, the next day he was received by the Regency [Council], and admitted into it with the uncontrolled command of the military affairs of this country and a share in the civil.

When Wellesley returned to Lisbon in 1813 for a four-day stay, crowds once again turned out to greet him.

General William Beresford was chosen by the British, with the blessing of the prince regent in Brazil, in 1809 to take over as head of the Portuguese army with the rank of marshal. He had a brief to modernize the local forces and make them compatible with their British counterparts. Beresford set up his headquarters in the Palácio da Ega in Alcântara, whose owner's wife had had an affair with Junot and which had later been used as a hospital during the fighting against the French. Beresford introduced new training methods and turned the Portuguese army into a stronger fighting force.

After Wellesley's defeat of Napoleon's forces in 1814, however, Beresford became a lightning rod for public resentment at what was seen as Britain's unofficial colonization of

Portugal. The mood soured as Beresford began meddling in Portuguese politics, and his overbearing manner caused friction with the Regency Council. Nevertheless, Beresford sailed to Brazil in 1815 and returned with broader powers granted to him by the prince regent. Beresford behaved like a viceroy and promoted only British officers, overlooking the Portuguese. The seeds of anti-British nationalism germinated.

Increasingly a target of scorn, Beresford's Waterloo in Portugal came in 1817. His brutal, ruthless crackdown on what he judged to be a Liberal conspiracy against the status quo was calculated to stamp his authority on the capital, but it would backfire.

The alleged ringleader of the supposed revolt was Gomes Freire de Andrade, a colourful character with a chequered history of adventure and shifting allegiances. Hard to pin down, he has been alternately described as a martyr, a heroic precursor of liberalism and a traitor. Gomes Freire, as he is known, was a palette of contradictions. He was born in Vienna, where his father was Portugal's ambassador to the Austrian court, and was an aristocrat. When the royal family sailed to Brazil, he was left in charge of some military units but cooperated with Junot. Gomes Freire's men were integrated into the French occupying force, becoming the famous Portuguese Legion which went on to fight elsewhere in Europe with Napoleon. Gomes Freire returned to Portugal after Waterloo in 1815. The British, unsurprisingly, eyed him with suspicion. Gomes Freire was also a founder of one of Portugal's biggest freemason lodges, which was created in a first meeting at his house.

Gomes Freire was one of twelve men rounded up in Lisbon in March 1817 on Beresford's orders. He was taken to the tower of the São Julião da Barra coastal fortress west of Lisbon and held incommunicado for three months. The others were taken to Limoeiro prison. On 15 October, after a trial fraught with procedural irregularities, the dozen were sentenced to death by hanging. The court also ruled that the bodies of eight of them, including Gomes Freire, should be beheaded and cremated, with their ashes thrown into the sea.

Three days later, the executions took place. Gomes Freire was hanged at the fort where he was being held. The eleven others were taken to the gallows at Campo de Santana. 18 October was a sunny day, according to the journalist and historian Raúl Brandão. At 2:00 p.m., after a lengthy and agonizing public reading of the sentence, the men were brought out. The coffins destined for the four who would not be burned were placed next to the gallows, beneath a blue sky. Soldiers kept back the crowds of people who turned out to watch the gruesome spectacle. The proceedings were carried out with harrowing slowness and lasted until after sunset. They were supervised by Miguel Pereira Forjaz, the Regency Council's secretary, a staunch royalist and a notoriously cruel man who was also Gomes Freire's cousin. As night fell and the executions continued, Pereira Forjaz famously uttered the chilling words, *Felizmente há luar* ("Fortunately, there is moonlight.")

The episode was not soon forgotten. Indeed, it was one of the factors that led to the 1820 Revolution. It also fuelled the animosity felt toward Beresford, who went to Brazil for more royal consultations but was denied entry back into Lisbon when he returned. In 1879 the Campo de Santana, long home to the city's open-air abattoir, was renamed Campo dos Mártires da Pátria (Field of the Martyrs for the Homeland).

Leading off it is Rua Gomes Freire, where the Polícia Judiciária has its headquarters.

For Britain, Portugal was a precious foothold on a sometimes hostile continent. Numerous treaties, agreements and conventions were signed from the Windsor Treaty of 1386 between Richard II of England and King João I onwards. A 1654 treaty, negotiated between Oliver Cromwell's administration and the court of João IV, granted broad privileges in Portugal to the British. Among them was somewhere in Lisbon to bury their dead, and this was where Protestant England crossed paths with the Portuguese Inquisition. Obstruction by the Inquisition meant that the cemetery did not come into being for more than fifty years.

St George's Cemetery was eventually created on a plot of land previously known as the military burial ground on Rua São Jorge, across from the Jardim da Estrela, and is today referred to as the British Cemetery. The novelist Henry Fielding was buried in this graveyard in 1754. The exact location of his grave is unknown, though a public subscription in 1830 raised enough money to build a monument to him there. The building of an Anglican church had to wait until the Inquisition's power had waned, in the early nineteenth century. The first St George's Church burnt down in 1886. The second one, consecrated three years later, still stands.

Despite some difficult moments in bilateral relations, British royal visits to Lisbon have delighted many Portuguese. In April 1903, King Edward VII's first trip abroad after acceding to the throne was to the Portuguese capital. He came to see King Carlos I, his second cousin. The Palácio das Necessidades merited a refurbishment for the visit, including new bathrooms. The British sovereign was received at the Ajuda Palace and attended a performance at the Teatro Nacional de São Carlos. After he left, Lisbon's largest city park was named after him—Parque Eduardo VII, at the top of the Avenida da Liberdade, behind the Marquês de Pombal roundabout.

Queen Elizabeth II made a bigger splash in 1957. The royal yacht sailed up the Tagus, with small fishing boats in trail sounding their sirens. The queen and the Duke of Edinburgh disembarked at the Praça do Comércio, where huge crowds awaited them. The vast square was fully occupied by a military parade, and there was a fly-past by the Portuguese Air Force. With rain threatening, the monarch went in a carriage up through the Baixa and the Avenida da Liberdade to the Parque Eduardo VII. The crowds were ten-deep on the pavements; men waved their hats, women waved white handkerchiefs and children waved small Portuguese and Union Jack flags. Elizabeth visited Lisbon's National Carriage Museum, had lunch at a spick-and-span City Hall and was given a Lusitanian horse as a present. At a banquet at the Ajuda Palace, President Craveiro Lopes said in his speech: "In a constantly changing world, the 600-year alliance between our two countries is a shining example of consistency. May it inspire future generations." Nobody was indiscreet enough to mention the Ultimatum.

France and Britain provided the century's bookends for the Portuguese, for whom the 1800s ended on a sour note. The outlay on all those infrastructure improvements drained the Treasury. Portugal's foreign debt went from 31 per cent to 75 per cent of GDP in the second half of the century. Interest payments consumed half of state revenue. In the Panic of 1890, international debt markets dried up after a crisis at London bank Baring Brothers. Portugal subsequently defaulted on its debts and declared bankruptcy. Lisbon had to postpone its ambitious plans for an underground railway. London opened the first one in 1863 and other European cities were keen to follow suit. In Lisbon, the idea was first discussed in 1885 and three years later an outline plan was drawn up. But there was no money. The city would have to wait another sixty years for the Metropolitano de Lisboa, because the next century would be tough as well.

SEVEN—A TALE OF TWO BRIDGES

You can search high and low in Lisbon for António Salazar but you won't find a mention of him. The man who ruled Portugal for more than three decades—and who was the country's most consequential political figure of the twentieth century—is unremembered in the capital. The man whose iron hand quelled incessant political strife by installing a dictatorship, who nimbly steered his neutral country unscathed through World War II but led it into protracted colonial wars in Africa, who kept the country out of the clutches of eager Cold War factions, who gripped the Portuguese in a chokehold of censorship, secret police and Orwellian propaganda, who wanted to preserve Portuguese culture in amber and banned Coca-Cola, who balanced the books and brought annual growth of 6 per cent even while most people scraped by in poverty and were illiterate, has been scrubbed from the city's history. Salazar has been put in a box in the attic.

The same cannot be said of the Carnation Revolution that ended the regime that Salazar built. The capital is strewn with emphatic reminders of that event. Naming streets and squares after the 25 April 1974 army coup that introduced democracy was a shorthand way of advertising a turning point, because one of Portugal's modern pieties is that the revolution was wholly good and Salazar was wholly bad.

The most blatant instance of this historic erasure is the name on Lisbon's 2-kilometre-long bridge over the Tagus between Alcântara and Almada. The bridge opened in 1966 and was baptized Ponte Salazar (Salazar Bridge), its sober symmetry befitting the staid nature of the man who wrote the cheque for it. In 1974 Salazar's name was unceremoniously stripped off the bridge. Workers from the Sorefame heavy industry company climbed a scaffold and, with sledgehammers, cheerfully knocked the black iron letters off the white concrete pillar. An S, an A, a Z dropped onto the grass after a few heavy blows. A new name went up: Ponte 25 de Abril.

A straight line can be drawn from that date to 1986, when Portugal joined the European Economic Community. The new times merited a new emblem. The Ponte Vasco da Gama was built 10 kilometres to the east of the older bridge. It possesses a sleek, wind-in-your-hair design, majestically sweeping kilometres across the Sea of Straw. It captures the late 1990s swagger of a country that had proved its critics wrong and made the grade for inclusion in the elite European class of the euro currency. The name was a safe pick. There was no chance of anybody grumbling about Vasco da Gama, in Portugal at least. It had the additional attraction of reminding the world about Portugal's glorious past.

These two bridges are not just busy physical links. They are also symbolic connections with the past and signature features of the modern city. Both are emblematic of Lisbon's twentieth century. But before either of them came into being,

Lisbon and Portugal strayed back into political quicksand and planted the seeds of Salazar's long rule.

* * *

The royal carriage was waiting for King Carlos, Queen Amélia, Prince Luis Filipe and his younger brother Prince Manuel when the steamer which had brought them across the Tagus docked at Praça do Comércio shortly after 5:00 p.m. on Saturday, 1 February 1908. The royal family was returning from a hunting trip in eastern Portugal to the capital, where revolutionary conspiracies were rife. A period of strikes and unrest had peaked with an aborted coup attempt in the capital four days earlier. Two bombs had gone off in Lisbon the previous year. The government supported by the king was broadly unpopular, and republican opposition to the constitutional monarchy was stiffening.

The royals climbed into the open carriage which proceeded at a trot along the western side of the square. It was heading to the Palácio das Necessidades. Men passing in the arcades along the square raised their hats in greeting as the landau passed. When the carriage turned left, into Rua do Arsenal, one of the most dramatic events in Portuguese history occurred.

Manuel Buíça, a thirty-two-year-old primary school teacher with a bushy beard, stepped out from behind a dark-green street kiosk, pulled a Mannlicher-Schönauer bolt-action rifle from beneath his cloak, crouched on one knee and fired. His shot hit the king in the throat and shattered his cervical spine, killing him instantly. His co-conspirator Alfredo Costa, a clerk aged twenty-four, leaped up onto the landau on the other side. He also shot the monarch, with a Browning revolver. Prince Luis Filipe, seven weeks shy of his twenty-first birthday and heir to the Portuguese throne, pulled out his Colt. Costa shot him in the chest. Another shot, from Buíça, hit the prince in the face. Queen Amélia made a desperate effort to protect eighteen-year-old Prince Manuel. She flailed at Costa with a bouquet of flowers she had received at the quayside. The driver whipped the horses and the carriage sped away at a gallop. He took it down Rua do Arsenal and turned into the wide gate of the Navy Arsenal. There, the king and the prince were pronounced dead. The queen and her youngest son survived, though he was wounded in the right arm as bullets flew.

Back in the square, police and mounted guards came running and shot the pair of assassins in the street. A bystander was also shot dead by mistake in the confusion. The attackers' bodies were dragged into nearby City Hall where they were put on display for photographs. Other conspirators, it is suspected, were involved in the regicide but got away as people scattered.

The slaying in a Lisbon street of Portugal's king and his first-born son made the front pages of newspapers across Europe. The carriage in which they were riding is today on display in Lisbon's National Carriage Museum, the bullet holes still visible. At the corner of Praça do Comércio and Rua do Arsenal, a stone plaque on a wall tersely announces that on that spot King Carlos and Prince Luis Filipe "died for their country". Oddly, the small plaque is too high up on the wall for most passers-by even to notice it.

Like the start of the nineteenth century, the early twentieth century was a bloody mess, with Lisbon providing the stage for Portugal's political and social chaos and consequent street violence. The 1908 regicide was the beginning of the end for Portugal's seven-century monarchy. King Carlos' youngest son became King Manuel II but he possessed neither the stature nor the wisdom to reverse the tide. The monarchy's credibility and popularity were damaged beyond repair. The Portuguese were fed up, too, with Lisbon's political squabbling, their country's backwardness, the Church's overbearing power and royal extravagance.

Indeed, a simmering row in Parliament over extra money granted to the Crown under the new monarch prompted a famous sword duel at Ameixoeira, in the outskirts of Lisbon, in July 1908. The republican Member of Parliament Afonso Costa accused the Count of Penha Garcia, a loyalist opponent in the chamber, of endorsing underhand payments to royals while he was in government. The contest took place at 11:00 a.m. on 14 July at the city's traditional duelling spot a few kilometres north of where Lisbon airport stands today. Eça de Queiróz mentioned in his works this preferred location for the city's duels. (Bizarrely, police halted a duel with pistols on the same spot in Ameixoeira in 2016. The antagonists, presumably, had a grievance to settle as well as a sense of history.)

Joshua Benoliel took photographs of the celebrated 1908 episode. Benoliel is regarded as the father of photojournalism in Portugal. Working mostly for the Lisbon newspaper *O Século*, he accompanied King Carlos on foreign visits, recorded Lisbon street battles between republicans and loyalists, and photographed Portuguese soldiers in the trenches of Flanders in World War I.

The Count of Penha Garcia was the better swordsman and won the duel, wounding Costa on the arm. The count's monarchist supporters said that he was unwilling to kill Costa because he feared turning his opponent into a martyr for the republican cause. But the following day, Costa returned to Parliament with his arm in a sling and resumed his verbal assault.

The Republic was not long in coming. Two years after King Carlos' violent death, the watershed moment arrived. Following thirty-six hours of intense street battles that rocked Lisbon, with barricades and artillery in the downtown city streets and navy frigates shelling the king's residence from the Tagus, the republicans declared victory at City Hall, and were photographed doing so by Benoliel. The triumph was not a foregone conclusion, however. For a long time the outcome was in the balance.

Years of frustrations and intrigue had come to a head in that autumn of 1910. Senior republican politicians and military sympathizers gathered at the Republican Party's headquarters, located in the square outside the Teatro Nacional de São Carlos, on 29 September. There, their minds were made up: they would take up arms against the regime. Four days later they held another meeting, on the third floor of 106 Rua da Esperança, the home of the mother of one of the conspirators. They agreed that the uprising would commence the following day, Tuesday, 4 October at 1:00 a.m., and that Lisbon would be their battleground.

The *Diário de Notícias*, Portugal's oldest newspaper, published four editions on 5 October as it attempted to reconstitute the chaotic events of the previous twenty-four hours. Its front-page timeline provided a blow-by-blow account from reporters and witnesses around the capital. There were terrifying night-time gun battles as infantry, cavalry and artillery units engaged in the Avenida da Liberdade, Avenida Fontes Pereira de Melo, Rossio Square and the downtown Baixa district. Explosions rattled buildings and echoed through the streets. Barricades were thrown up. Few people dared venture out, and some who did were injured in the crossfire, while shops stayed closed.

Troops loyal to the regime set up their headquarters in Rossio, on the *Mar Largo* paving. The heavily outnumbered republicans made their stronghold at the top of the Avenida da Liberdade, at the Rotunda (roundabout). Initially, only the Regimento de Infantaria 16 (16th Infantry Regiment) and the Artilharia Um (1st Artillery Regiment) joined the mutiny. Just a few hundred of them stood firm at the Rotunda, which became the ground zero of the uprising, and the few triumphed against the odds. They were aided by civilians who brought guns and lined up alongside the mutineers behind park benches, planks and felled trees used to create barricades. Local people brought them food and water.

Key to the republican victory were the navy cruisers *Adamastor* and *São Rafael*, which were anchored in the Tagus. Their crews joined the uprising and at mid-afternoon on 4 October they moved into position opposite the Praça do Comércio and began shelling the loyalists in Rossio. The troops there dispersed in confusion, easing the pressure on the Rotunda. At the same time, increasing numbers of loyalist troops deserted and joined the republican side.

The *Adamastor* was ordered to move west and take up position across from the Palácio das Necessidades, which sits on a hilltop. The handwritten order gave the ship's captain instructions to shell the palace. It added: *Cuidado com pontarias* ("Be careful with your aim") because homes were situated all

223

around it. The bombardment of King Manuel's residence damaged the façade and some rooms of what today is the home of the Foreign Ministry. The mark of one of these cannon shells can still be seen on a wall of the room where the head of protocol currently works. Another shell symbolically struck a flag pole where the royal banner flew. King Manuel fled out of the back door and was taken by car to the palace at Mafra, 40 kilometres north of the capital. He later sought refuge in Gibraltar.

At daybreak loyalists played a trump card, placing a cannon on the Torel slope overlooking the Avenida da Liberdade. It opened fire on the Rotunda and the Parque Eduardo VII below, unnerving the republican combatants. But by now all the ships in the river had embraced the republican cause and threatened to open fire on the Baixa, as well as to disembark troops who would attack the loyalists' rear in Rossio.

Faced with the monarch's flight and increasing numbers of soldiers and sailors joining the republicans, the loyalists did not last long. The battle ended with more than sixty dead and more than 700 wounded, many of them civilians, on the streets of Lisbon. The republican flag was raised over St George's Castle. The Republican Party's leaders proceeded to City Hall. From its balcony, at 11:00 a.m., José Relvas, one of the party's oldest members, told the crowd below: "With everyone united behind the same ideal aspiration, the people, the army and the navy have now, in Portugal, proclaimed the country a republic." 5 October remains a national holiday.

The momentousness led the *Diário de Notícias* into a bout of both hyperbole and amnesia:

The city of Lisbon, this beautiful and cherished land, with such peaceful traditions, was the stage of the most distressful, the most painful scenes, in which was spilled since Monday night—a lot of Portuguese blood, only Portuguese blood—the blood of brothers, the blood of bygone and future heroes on the path of progress and the triumph of peace.

The victors wasted no time. On 6 October, at a special session of the City Council, the names of some Lisbon streets were changed (foreshadowing what would happen after the 1974 Carnation Revolution). Avenida Ressano Garcia became Avenida da República, and Rua António Maria de Avelar was renamed Avenida 5 de Outubro. A week later, more alterations were made at another session: Rua d'el-Rei (King's Road) became Rua do Comércio (Commercial Street), and the city avenue named after Queen Amélia became Avenida Almirante Reis, after Admiral Carlos Cândido dos Reis, who committed suicide when only two regiments initially joined the mutiny and he presumed the uprising was doomed.

Portugal acquired its new national anthem, called *A Portuguesa*, but the new republic also needed a human face as a symbol, like France's Marianne. Portugal's poster girl was Hilda Puga. This sixteen-year-old girl was a sales assistant in a shirt shop in Rua Augusta, in the Baixa. She was chosen by the sculptor Simões de Almeida, who encountered her by chance. She turned out to be quite a character. Her grandson, Nuno Maia, told *Expresso* newspaper in 2016 that his grandmother was in fact "deeply monarchical, very Catholic and reactionary" but accepted the job out of a sense of patriotism. Hilda's father had a successful brick factory but lost his business and went to Brazil in search of better fortune. Hilda's mother went with her as a chaperone to the modelling sessions at Simões de Almeida's studio. The artist produced a bust with bare breasts. Hilda, whose likeness was on Portuguese coins until the 1970s, was married and then divorced at a time when it was scandalous. She died in 1993, aged 101.

Anti-clerical sentiment was rife among the population. After the republican victory, at least four convents and religious colleges in Lisbon were attacked and two priests were killed. The government gave instructions to the police to take priests off the streets in order to "avoid abuse". On 20 October several priests in detention at Limoeiro prison were subjected to anthropological measuring as part of pseudo scientific tests profiling links between criminality and physiognomy.

On 24 August 1911 the Portuguese were given their first president of the republic, Manuel de Arriaga, who was elected by Parliament. The front-page headline of *A Vanguarda* decided that it was "a historic day". Regarded as one of Lisbon's top lawyers, an eloquent public speaker and a dyed-in-the-wool republican, Arriaga was an endearing intellectual. He had kind eyes, a goatee and, beneath his top hat, grey hair that came below his ear lobes. This seventy-one-year-old amateur poet began his stint as head of state by living in the Palácio da Horta Seca, which today houses the Industry Ministry, next to Camões Square in the Chiado district. That was because Lisbon's population had grown to house around 450,000 people, and the carriage ride out west along the river to his official workplace, the Palácio de Belém, took too long.

This palace dates from the eighteenth century and is where King João V was staying when the 1755 earthquake struck. Though the national monument has long played second fiddle to the larger and more exuberant Ajuda Palace, further up the hill, the Palácio de Belém has its own charms: it is on the riverside, is painted a charming pink colour, and the Guarda Nacional Republicana cavalry on guard duty outside wear full dress uniforms featuring a gleaming sword and helmet. The room where nowadays the Council of State, an advisory body to the president, convenes was once a ballroom created by Queen Maria II. When the head of state is at the palace, the presidential standard—a green flag with the national shield in the middle—is flown.

When President Manuel de Arriaga and his wife and daughter moved into the Palácio de Belém to save time on his commute to work, he had to pay rent. He did so for four years, until a political crisis compelled his resignation in 1915 and he walked out of the palace escorted by the Guarda Nacional Republicana. In 2004 his remains were moved to the National Pantheon.

The First Republic brought turbulent times. As the military historian Nuno Lemos Pires has commented, "The real situation in Portugal from 1908 until 1926 was an ongoing, and increasingly worse, intermittent Civil War." Over those sixteen years, there were eight presidents and forty-five governments. President Sidónio Pais was assassinated at Rossio train station. Between 1920 and 1925 there were more than 300 incidents involving bombs. Riots in the streets were not uncommon. In 1915 a military coup in Lisbon ousted the government of Pimenta de Castro. That government's leaders hastened to shelter at the Guarda Nacional Republicana's barracks at the Largo do Carmo in Chiado (also the preferred bolthole for a deposed dictator in 1974). After the dust settled, there were about 100 dead and hundreds of injured in the city's streets.

Indeed, the World War I period was especially rich in turmoil. The Great War in its early years was a very distant rumble for neutral Lisbon, though people felt the impact of acute food and fuel shortages. The country's leaders realized that they needed to be in the conflict in order to be at the victors' table when the postwar geopolitical map of the world was drawn. So, on 23 February 1916, Portugal seized German and Austrian warships in Portuguese ports. The result: Germany declared war on Portugal on 9 March.

In January 1917 three British steamships carrying the first contingent of Portuguese soldiers for the war sailed out of Lisbon and turned north. Thousands of newly trained troops from around the country had arrived in the capital by train. Horse-drawn wagons carried supplies and equipment to the Alcântara docks. Tugboats took the soldiers, equipment and supplies out to the ships, and the Corpo Expedicionário Português (Portuguese Expeditionary Corps) departed in search of glory. In all, around 55,000 Portuguese soldiers went to the western front to fight the Germans. Others went to Mozambique to do the same.

All told, 2,288 Portuguese men died during the 1917–19 military campaign, according to historian Isabel Pestana Marques. At the infamous Battle of the Lys, in April 1918, almost 400 were killed and more than 6,500 taken prisoner. Fifteen died in the mouth of the Tagus, too, when the minesweeper *Roberto Ivens* became the first Portuguese naval ship to be sunk in the conflict when, on the afternoon of 26 July 1917, she hit a mine laid by German submarine *UC54* 4 nautical miles south of Bugio, in the shipping lane. The blast broke the ship in half and it quickly sank, though seven crew members survived. It was the nearest the war got to Lisbon.

Amid the fog of political and social turmoil in the early twentieth century, a Lisbon confidence trickster pulled off one of Europe's biggest financial swindles of the age. The celebrated 1925 case became known internationally as the Portuguese Bank Note Crisis. The scandal made a huge splash, and its ripples undermined faith in the Portuguese financial system and cast a cloud over one of London's most distinguished printing companies.

The scheme's mastermind was Artur Alves dos Reis. This bankrupt undertaker's son from Lisbon broke free of his humble background by dint of his seductive charm, a silver tongue and brashness to spare. He also married well, tying the knot at the age of seventeen with Maria Luísa Jacobetty de Azevedo. Her well-to-do family looked down on him, however, and he was determined to show them his worth.

Breathtakingly bold, while in his twenties Alves dos Reis forged a university diploma and went off to make his fortune in Africa. He finagled his way into becoming the acting head of Angolan railways and inspector of public works. Returning to Lisbon with prestige and money in his pocket, he went a step further and started writing bad cheques. That landed him in jail on fraud charges, though due to a technicality he served only a month and a half. And those six weeks were enough for Alves dos Reis to dream up his biggest and most daring scam. It was a stroke of genius: he would not forge bank notes but would forge the letter that ordered authentic bank notes to be printed—and sent to him.

With a group of international accomplices, Alves dos Reis forged signatures and letterheads from the Bank of Portugal, Portugal's licensed currency issuer, to Waterlow & Sons Limited, which printed Portuguese bank notes. The Bank of

Portugal, now the country's central bank, was then a private institution, headquartered as it is today in the Baixa, in Rua de São Julião. Alves dos Reis conned the London printers into issuing 200,000 notes of 500 escudos. They were genuine bank notes, featuring Vasco da Gama on one side. The total amount issued was equivalent to a staggering 1 per cent of Portugal's annual GDP.

At the age of twenty-eight, this consummate con man was suddenly mega-rich. Living the high life suited him. A famous photograph suggests that Alves dos Reis was something of a dandy, with his white hat cocked back, a bow tie and a primped handkerchief in his top pocket. He bought a mansion in Rua de São Marçal, a building today occupied by the British Council, but he never actually lived there. He collected prestige properties. For his wife, he purchased expensive jewels (one necklace reportedly cost half as much as the Rua de São Marçal mansion) and *haute couture* finery. Then, forging contracts, he launched on a buying spree of motor vehicle and mining companies and established a bank that eyed a takeover of the Bank of Portugal.

His downfall was his ostentatiousness. His showy behaviour attracted the attention—and envy—of some powerful people in the capital. The press started taking an interest and looked into how Alves dos Reis had made his fortune. In December 1925, ten months after the first batch of his illegitimate bank notes from Waterlow & Sons had arrived, the Lisbon newspaper *O Século* published an investigative report that brought the phoney empire tumbling down.

The master swindler was arrested and kept in prison for five years. His trial began at Lisbon's Santa Clara courthouse in May 1930. The scarcely credible story of Alves dos Reis and his exploits caught the public imagination and drew huge interest. Newspapers sent twenty-two reporters to cover the trial, according to lawyer Francisco Teixeira da Mota's 2008 biography. While incarcerated, Alves dos Reis tried to commit suicide, converted to Protestantism and then confessed to the crimes, saying his eight alleged accomplices were innocent. He was sentenced to twenty years in prison but was released in 1945. A heart attack ended his life in 1955. Alves dos Reis died poor.

The undertaker's son almost broke the Bank of Portugal. His scam skewed the country's economy. By striking at the heart of the state—its capacity to print money—it also undermined the credibility of the national currency and the government. The episode, along with much else, helped to discredit the First Republic. Some have argued that Alves dos Reis contributed to the 1926 military coup that ended the republic and opened the door to Salazar's rule.

The 28 May 1926 revolt—bloodless, remarkably—exploded in Braga, in northern Portugal. From there, its leaders headed a "March on Lisbon" that took them to the centre of power. Propelled by broad popular support, they quickly triumphed and on 6 June General Manuel Gomes da Costa celebrated his taking of power by marching more than 10,000 soldiers up the Avenida da Liberdade to the cheers of crowds.

Salazar came from his post as professor at the University of Coimbra to take on the daunting task of finance minister in the first post-coup government, which had a choking economy to resuscitate. Salazar lasted barely two weeks. The political mess was too much even for his uncluttered mind. He returned to government in 1928, however, after being granted his demand for veto power over public spending. The concentration of power in his hands had begun.

That was the same year that Portugal won what was seen as a kind of back-handed revenge on Britain for the humiliating Ultimatum three decades earlier. On 1 June, from 5:00 a.m., vehicles on Lisbon streets started driving on the right instead of the left. In the rest of the country, the change happened at midnight. The *Diário de Notícias* devoted its back page to a light-hearted story about how Lisbon handled the changeover. It noted that no damage was reported, adding that "everybody finds it greatly entertaining." Traffic in the city, the paper said, was "like a dance where the partners don't recognize each other's steps".

Salazar tendered his resignation again in 1929 but he was talked out of it on his hospital bed, where he was laid up after tripping over a carpet at the Finance Ministry and breaking his leg, by President Óscar Carmona. Nobody in Lisbon's corridors of power thought that Salazar would amount to much. He was thirty-nine, dry and gaunt, with a pinched voice and the bearing of a rural clergyman. But the capital's sophisticates made the same mistake that international leaders would later repeat: they underestimated him. Salazar would stay in government until the late 1960s.

Even the great poet Fernando Pessoa saw the need, after almost two decades of unrelenting and deadly strife, for benign authoritarian rule. "A military dictatorship in Portugal," he wrote, "is today both legitimate and necessary." Pessoa initially looked kindly on Salazar, too, for being upright and knocking Portugal into shape, though his enthusiasm later cooled.

Pessoa is to Lisbon what James Joyce is to Dublin and Franz Kafka is to Prague. Pessoa poetically sighed, *Oh, Lisboa, meu lar!* ("Oh, Lisbon, my home!") in a swooning declaration of love. The city was Pessoa's muse, just as it was for the poet Cesário Verde in the previous century. Pessoa was a city portraitist, a pointillist almost. The capital takes on the life of a character in his *Livro do Desassossego* (Book of Disquiet), one of Portugal's twentieth-century literary masterpieces. Unfinished during his lifetime, it was compiled from fragments of writing he kept in trunks and was published in 1982, forty-seven years after his death. It is in diary form and is shot through with fidgety, unsettled ruminations. The city constantly insinuates itself, slithering between the characters or barging them out of the way. "I owe much of what I feel and think to my work as a book-keeper, since the former exists as a negation of and escape from the latter," the author writes.

> If I had to fill in the space on a questionnaire listing formative literary influences, I would write on the dotted line firstly the name of Cesário Verde, but the list would not be complete without the names of Senhor Vasques, Moreira the book-keeper, Vieira the cashier and António the office boy. And after each one I would write in capital letters the key address: LISBON.

Pessoa and his poetical heteronyms commonly rode on the famous tram No. 28, nowadays crammed full of tourists, which runs from Martim Moniz Square in the downtown to the delightfully named Cemitério dos Prazeres (Cemetery of Pleasures), up the hill from the Palácio das Necessidades. Pessoa adored the snug, village-like feel of the city of his birth, even around the downtown offices where he worked:

> How good it does the soul to watch, beneath a high, unmoving sun, these carriages with their loads of straw, these empty boxes, these slow passers-by, transported here from a village!

I myself, seeing them through my office window, where I am
alone, am transformed: I am in a quiet provincial town, I am
idle in an unknown hamlet, and because I feel outside myself,
I'm happy.

It exasperated Pessoa that Lisbon, and Portugal in general,
weren't more widely known abroad. At Durban High School
in South Africa, which he attended as a teenager before
returning to his homeland, he was infuriated by the general
ignorance about Portuguese history—in a country whose
most famous cape had been named by Portugal. In 1988,
researchers discovered Pessoa had tried to put that right. A
Lisbon guidebook he had written in English was discovered
among his thousands of pages of unpublished papers. It was
entitled *Lisbon: What the Tourist Should See* and ran to about 100
pages. It was finally published in 1992, by Livros Horizonte,
as a kind of novelty. It is not, truth be told, much of a book.
Indeed, for a work by one of Europe's foremost poets, the
purchaser might feel short-changed. It leads visitors by the
hand across the capital's main sights, amid the "masses of
houses [that] cluster brightly over the hills." It is a serious
work, providing ticket prices and opening hours of venues,
and is absent of poetic flourishes. In his eagerness to turn
attention to Lisbon, he lingered on descriptions of Portuguese
heroes and seafaring adventures. Like Damião de Góis in his
sixteenth-century *Description of the City of Lisbon*, Pessoa at
times overegged his eulogy:

> For the traveller who comes in from the sea, Lisbon, even
> from afar, rises like a fair vision in a dream, clear-cut against
> a bright blue sky which the sun gladdens with its gold. And
> the domes, the monuments, the old castles jut up above the
> mass of houses, like far-off heralds of this delightful seat, of
> this blessed region.

Lisbon possesses ample remembrances of Pessoa. There are plaques, paintings and a statue, and one of the houses where he lived is a museum. The sights include Pessoa's birthplace in the Chiado district, in a fourth-floor apartment, across from the Teatro Nacional de São Carlos, where he lived until he was five; the nearby Igreja dos Mártires, where he was baptized and whose church bells enchanted him; A Brasileira café, a bohemian hang-out in the Chiado, and the Martinho da Arcada café in Praça do Comércio, where the hard-drinking poet was three days before his death with Almada Negreiros; and the Casa Fernando Pessoa in the Campo de Ourique neighbourhood, where he spent the last fifteen years of his life.

At the end of November 1935, Pessoa was admitted to the Hospital de São Luís in the Bairro Alto with a gallstone attack and quickly died. He was forty-seven. Pessoa was buried at the Cemitério dos Prazeres and in 1988 moved to the Jerónimos Monastery. A 1954 portrait in oil by Almada Negreiros, painted for the Lisbon restaurant Os Irmãos Unidos, where the bohemians often ate, depicts Pessoa, with his distinctively slender build, in his trademark hat, moustache and round spectacles, seated at a table. It is on display at the Fernando Pessoa House. A life-size alternative is a bronze statue of Pessoa outside A Brasileira.

Right at the start of his political career Salazar pulled a rabbit out of the hat: in the 1928–29 financial year he delivered a budget surplus. Lisbon's elite gasped. Salazar looked like a miracle worker. The success propelled him into the seat of power. The military appointed him head of government in 1932 (he would stay in that post until 1968), and Salazar had a new Constitution drawn up. It won broad support and, when it came into force in 1933, it established the *Estado Novo* (New State), which would run things for the next forty-one years.

Not everyone was happy. In 1937 an attempt was made on Salazar's life. He was living in a rented Lisbon house with Maria, his long-time housekeeper, and a child called Micas, her ward. Both of them came with Salazar from Coimbra. (Salazar never married.) The two-storey house was in Rua Bernardo Lima, not far from the Marquês de Pombal round-about. They kept chickens and rabbits in the back yard. One of Salazar's neighbours, well-known singer Maria Fernanda Mella, said of him: "He never spoke to anyone. He was a very cold person ... He always looked very serious. He never smiled or anything." Indeed, social niceties were not Salazar's forte and he would never possess the popular touch.

Salazar used to go from there to worship at a private chapel at the house of a friend, Josué Trocado. On the morning of Sunday, 4 July, he escaped death by the skin of his teeth. Salazar was about to step out of his official car, a Buick, when a powerful bomb was detonated. Stones and roof tiles flew, and smoke filled the air. People screamed and ran. The explosion left a deep crater in the street. The bomb's target survived unscathed due to a miscalculation by his attackers, according to Joaquim Vieira, who wrote a book about the episode. Vieira believes that the escaped perpetrators belonged to the Frente Popular—a coalition of communists, anarchists and trade unionists angered by Salazar's support for General Francisco Franco in the Spanish Civil War.

The incident brought home the need for proper security. The government expropriated a nineteenth-century mansion in the walled gardens behind the parliament building in São

Bento, and Salazar moved there in May 1938 after renova-tions were completed. He spent most months of the year there until his death in 1970, and it remains the Portuguese prime minister's official residence. Salazar's old house, in Rua Bernardo Lima, was put on the market in 2014 with a price tag of 5.5 million euros.

World War II tested Salazar's political and diplomatic skills, but he was shrewd enough to steer his country through it rela-tively unscathed. Portugal stayed out of the conflict, maintain-ing neutrality as it sold tungsten and canned sardines to both sides. Lisbon, on the other hand, was very much in the thick of it. A heavy contingent of spies meant that developments in the Portuguese capital influenced world events.

The Nazi occupation of France in 1940 sent tens of thou-sands of refugees hurrying to Lisbon—the only free and neutral port on the continent—where they waited for passage across the Atlantic to the United States. The 1942 film *Casablanca*, starring Humphrey Bogart and Ingrid Bergman, mentions this escape route when, at the end, Rick makes Ilsa board a plane to Lisbon and freedom.

A who's who of early twentieth-century cultural figures passed through the city. They included the actors Tyrone Power and Robert Montgomery, the directors Alexander Korda, Jean Renoir and King Vidor, the writers Antoine de Saint-Exupéry, Arthur Koestler and Thomas Mann (who described Lisbon as "a waiting room"), artists such as Marc Chagall and Max Ernst, the celebrated collector Peggy Guggenheim (whose jewellery reportedly turned heads at the Café Leão d'Ouro next to Rossio's Central Station), and intellectuals including José Ortega y Gasset and Hannah Arendt, who lived with her husband for four months at 6 Rua da Sociedade Farmacêutica. European royalty also came and, in some cases, stayed.

Pan American Airways had started the first trans-Atlantic air mail service, from New York via Lisbon to Marseille, in 1939. The *Yankee Clipper* could also carry a handful of passengers and flew via the Azores to Lisbon, where the flying boat landed on the Tagus and taxied to Cabo Ruivo Maritime Airport, on the eastern side of the city. The Boeing hydroplanes moored close to the end of a long wooden pier that stretched out into the river, and small boats went to fetch the passengers. Most of the refugees left on ships, however, and local people referred to their city as "Europe's quayside".

Lisbon, poor and behind the times, suddenly came face-to-face with modernity. On the streets of Salazar's isolated capital, a hodge-podge of European languages could now be heard. Foreigners sat outside cafés and read foreign newspapers. The influx of foreign currency brought a financial windfall. From sleepy and remote city, Lisbon was transformed into a busy wartime hub.

"For anyone who knew this city before, it is immediately striking how it has changed so much in such a short space of time," Eugene Tillinger, a journalist from Berlin, wrote in 1940.

> The way of life here gathers pace each day. More and more emigrants from France and from German-occupied lands are arriving. In Rossio square, in the city centre, you hardly hear a word of Portuguese. On the other hand, you overhear so many other languages, mostly French, English and German, but also Polish, Dutch and Flemish. Lisbon is sold out … the hotels are overcrowded, bathrooms are rented out with mattresses laid on the floor. Cafés and restaurants are packed.

The city hasn't seen anything like this for a long time. The city is teeming with life.

Many local people were initially aghast at what they saw. There were suddenly men walking around Lisbon without hats on and women in short skirts and lipstick who smoked and sat alone outside cafés. Several fashions, the historian Maria João Castro says, caught on. Some Lisbon people went to the hairdresser and demanded "a refugee cut"—that is, short. Other Lisbon women began wearing short-sleeved dresses and shorter skirts, mimicking the foreigners. Salazar's regime frowned on all this. It indicated it was displeased by a law in 1941 forbidding men and women from showing too much flesh at the beach. The government claimed that it was acting in the interests of "public morality" and in an attempt to prevent the "corruption" of local customs. It established the areas of the body that could be shown or must be covered up, down to the centimetre. The rules, posted on beaches, allowed men to bare their back down to the waist, but women could only go as far as 10 centimetres above their waist, and ladies' bathing costumes had to include a skirt that covered their thighs to at least a centimetre below the bottom of the suit.

One refugee left a longer-lasting mark on Lisbon. Calouste Sarkis Gulbenkian, who was among the world's richest men due to his oil interests in Turkey and Iraq, also sought personal peace in this haven amid Europe's destruction. From 1942 until his death in 1955 he lived at Lisbon's famous Hotel Aviz, where he was the star guest despite competition from overnighting monarchs. Gulbenkian was, indeed, known among the hotel staff as *O Rei* (The King). Wealthy but miserly, with a reputation as a difficult man, he stayed in room 52, the hotel's best. In his later years, when he was in ill health, he occupied ten of the hotel's twenty-five rooms, making space for his secretaries and nurses, as well as his cats.

As thanks to the city that gave him a home, Gulbenkian bequeathed part of his vast fortune for the creation of a Lisbon-based institution bearing his name. The Gulbenkian Foundation remains one of Lisbon's most prestigious cultural institutions. His collection of around 6,000 works of art went, after lengthy negotiations between the Portuguese and French governments, to the Gulbenkian Museum that is part of the foundation's Lisbon premises. The Amigos de Lisboa (Friends of Lisbon), an earnest association of people who aim to protect the city's cultural wealth, made Gulbenkian a posthumous honorary member a year after his death.

Gulbenkian's son Nubar became engaged in an endeavour that was gripping the capital. Lisbon was a hotbed of intrigue and was once described by American historian Douglas Wheeler as "spyland". Secret agents from both sides gathered in the neutral city and ran competing underground networks. Conspiracy and subterfuge, double-dealing and disinformation were their daily bread. By the war's end, MI6 had identified 1,900 enemy agents and 350 suspected ones in Lisbon.

There were spooks from Britain and Germany as well as from France, Italy, Russia, Poland and Japan. The FBI and the OSS (later CIA) were also represented. A club called Cabaret Maxime in the Praça da Alegria, just off the Avenida da Liberdade, was a nest of spies and a kind of Lisbon version of Bogart's "Rick's Café". German agents gathered at two hotels on the Avenida da Liberdade: the Hotel Tivoli and the Avenida Palace, which on its fourth floor had a passage leading directly—and unseen—to the Rossio train station.

The British were at the Hotel Metrópole and the Hotel Aviz. As well as providing a home for Calouste Gulbenkian, the Aviz was for a time the residence of kings Carol II of Romania and Umberto II of Italy, and of Don Juan of Spain. It was also where the Duke of Windsor gave a farewell dinner before sailing with Wallis Simpson on the SS *Excalibur* for the Bahamas. The hotel closed down in 1961.

Skullduggery was rife. Walter Schellenberg was dispatched to Lisbon by Adolf Hitler to assist in kidnapping the Duke of Windsor before he left. Dusko Popov, who also stayed at the Aviz, was codenamed Tricycle and was run as a double agent by MI5 whose Lisbon office was in Rua da Emenda, in the Bairro Alto. The local Special Operations Executive unit was attached to the British Embassy in the Lapa district. Berthold Jacob Salomon, a Jewish journalist, was abducted in downtown Lisbon at the Gestapo's request and sent to Germany, where he died in jail. Juan Pujol, a famous double agent working for MI5 who helped trick Hitler about the site of the D-Day landings, also set up his stall in Lisbon. Ian Fleming stopped over while he was shadowing Popov, and it is said that nearby Estoril's casino and its Hotel Palácio inspired parts of his first James Bond novel, *Casino Royale*.

Donald Darling, a Secret Intelligence Service officer who ran Allied prisoner escape operations through MI9, operated with the support of the British Consulate in the Portuguese capital and carved out escape routes through Lisbon to Britain. Darling ran Nubar Gulbenkian as a courier to maintain contact with those involved in the escape network. Calouste Gulbenkian had been the Iranian ambassador in Vichy France, and Nubar was the commercial attaché. That meant Nubar could travel in and out of the occupied zone. Harrow-educated Nubar was a flamboyant personality and an unlikely secret agent, which was perhaps the secret of his success.

The passing visitors recorded some perceptive observations of Lisbon. The German political journalist Karl Paetel noted the gulf between the rich and poor. "Lisbon was beautiful," he remarked in his 1982 autobiography, "as long as you stayed on the Avenida [da Liberdade] and didn't stray into the dark side streets where on the doorstep of miserable houses men and women cooked meagre meals on open fires." Saint-Exupéry picked up on the local glumness that contrasted with the sense of safe haven and degree of relief felt by the foreigners. "When in December 1940 I crossed Portugal to go to the United States, Lisbon seemed like a kind of clear and sad paradise," he wrote. What truly left the French writer agog, however, was the Portuguese World Exhibition. It was like something out of a fairytale, far removed from the grim reality of the moment: "Lisbon partied in defiance of Europe," he remarked.

This six-month event was a calculated propaganda exercise by Salazar. Its goal was to bond the Portuguese and stiffen their national resolve in the times of shortages, when olive oil, bread, rice and sugar were rationed. It marked the anniversary of the founding of Portugal in 1140 and the restoration of independence in 1640. It took place in Belém, the symbolic root of Portugal's greatness, in front of the Jerónimos Monastery and next to the treasured Tagus, and a new part of the city would grow out of it. The exhibition was supposed to be temporary and was built in plaster and wood. Nevertheless, the scale was in the monumental style favoured by dictators. It opened on 23 June 1940—the same day Hitler toured Paris and had his photograph taken in front of the Eiffel Tower. No wonder Saint-Exupéry was astounded.

The exhibition had a wow factor. Even the extravagant night-time lighting was something to behold for the people of Lisbon. The *Diário de Notícias*, in a front-page story above news of the Franco-German armistice, said it was *um grande momento nacional* ("a great national occasion") that would provide the Portuguese with "a tonic of joy and self-confidence". Hitler sent a message of congratulations on the double anniversary and his wishes for Portuguese prosperity. Winston Churchill is not known to have sent anything.

The event was a huge success. Official statistics claimed that some three million people visited between June and December. For a 2016 exhibition recalling the happening, elderly people who had visited the event as children recalled marvelling at parades and firework displays. They remembered the loud tannoys of the public address system and its advertising jingles, the smells of wet paint and plaster, seeing black people, some for the first time, and the lions, crocodiles and monkeys. Appearing in the black-and-white home movies was a parade with the inevitable elephant, draped with the Portuguese flag.

The only exhibits that have endured are the Museum of Popular Art, which was adapted from the Everyday Life section, and the Padrão dos Descobrimentos (Monument to the Discoveries). This monument had, in 1940, an iron and cement structure which was then plastered over. The architect was Cottinelli Telmo and the sculptor of the thirty-two lateral figures was Leopoldo de Almeida, one of the dictatorship's favourite artists. The statues are massive in scale—appropriately so, for these are giants of Portuguese history.

The monument was demolished, despite talk of keeping it, but in 1960, on the 500th anniversary of the death of Henry the Navigator, it was rebuilt, bigger, using concrete and pink-tinted stone cladding. The stone does not come alive until it catches the sun and gleams white against the blue sky or smoulders with a pale ochre hue at sunset.

The monument mimics a caravel with billowing sails jutting over the riverbank onto the Tagus and facing, naturally, south. It stands 56 metres high and the sculptures in limestone invite a game of Identify Famous People from Portuguese History. You can spot Vasco da Gama, Bartolomeu Dias, Camões and Phillipa of Lancaster as well as less glamorous map-makers, chroniclers, warriors and evangelizers. The facial expressions on the statues look suitably noble and resolute. The monument has become one of the city's best-known, and most photographed, features.

The war and the Catholic Church, which after years of being assailed by the republicans was on a much surer footing with Salazar, contributed another Lisbon hallmark. In 1940 Portuguese bishops decreed that if the country was spared from World War II, "there would be built over Lisbon a monument to the Sacred Heart of Jesus". They wanted something like Rio de Janeiro's Christ the Redeemer statue. A postwar fundraising campaign proceeded slowly until the first stone was laid on the south bank of the Tagus in 1949. Construction of the rest began in 1952. The Cristo Rei (Christ the King) statue was built *in situ* using plaster casts, and some 40,000 tonnes of concrete were poured into it. In 1959 around 300,000 people attended the inauguration of the statue whose open-armed, come-hither pose looks over to Lisbon from Almada. Up close, however, the effect is weakened because the long-haired, bearded Jesus is in fact looking pensively down at the river, as if something has just crossed his mind and he's thinking about it.

244

Though Salazar's name can be found on no Lisbon building or monument, his regime's architectural legacy is all around the capital. His presence is woven into the city's fabric, and there is just too much of it to erase. After taking power, the New State swiftly set in motion a vast public works programme. It was not just a matter of propaganda. The plan also soaked up labour left idle by the international financial crisis of the 1920s. Salazar also fretted that his impoverished, poorly educated people might be vulnerable to the seductions of communism, which he loathed.

Salazar's master builder was a man who, despite being killed in a car accident in his prime, went down in history as one of the country's greatest ever public works ministers. Duarte Pacheco brought about a substantial improvement in the national infrastructure in the space of roughly ten years, and he is regarded as a pioneer of modern urban planning in Portugal. Salazar appointed Pacheco to his first Cabinet, in July 1932, as minister for public works and communications. It was a newly created government post intended, in part, to help bring order to the capital's housing chaos.

Pacheco and his ten brothers and sisters were orphaned early, and he had to work from a young age to support the family. Gifted in mathematics, he gained entry aged seventeen to the electrical engineering course at Lisbon's Instituto Superior Técnico. He gave one-on-one private classes to students at cafés in the city's Baixa district to make ends meet. By the time he entered government, Pacheco was the prestigious institute's thirty-two-year-old director. Pacheco's work rate was astonishing, and his list of accomplishments is staggering. He was perhaps Salazar's most visible and dynamic minister. He was also the only person who has ever held the posts of minister for public works and mayor of Lisbon simultaneously.

When Pacheco joined Salazar's Cabinet in 1932, Lisbon was in the grip of a severe housing shortage. Governments during the First Republic had neglected the issue, barely adopting housing policies worthy of the name. The city plan had not even been updated since 1911. At the same time, a spurt in the capital's demographic growth had brought the anarchic contruction of new houses and burgeoning unofficial—and unhygienic—neighbourhoods. Lisbon's population shot from almost 600,000 in 1930 to almost 700,000 in 1940. Pacheco became mayor of Lisbon on 1 January 1938 and set about tidying things up.

At the heart of his endeavour was the *Plano Geral de Urbanização e Expansão de Lisboa* (General Plan for the Urbanization and Expansion of Lisbon). This project was principally the work of Étienne de Gröer, a Warsaw-born Frenchman persuaded by Pacheco to move to Lisbon from Paris, where he was a renowned urban architect. The plan Gröer authored established how the city would grow and be improved over an initial ten-year period, up to 1948. It involved building housing estates, roads, schools, parks and gardens, and sanitation systems. It focused on expanding the city once more northwards, with new avenues stretching like fingers out into the countryside, picking up where Ressano Garcia had left off. Pacheco, in his simultaneous role as public works minister, oversaw some landmark administrative and legal reforms, such as the laws on planning permission and expropriations, which cleared a path for Gröer's designs. The plan cast the broader city in roughly the shape it possesses today. In this and other ways, Salazar stamped his mark on Lisbon.

Pacheco was the brains behind new low-cost housing estates, called *bairros de casas económicas*, which sprang up in Lisbon in the 1930s. They were made up of single-family houses which were inspired by the famous twentieth-century architect Raul Lino, who designed the Teatro Tivoli in the Avenida da Liberdade. Lino argued for family houses instead of apartment blocks as he sought to reconcile Portuguese traditions with modern trends. His 1933 book *Casas Portuguesas* (Portuguese Houses) defended the case for plain, sober architecture. These houses went mostly to lower-paid workers, whose rent was calculated according to their income. They included clerical workers and, mostly, civil servants. Not a wholly benevolent gesture by Salazar's regime, it was intended to help keep working-class radicalism in check, at a time when it was spreading across Europe. It aimed at cementing the government's popularity and preventing the backbone of the state's employees—its enforcers, in fact—from being seduced by radical ideas by granting them property rights. After twenty-five years of paying rent, they were awarded ownership.

The most famous of these estates were those in the districts of Ajuda, Alvalade, Arco do Cego, Encarnação and Madredeus. The Alvalade *bairro*, for example, covered 230 hectares and was intended to house around 45,000 people. Building began in 1947 and people started moving in the following year. Alvalade was designed by the City Council architect João Faria da Costa, who worked closely with Gröer, and remains popular.

The *Diário de Notícias* of 11 March 1935 waxed lyrical about these new dwellings. They were the "comfortable, cheerful and sun-filled little houses that the New State built," the newspaper wrote. (The all-powerful regime had also introduced censorship to "oversee the exercise of freedom of thought".) In the Arco do Cego neighbourhood, for example, almost 500 simple two- and three-storey houses were built. They are symmetrical, virtually identical, terraced or semi-detached, some with slender gardens. They are pretty houses painted in delicious yellows, blues and pinks along short, narrow streets. There is a school, several cafés and a quiet and pleasant little public garden. Walking into this neighbourhood has something of a "through the looking glass" feel to it because it is unusual to come across such an agreeable sanctuary in the middle of a busy western European capital. And that is how these new areas were supposed to feel: like little villages, with a rural flavour. Thus, Pacheco successfully translated into the urban landscape Salazar's conservative ideas for his people and his country. Salazar dreamed of *um quintal para cada português*—a *quintal* for every Portuguese. A *quintal* is a kind of backyard that is large enough to keep chickens and rabbits and plant greens, and he wanted every Portuguese to have one, even in the capital. However, in the 1940s, faced with the pressing demand for housing, the government opted to start building four-floor apartment blocks with modestly priced rents. It also broadened the scope of who was eligible to live in them.

Pacheco's City Council carefully spread the city's wings to the north. He developed housing, for example, along and around the Avenida de Roma and to the east of the Avenida da República, which was largely fields. The Avenida Almirante Reis would become one of the main roads northwards out of the city, towards Sacavém. At the top of that avenue an imposing square was built, known as the Praça do Areeiro. It offered upmarket apartments, with one tower climbing eleven floors. Avenida Sidónio Pais, running alongside the Parque Eduardo VII, became another prestigious address.

In 1941 the weekly paper *A Acção* eulogized Pacheco's "new and modern Lisbon", the "big village being transformed into a big and superb city", waving farewell to the "provincial city". Pacheco's makeover included the building of the Alcântara docks, which modernized the capital's port facilities, and of the Belém river station, which provided ferry services across the Tagus. He opened a door for the city's expansion to the west with the Marginal coast road along the river and a four-lane motorway—one of the world's first— from Lisbon as far as the National Stadium. It was completed, reaching Cascais 30 kilometres away, only in 1991. The motorway is reached from the Marquês de Pombal roundabout and crosses the Alcântara Valley over what came to be called the Viaduto de Duarte Pacheco. It was begun in 1937 and inaugurated by Salazar in 1944, a year after Pacheco's death. The viaduct, roughly parallel to the aqueduct, is 471 metres long and up to 27 metres high. (Pacheco did make one mistake: building the Marginal, with a suburban train line alongside it, blocked off Lisbon from the Tagus and was regretted for decades afterwards.)

He also oversaw the building of a new airport. International flights had previously landed at an airfield near Sintra, but from 1942 they arrived at Portela airport close to Lisbon. Today, it is one of the few European international airports which is inside the city and where landing planes skim with a mighty roar over rooftops, including over the Biblioteca Nacional (National Library) where visitors in the Reading Room are asked to be quiet.

Three years after Portela opened, the national airline TAP—Transportes Aéreos Portugueses—was created, with its headquarters in Lisbon. The flag carrier started out with three DC-3 Dakota aircraft, which could carry up to twenty-one passengers and served just one route, Madrid. Three months later the state-owned company launched the 25,000-kilometre Linha Aérea Imperial (Imperial Air Route), a colonial service which went from Lisbon to the Angolan capital Luanda and crossed the African continent to the Mozambican capital Lourenço Marques (now Maputo). It was a fifteen-day round-trip with twelve stopovers. By the end of the 1940s, TAP was also flying to Paris, London and Seville. When the airline went through difficult times later in the century, wags unkindly commented that TAP stood for Take Another Plane.

Pacheco also improved city sanitation, by collecting more water from the Tagus Valley. He created and took part in tree-planting ceremonies in the extensive Monsanto Park on the west side of Lisbon which is nowadays appreciated for the biking and hiking tracks that wind through its forest. He was one of the prime movers behind the hefty and imposing Fonte Luminosa (Luminous Fountain) near his beloved Instituto Superior Técnico. Across the country, he was behind the construction of new roads, post offices, courthouses and prisons. In Lisbon, he was also responsible for a series of other buildings that remain prominent: the Casa da Moeda (National Mint), the National Statistics Institute building, the Hospital Santa Maria and the Lisbon University campus. The common denominator of these landmarks of a quasi-totalitarian state is that they are utilitarian and graceless, without elegance or subtlety. The architectural style lacks warmth, and the buildings have lines as rigid as a dictatorship, but they were at their time fashionable. The influence of Albert Speer, Adolf Hitler's chief architect, is also clear. Speer came to Lisbon in 1941 for the inauguration of his travelling urban architecture exhibition called *Neue Deutsche Baukunst*. Pacheco, with President Óscar Carmona, attended the opening of the exhibition, which drew more than 100,000 visitors during its two-week stay.

Wearing his communications hat, Pacheco founded the Emissora Nacional (National Broadcaster). This public radio began a test phase in 1934, when it broadcast a stodgy diet of classical music and New State propaganda. That earned it the nickname Maçadora Nacional (National Bore). It was inaugurated in 1935 when it had two daily broadcasts, one at lunchtime and the other in the evening. Its first premises were in Rua do Quelhas, just south of the parliament building and the Estrela Garden.

Arguably the best-known project that Pacheco oversaw was the Estádio Nacional (National Stadium), which is still used to host the Portuguese Cup final. This sports complex was first mooted in 1933. Portuguese sports clubs asked Salazar for a central stadium for major events, and he granted their wish. The venue's site in Lisbon was much discussed. It could have gone to Campo Grande, close to the city centre, or to the Monsanto Park. In the end it went to the Vale do Jamor, on the west side of Lisbon, which the nineteenth-century writers Almeida Garrett and Cesário Verde had mentioned in their works and which was known as a rural and bucolic area. The stadium was inspired by the Olympiastadion Berlin, built for the 1936 Summer Olympics, and is a Greek-style construction, with a central field and running track around it, scooped out of the landscape amid a park and woodland. The neoclassical design can also be detected in the monumental tribune, where Portugal's president hands the winning team's captain the trophy on Cup final day.

The opening was initially planned to coincide with the 1940 Portuguese World Exhibition, which Pacheco also oversaw, but it took place only on 10 June 1944. That was four days after the Allied landings in Normandy and on the public holiday the New State had decreed to celebrate the Dia da Raça (Race Day—that is, the Portuguese race). This was a woolly concept that had no scientific authority. It was, in essence, just more propaganda devised to carve out a unique place for the Portuguese and make them feel special. After the Carnation Revolution, it became Portugal Day.

The stadium's inauguration ceremony pulled out all the stops. Watched by around 50,000 spectators, it began with a calisthenics display by the Mocidade Portuguesa (Portuguese Youth), an organization which had initially taken its cue from the Hitler Youth. Some 4,000 boys in white shorts, socks and plimsolls and with bare chests showed off their synchronized moves. Then came a women's gymnastics performance by the National Foundation for Joy at Work, an unimprovable New State name. To cap it all off came the highlight of the day: a friendly football game between Lisbon rivals Sporting, the national league champion, and Benfica, the Portuguese Cup winner. Such a day of spectacle the Portuguese had never witnessed. António Ferro, Salazar's propaganda chief, told the Emissora Nacional that the event represented "the apotheosis of the New Portugal, confidence in today and certainty in what tomorrow brings." Clearly, the regime was terribly worried about the outcome of the war.

Pacheco's overhaul wouldn't have been felt so keenly, even today, if not for his key associate: Porfírio Pardal Monteiro. This Lisbon architect translated the government minister's new ideas for Portuguese urbanism into concrete and stone. He was dutiful, pragmatic, technically accomplished and one of the pioneers of architectural modernism in Portugal. He was appointed to design many of the city landmarks that became Pacheco's legacy: the Biblioteca Nacional, the Cais do Sodré train station, the Instituto Superior Técnico, and the *Diário de Notícias* newspaper's celebrated headquarters in the Avenida da Liberdade, among others.

Perhaps Pardal Monteiro's most striking original design, however, was Portugal's first modernist church. In 1933, the Catholic Church sold the downtown district's Igreja de São Julião to the Bank of Portugal, which wanted to expand its nearby premises. It used the money to build a new church in the area of the "new avenues," close to where the Gulbenkian Foundation now stands. It would be called the Igreja de Nossa Senhora de Fátima, in a reference to the holy shrine 130 kilometres north of the capital. The Cardinal Patriarch of Lisbon, Manuel Gonçalves Cerejeira, told Pardal Monteiro he wanted the project to meet three conditions: it must be "a church, a modern church, and a beautiful modern church." The architect complied, and the finished work sparked a loud and public clash between traditionalists and modernists.

The church's stark, functional external design in reinforced concrete was daring. Inside, with seating for around 800 worshippers, it uses no pillars that might block the view of the altar and possesses a neo-Gothic flavour, with mosaics and marble, sculptures and stained glass designed by Almada Negreiros. Its inauguration in 1938 was attended by the

Cardinal Patriarch and the Portuguese President Óscar Carmona. The design earned gushing reviews in Lisbon newspapers, which were unlikely to be sniffy about a project overseen by the Cardinal Patriarch. The church won the Valmor Prize, Portugal's main architectural award, and became a twentieth-century monument.

The word on the street, though, was different. Tomás Ribeiro Colaço, a writer and lawyer, recounted in the pages of *Arquitectura Portuguesa* magazine: "The whole of Lisbon is going round whispering that the church is ugly." Nobody dared speak up for fear of drawing the authorities' ire, he said. The most common complaint was that the building didn't look Portuguese, it looked foreign, and indeed Pardal Monteiro had drawn his inspiration from ecclesiastic fashions in France. The Cardinal Patriarch came to the architect's defence. "As regards [the building] being modern, we cannot even begin to imagine it being anything else. All forms of art in the past were modern in relation to their time," he wrote.

Pacheco died from injuries he sustained in a car accident while on his way back to Lisbon for a Cabinet meeting in 1943, at the age of forty-four. He was widely popular with the Portuguese, in part because of his swift and sure response to a 15 February 1941 cyclone that tore across the country, killing scores of people and wrecking infrastructure. Pacheco's funeral procession began at City Hall, where the vigil was held and where a black flag flew. His coffin was carried by students from the Instituto Superior Técnico and placed on a horse-drawn carriage. Soldiers and local people lined the square outside City Hall and the streets of the Baixa. Pacheco was buried with military honours at the Alto de São João cemetery.

Pacheco, due to his early death, never saw Lisbon's dream come true: the building of an underground railway, which had been repeatedly postponed since the 1890s. Digging finally began in 1955, and the Metropolitano de Lisboa opened to the public four years later, on 30 December. It was like a late Christmas present for the city and a culmination of the anticipation felt by local people who had been watching the work progress at gaping holes in the streets. On opening day, people started queueing to get in at 3:00 a.m. Even the escalators were a novelty for many.

A day earlier, the inaugural train had left Restauradores station at 11:07 a.m. It carried President Américo Thomáz, the Lisbon Patriarch Cardinal Manuel Cerejeira and other illustrious guests. The Y-shaped line was a private concession, ran 6.5 kilometres through eleven stations and, in 1960, passengers made almost 16 million trips. In 2016, there were more than 153 million trips; the network ran on four lines covering 44 kilometres and had fifty-six stations. The Olaias station, designed by Lisbon architect Tomás Taveira and opened in 1998 during an expansion, has been considered one of the world's most attractive. In the trademark garish and flamboyant style of its famous architect, who also produced the city's conspicuous Amoreiras shopping and office complex in 1982, it is visually stunning, with multi-coloured, soaring columns and iron arches in a cavernous setting.

Salazar, who had tacked close to Hitler in the 1930s and even adopted the stiff-armed Nazi salute, artfully secured an accommodation with the winners of World War II. Portugal even became a founder member of NATO in 1949. But there were clouds on the horizon.

The man known as the Fearless General arrived back in Lisbon on 16 May 1958 at Santa Apolónia station. Cheering crowds met him off the train. They stood in anticipation all along his planned route to the Avenida da Liberdade. It was the kind of euphoric welcome that Air Force General Humberto Delgado, who was running for president, had also received during his trip earlier that week to Porto. But the regime did not want a repeat performance in Lisbon. Mounted police with swords drawn charged the crowds, scattering them and sending dozens to hospital.

Delgado, after whom Lisbon's Portela airport was renamed in 2016, had endeared himself to the Portuguese with his answer to a journalist who asked him what he would do, if he were elected, with Salazar. "I shall sack him, of course," Delgado dryly replied. The head of state, who possessed no executive power and was a figurehead, was still chosen by ballot at that time, though voting rights were strictly limited. Salazar, as head of government and *de facto* national ruler, rigged the 1958 election and after that changed the electoral process because of the embarrassment caused by Delgado's fearlessness. The secret police, which became known by its acronym PIDE, caught up with Delgado in 1965, luring him into a trap and shooting him dead on the Spanish border.

Iva Delgado, his daughter, recounted how the Brazilian ambassador's residence used to be across the narrow street from the secret police's headquarters in the Chiado district. When the ambassador's wife complained about screams coming from the building, Delgado said, the police told her it was the screech of the trams passing by outside.

Delgado's brave defiance of Salazar was an ominous warning for the New State. Alfredo Barroso, a co-founder of the outlawed Socialist Party, saw 1958 as a milestone, as the year the New State "began truly to shake", largely thanks to

Delgado. The following year, in what became known as the Revolta da Sé (Cathedral Revolt), military officers, in league with civilians and a priest, hatched a plot to topple Salazar. Some of their secret meetings were held at Lisbon's cathedral. Most were arrested when the secret police broke up the ring before the planned coup could take place on the night of 11 March. In 1960 there was a brutal police crackdown on a march in Lisbon marking the 5 October anniversary of the Republic.

In January 1961 leading moderate politicians published a "Programme for the Democratization of the Republic". Over thirteen chapters, it proposed comprehensive, democratic and peaceful reforms. The next day, many of them were rounded up and interrogated by the secret police. Some were jailed. Dissent, under Salazar, invited a brutal response. The jail of choice for Salazar's henchmen was Aljube, near the cathedral and today a museum. Aljube had always been a prison of one kind of another. Before the *reconquista*, the Moors used it as a jail and it subsequently became an ecclesiastical prison. After the Liberal Revolution it was used for those convicted of common crimes, and later was a women's prison. From 1928 it was used by the New State for political prisoners, who were held there without trial. Its isolation cells where prisoners were tortured, commonly through sleep deprivation, were nicknamed *curros*, which is the name for a pen where bulls are held at arenas.

The problems started coming thick and fast for Salazar. In February 1961 the colonial war erupted, starting in Angola, and over the next thirteen years the campaigns would kill around 9,000 Portuguese and absorb close to half of the country's GDP. In November of that year, Hermínio da

Palma Inácio, a swashbuckling enemy of the regime and ex-Aljube inmate, and a group of five cohorts hijacked a TAP Super Constellation plane flying from Casablanca to Lisbon. Palma Inácio ordered the pilot to fly low over the capital while he and his men flung out of the door leaflets calling for people to rise up against Salazar.

Student revolts, called *crises académicas*, gathered pace in the 1960s. Lisbon University students went on strike. The secret police recruited the help of the Legião Portuguesa militia to brutally smash one demonstration. In 1967 Portugal faced its own *"ballets roses"* scandal, similar to the one that had gripped France in 1959—except that this was a dictatorship and the affair was covered up. Powerful politicians and aristocrats were having orgies with prostitutes and girls as young as eight, who danced in a pink spotlight. The following year, opposition to Salazar's regime emerged from an unexpected quarter, when about 200 Catholics held a night-time vigil in the São Domingos Church, the site of the 1506 Easter Massacre, to protest the colonial war.

Foreign visitors, like American writer Mary McCarthy who remarked on the "medieval" poverty of Alfama, could not help but notice the Dickensian hardship confronting many people in Lisbon. Barefoot street urchins were a common sight in the capital. Social care was scant and illiteracy was rife. From the mid-1950s onwards, a huge wave of emigration provided a damning indictment of the standard of living Salazar was providing for his people. An estimated 1.6 million Portuguese—more than 10 per cent of the population—left the country legally and illegally. Others migrated from the countryside to the capital. Lisbon's population stood at around 700,000 in 1940, but by 1960 it was more than 800,000.

The population growth, especially on the south bank of the Tagus, was the cue for the New State's most eye-catching project and its most enduring physical legacy: a suspension bridge that was the biggest in Europe at the time. It was said to be the biggest public works project ever undertaken in Portugal. It also advertised Portugal's robust economic growth after it became a founder member of the European Free Trade Association and used its low-paid workforce to ramp up exports. Between 1960 and 1973, Portugal's economy grew at an average rate of 6.9 per cent, similar to those of Spain and Greece.

Pacheco, the former public works minister, had once suggested building a bridge over the Tagus. He had favoured linking Lisbon with Montijo, which is about 20 kilometres from the mouth of the river, across the Sea of Straw. But the government in the end opted for a much shorter crossing from Alcântara to Almada, close to the river mouth where the Tagus tapers. The tender was won by the American Bridge Company, a division of the United States Steel Corporation. The company had previously built the Oakland Bay Bridge in San Francisco.

Up to 3,000 men worked on the construction at any one time, and the bridge took almost four years to complete. It sits on bedrock some 82 metres below the river's surface. Tests performed in the 1990s showed that it would withstand an earthquake like that of 1755. Completed six months ahead of schedule and within budget, the bridge was regarded as a feather in the cap of the dictatorship and partly explains why some people even today express a longing for Salazar's firm hand.

The bridge's August 1966 inauguration was a grand occasion. There were 12,000 guests, live television coverage and a religious blessing. The navy band played the national anthem, three navy ships on the Tagus gave a twenty-one-gun salute, and Handel's "Hallelujah" chorus was performed. The *Diário de Notícias* went overboard in its coverage, with a black-and-white photograph occupying the top half of the front page that showed Salazar's cortège, with motorcycle outriders, crossing the bridge with the Cristo Rei statue in the background. In an unchallenged overstatement befitting a dictatorship, the paper reported that "100 million Europeans saw on TV the biggest and most beautiful bridge on the Old Continent." The article was somewhat overegged as it referred to the bridge as "a dream that fed the imagination of Portuguese children through the centuries." Salazar cut the ribbon, proclaiming: "I thank God and declare open to traffic and at the service of the nation the Salazar Bridge."

Despite all the opening day bells and whistles and the relatively grand scale of the undertaking at the time, this was no vanity project. Salazar frowned on the cult of personality adopted by other leaders. He found it distasteful. He regarded dictatorship as his duty.

Just over one million vehicles crossed the bridge that inaugural year. Nowadays it receives on average around 150,000 vehicles a day. The bridge embellished the beauty of Lisbon and its estuary, rather than subtracting from it. The long, looping suspension cables possess graceful and dignified curves. The steel structure appears to be red, but officially the colour is "international orange". The bridge also altered Lisbon lifestyles. The south bank suburbs grew, as did commuter traffic into the city, and the beaches at Caparica came within easy weekend reach of city-dwellers. On a bleaker note, the bridge became known for suicides, with people abandoning their car in the middle of the deck and leaping to their death. Also, residents of the Alcântara neighbourhood, which lies under the north side of bridge, for years complained about falling debris, including tyres, hub caps and—most dispiritingly—dogs. Authorities eventually erected a fence.

Renaming the bridge after the date of the 1974 revolution was a symbolic gesture, marking the demise of the dictatorship. But anyway, Lisbon people had always referred to it as the Ponte Sobre o Tejo (Bridge over the Tagus), not the Ponte Salazar.

Salazar died in 1970, two years after a chair collapsed beneath him at his summer residence in Estoril and left him impaired. The state funeral was at the Jerónimos Monastery, after which he was taken for burial to the rural town 250 kilometres north of Lisbon where he was from. Marcello Caetano, a university professor, replaced Salazar as head of government, but the regime's days were already numbered. It was a spent force. Its strength was sapped by the patently unwinnable colonial wars that had dragged on for more than a decade. Deep cultural changes in Western Europe also chiselled at the New State's foundations. Meanwhile, unrest was percolating among junior army officers. The discontent spectacularly broke the surface one Thursday before dawn.

* * *

On 25 April 1974 Lisbon woke up to troops on the streets, just like sixty-four years earlier when republicans had risen up against the constitutional monarchy. Discontent among the army had quietly coalesced into what became known as the Captains' Revolt. After four decades in power the weighty New State shattered, astonishingly, like thin glass at the first tap. The cloak-and-dagger operation took the Portuguese by surprise and caught foreign governments napping. The Carnation Revolution was something of a historical peculiarity: soldiers rose up against a civilian dictatorship to install democracy, not to seize power themselves, and though society was stood on its head in the space of twenty-four hours only five people were killed.

At the time of the rebellion, around 80 per cent of the army was deployed in Africa. An estimated 150 officers and 2,000 soldiers took part in the coup, with the navy and air force initially staying on the sidelines. The conspirators set their plan in motion on the night of 24 April through codes broadcast on public radio stations. At 10:55 p.m. the first signal went out when Lisbon radio station Alfabeta played Paulo de Carvalho's song "*E depois do Adeus*" (And After We've Said Goodbye), meaning: it's on, it's tonight. The DJs were involved in the conspiracy, too, though they did not know exactly what playing that song would unleash.

At twenty minutes after midnight, another song pulled the trigger for action as the *Limite* late-night show on the Renascença radio station broadcast the song "*Grândola, Vila Morena*" (Grândola, Dusky Town). It was the green light for army units to leave their barracks and move on their pre-established targets.

By 4:00 a.m. the coup had achieved its early objectives. The mutineers in Lisbon took charge of public television RTP's studios, the Emissora Nacional public radio headquarters, and the premises of Rádio Clube Português, the country's main private radio station. Twenty minutes later, Lisbon airport fell into their hands and six minutes after that a first communiqué from the rebels was read out over the microphones of Rádio Clube Português, asking people to remain calm and stay indoors, followed by the national anthem.

Luís Pimentel, a conspirator who at the time was a thirty-year-old army captain, recounted one of the many unlikely, not to say bizarre, episodes that occurred that day. He was in a military column that entered Lisbon from Carregueira, 140 kilometres to the north, with orders to seize the Emissora Nacional. When he and his men got there at around 3:00 a.m., two policemen with machine guns were outside the building on sentry duty. Pimentel feared a shoot-out in the street and approached them with trepidation. But to his astonishment, the policemen knew nothing about what was afoot. Pimentel showed them his forged orders instructing him to occupy the national radio station's headquarters. One of the policemen calmly replied and pointed, "It's through that door down there, on your left." Pimentel thanked him and rang the bell. The door opened and he walked in. He asked to use a telephone, called his command post and gave the code message: "We're in Tokyo."

At around 5:00 a.m. the head of the secret police, Major Fernando da Silva Pais, called Marcello Caetano. "Mr President," he said, "there's a revolution going on." He advised Caetano to seek safety at the garrison headquarters of the Guarda Nacional Republicana, traditional loyalists, in the Chiado district's Largo do Carmo, just as the 1915 government had done. Maria de Lurdes Rocha, the garrison's head of cleaning and laundry services, made up five rooms to receive the country's leader and his entourage. Caetano arrived at about 5:30 a.m. Just over an hour later, the revolutionaries found out he was there.

Before dawn, armoured cavalry units took up position in Praça do Comércio and surrounded the government ministries in the square as well as nearby Lisbon City Hall, the Bank of Portugal and police headquarters. The rebels guarded the Salazar Bridge, too, to prevent any government reinforcements reaching the capital from the south. In an echo of 1910, the frigate *Almirante Gago Coutinho* received orders from the navy command, which was considering a counter-attack against the insurgents, to take up position by the Praça do Comércio. But rebels in positions on the south bank of the river threatened to sink the ship with their artillery if it opened fire. The ship withdrew to the Sea of Straw.

At the Defence Ministry in Belém, staff used a pick-axe to hack a hole in an office wall. Through it, the ministers of defence and of the navy and their chiefs of staff escaped into the Navy Ministry library next door. From there they made their way to the 2nd Lancers Regiment in nearby Ajuda where they established the loyalist HQ at 9:40 a.m.

Meanwhile, tens of thousands of people ignored the call to stay indoors. They at first emerged warily, as if coming out of burrows into the light, but soon thronged the Lisbon streets. There were scenes of joy and spontaneous jubilation. Salazar's New State was gone! Strangers hugged each other and the soldiers. Flower-sellers slotted carnations, which were in bloom, into the soldiers' gun barrels. It was like the Summer of Love which the Portuguese had missed out on. People out that day recall the rebels' tank tracks chewing up the tarmac on downtown streets. They remember taking water, sandwiches and cigarettes to the insurrectionists. They recollect punching the air and shouting the slogans of the day: *Viva a Liberdade!* ("Long live freedom!"), *Abaixo o fascismo!*

("Down with fascism!") and *Morte à PIDE!* ("Death to the secret police!")

The thickening crowds meant that a military column dispatched to the Largo do Carmo made slow progress, and in any event tanks are hard to manoeuvre in Lisbon's old streets. Loyalist troops tried to halt the column, but civilians swarmed around in celebration and the loyalist troops ended up joining the impromptu party. Army Captain Fernando Salgueiro Maia was handed the task of surrounding the garrison where Caetano, Foreign Minister Rui Patrício, and Information Minister Moreira Baptista were holed up. The small, leafy square became the unanticipated epicentre of the uprising and the place where Portugal's fate would be decided.

There was more drama a few hundred metres away. Hundreds of people had surrounded the hated secret police's headquarters in the Chiado's Rua de António Maria Cardoso. They chanted *Morte aos PIDEs!*, sang the national anthem and feted the armed forces who had set them free. The agents hid inside behind locked doors.

Back at the Largo do Carmo, meanwhile, troops had to form a cordon to keep back the growing crowds of civilians for whom seeing was believing. People climbed up trees, lamp posts, the square's eighteenth-century stone fountain and onto tanks to watch the stalemate unfold. At 3:10 p.m. Captain Salgueiro Maia received orders to deliver an ultimatum to Caetano. He picked up a megaphone and, with hundreds of people intently watching his every move and hanging on his every word, said: "Attention Carmo garrison, attention Carmo garrison. You have ten minutes to surrender. Everybody inside the garrison must come out unarmed, with a white flag and with their hands up. If you don't, we will destroy the building."

The warning elicited no reaction, so Lieutenant Santos Silva fired a machine gun burst from the turret of his armoured personnel carrier across the garrison's façade. Negotiations for the surrender of Caetano began. Caetano refused to capitulate to a junior officer, so General António de Spínola, a monacled soldier's soldier who had fought on the front lines in Africa and urged an end to the colonial wars, was called to the scene. When he arrived, in an unmarked car, he was mobbed by the ecstatic crowd. His arrival was taken as a sign that the revolution had succeeded. Francisco Sousa Tavares, a politician, journalist and lawyer who had spoken out against the regime, climbed onto a sentry box and addressed the crowd through a megaphone. "People of Portugal," he said, "we are witnessing an historic moment, one that hasn't been witnessed perhaps since 1640: the liberation of our homeland."

Captain Salgueiro Maia asked the crowds to leave the square so that Caetano could be taken away in safety. But nobody budged. The genie was out of the bottle, and there was too much at stake. An armoured personnel carrier had to back up to the garrison's gate so that Caetano and his officials could get into it unseen at around 7.30 p.m. According to twenty-two-year-old Sergeant Manuel Silva, who was in charge of the vehicle and had only ever seen Caetano on television, the deposed leader climbed calmly inside and sighed, "Well, that's life." The crowd banged on the sides as it slowly pulled away, chanting *Vitória! Vitória! Vitória!* Caetano was taken to the rebel headquarters at the 1st Engineer Regiment in the suburb of Pontinha. He later went into exile in Brazil.

The secret police were still barricaded inside their nearby headquarters, however. They probably feared for their lives after mistreating people so badly—or suspected they would be treated in the same fashion. At dusk, in a final desperate act, they opened upper windows and fired machine guns and threw tear gas grenades down into the crowd in the street. Four people were killed and forty-five injured. Soldiers shot one secret policeman in the back as he tried to escape. The building, now converted into luxury apartments, has a plaque outside stating, "Here, on the evening of 25 April 1974, the PIDE opened fire on the people of Lisbon and killed Fernando Gesteira, José Barneto, Fernando Barreiros dos Reis and José Guilherme Arruda."

A communiqué, signed by the Movimento das Forças Armadas (Armed Forces Movement), at 7:50 p.m. announced that the government had fallen. It had been a long day for the soldiers, kept going by fear, adrenaline and euphoria. It had been an even longer one for Portugal. "Never has a single day been so long," said an RTP reporter. People still talk about it being the happiest day of their lives.

Over the following weeks and months, the revolutionary fervour boiled over. Farm workers collectivized the land they tilled, and blue-collar staff seized control of the companies where they worked. Hopes of building a new and fairer society ran high. Jean-Paul Sartre, Simone de Beauvoir and Gabriel García Márquez came to Lisbon for a look at the experiment. So did Romanian President Nicolae Ceausescu.

The British journalist and commentator Bernard Levin, writing in *The Times* of 2 July 1974, described the revolution as "the second Lisbon earthquake". He also noted that "before the sun went down on the first day of the new era, the entire edifice of a regime that had existed without serious internal challenge for over half a century had vanished as though it had never existed at all."

Changing the names of streets was part of drawing the curtains on that distasteful past. In Lisbon, the avenue called 28 de Maio, in reference to the 1926 military coup that heralded Salazar's rule, became Avenida 25 de Abril. A municipal edict explained that names that "affronted" people must be removed. A city square, for example, received the new name Praça Marechal Humberto Delgado, in remembrance of the Fearless General. One suggestion, presented by the Association of Former Anti-Fascist Political Prisoners, to change Rua de António Maria Cardoso, where the secret police HQ was located, to Rua da Leva da Morte (something like, Dragged to Your Death Street) was considered too macabre. Another rejected proposal was to rename the Praça do Comércio as the Praça do Povo (People's Square).

Inspirational political leaders who had been banished by the New State returned from exile. Two of them stood out due to their charisma, eloquence and impeccable anti-fascist credentials: Socialist leader Mário Soares, a graduate of Lisbon University's Faculty of Law who had specialized in defending critics of Salazar's rule, and Communist Party Secretary-General Álvaro Cunhal, a dyed-in-the-wool Stalinist. Soares and other exiles were the first to arrive, travelling from Paris on what became known as the Freedom Train. At Santa Apolónia station, where the police had once beaten the supporters of Humberto Delgado, Soares went up to a veranda to address the great crowd that had gathered to greet him. He then gave an impromptu press conference in the station's waiting room. Two days later, Cunhal arrived on an Air France flight at Lisbon airport after fourteen years' exile in the Soviet Union. He gave a speech from the top of a *chaimite* armoured personnel carrier—a vehicle that, along with red carnations, was one of the revolution's symbols. Cunhal was a canny politician.

Soares and Cunhal marched together at one of the most memorable events in the weeks following the revolution. A massive crowd, estimated at around one million, turned out for the annual 1 May parade. It was the first Workers' Day celebrated in freedom, and people savoured the deliciousness of the occasion. Crowds began gathering before dawn at the Alameda Dom Afonso Henriques, a large grassy area between the Instituto Superior Técnico and the Fonte Luminosa, where the march was due to start at 3:30 p.m. It was an exhilarating celebration. After being held for decades in a straitjacket, people trumpeted their release. Liberty amplified their voices. They shouted slogans about freedom and democracy, they chanted and sang together. Strangers hugged. Some wept with joy.

The great mass of people marched for two hours along city avenues, with Soares and Cunhal side-by-side near the front and ringed by navy personnel who kept back the many well-wishers. The loud procession made its way to a sports stadium in the Alvalade neighbourhood that had belonged to the National Foundation for Joy at Work and had been renamed Estádio Primeiro de Maio (First of May Stadium). Many people couldn't get in. Soares and Cunhal gave rousing speeches. "Comrades," Soares said, "it was worth suffering for so many years to come to a party like this."

Relations between the two party leaders would soon sour, however, as they became rivals in a democratic quest for power. Soares, with his moderate policies, was destiny's child. Over the next two decades he would occupy, at different times, the posts of foreign minister, prime minister and two-term president. In any other place at any other time, Soares would probably have remained just a successful city lawyer and a gourmet raconteur with a taste for the arts. But the times destined him to become a European statesman. Cunhal had a mane of white hair and jet-black eyebrows, with piercing charcoal eyes that hinted at his uncompromising nature. Cunhal led the Portuguese Communist Party for thirty-one years, up to 1992. He was hidebound, and that was his undoing, though he would not see it like that. He was stuck in a Brezhnevian time warp while Portugal moved on. After his 2005 death aged ninety-one, it was revealed that Cunhal had also been a secret novelist, publishing books under the pseudonym Manuel Tiago.

The tension between them came to a head in a decisive moment just over a year later, in the so-called *Verão Quente* (Hot Summer) of 1975, a few months after the country's first free elections, to a Constituent Assembly. Soares addressed a huge Socialist Party rally on a Saturday from the top of the Fonte Luminosa, with about 100,000 people filling the grassy Alameda Dom Afonso Henriques below. Some people had been coerced and even physically prevented from attending the event. In a famous speech, Soares described the Communist Party leadership as paranoid and accused senior members of the Armed Forces Movement of supporting its political ploys. The massive crowd that turned up at the rally despite the intimidation helped prove that the Portuguese were not minded to be radical—as shown at the ballot box for the following year's first parliamentary elections, which the Socialists won while the Communist Party came third.

Ending the deeply unpopular colonial wars and granting the five African colonies their independence was a top priority for Portugal's new leaders. It was such a pressing issue that, in some important aspects, the process was rushed. Almost at once, hundreds of thousands of Portuguese living in the African colonies clamoured to leave. The biggest exodus was from Angola, the jewel in Portugal's African crown, which had witnessed horrific violence on both sides during the war and where the Portuguese feared retribution.

An air bridge was established between Lisbon and Luanda, the Angolan capital, with the United States and Soviet Union providing planes and crews to help overburdened TAP. The first flight arrived back in the capital on 13 May 1975 and the last one on 13 November. At the same time, ships carrying the *retornados* docked in Alcântara. Wooden crates and trunks with names scribbled on the side in chalk were piled above head height along the quayside, recalling the royal flight to Brazil in 1807.

The Institute for the Support of Returning Nationals, created by the government, recorded more than 505,000 people coming home from the colonies, some of them penniless and homeless. The government requisitioned entire hotels in Lisbon to provide temporary accommodation. Even the Ritz, Lisbon's first big European-standard luxury hotel, was required to help out. Salazar had not been keen on luxury, ostentation and modernity, but he allowed the Ritz, which became a 1950s landmark. Located on a high point next to Parque Eduardo VII, it employed cutting-edge architecture, used 15,000 tonnes of marble, rose fifteen storeys high and still possesses many memorable works of modern art, including tapestries and murals by Almada Negreiros.

Portugal almost came unglued during the post-revolution frenzy. Authority frayed. Political parties broke up into factions which, amoeba-like, divided into sub-factions. Splinter groups fragmented. At one point, there were thirty-two registered political parties. Many of them had communist leanings and tried to "out-left" each other. In this battle, walls along Lisbon streets were co-opted for huge political murals. The Frente Eleitoral de Comunistas (Marxista-Leninista) (Communist Electoral Front [Marxist-Leninist]), for example, known by its acronym, FEC (m-l), commandeered the high walls of the large Alto de São João cemetery. In red writing on the white wall, with a Soviet flag and a shirtless man at an anvil as decoration, it proclaimed "Down with capitalist exploitation" and "We support the just fight of the farm workers against fascist reorganization."

Escalating tensions during the eight months of the Hot Summer brought Portugal to the brink of civil war. Everything and nothing seemed possible in that incendiary atmosphere. Grievances were freely and loudly aired. Strikes and protest marches demanding broader legal rights or substantial pay rises were an everyday event in Lisbon. Strikers sometimes threw up barricades on roads into the capital. Governments came and went, lasting weeks or a few months. One government even went on strike for ten days. People, it said, were demanding too much too quickly from their new leaders. Lawmakers elected to draw up a new Constitution were unable to leave the São Bento parliament building for forty-eight hours when they were held under siege by workers in overalls who lounged on the generously upholstered sofas in the parliamentary corridors. Some wits remarked that the scene bore a passing resemblance to the Bolsheviks in the Winter Palace in 1917.

The uncertainty stretched into the next decade, when a succession of violent deaths tested the country's nerves. The first of these came on the evening of 4 December 1980, when a twin-engine Cessna aircraft carrying Prime Minister Francisco Sá Carneiro and Defence Minister Adelino Amaro da Costa crashed into the Camarate suburb of Lisbon forty-three seconds after taking off from the capital's airport. They were killed instantly. Their wives, the prime minister's chief of staff, the pilot and co-pilot also perished. A joint investigation by Portuguese police and accident investigators decided it was an accident caused by engine failure. Many experts have argued persuasively, however, that the official explanation is implausible. Contradictions in the official investigation have fuelled speculation of sabotage, sinister cover-ups and international conspiracy. The murky circumstances surrounding the accident have kept alive the public's fascination.

One theory has it that Amaro da Costa's briefcase, which was lost in the crash and subsequent fire, contained secret evidence of top-level Portuguese army involvement in arms trafficking from the United States through Portugal to the Middle East and Africa. The cover-up, according to that theory, was an attempt to preserve a minimum of political stability in the stormy years after the revolution. Sá Carneiro, a widely respected leader of the moderate Social Democratic Party, had been elected as head of a right-of-centre coalition government in 1979 and was credited with restoring a degree of order. Authorities, some believe, entered into a pact of silence about the true causes of the plane crash because they feared tipping the country back into political chaos, even civil war.

Other trouble surfaced. In June 1982 the Turkish chargé d'affaires was gunned down by an Armenian commando unit in a Lisbon suburb. The following year, another Armenian commando unit overran the Turkish Embassy in Belém. The five attackers in that assault were killed, as were a Portuguese policeman and the wife of a Turkish diplomat, after the attackers apparently detonated their explosive device by mistake.

Meanwhile, a home-grown terrorist group sprouted. The Forças Populares 25 de Abril, known as FP-25, was an extreme-left-wing terror group that was active across the country from 1980 until 1987. It was blamed for more than a dozen deaths, mostly company executives and police officers. The group financed itself through robberies and the kidnapping of wealthy entrepreneurs for ransom.

In 1981 the group fired a rocket against the Royal British Club premises in the Bairro Alto district in what it said was an expression of support for the IRA. The FP-25 was blamed for two night-time bombs that went off the following year in Lisbon, destroying the Air France and Lufthansa offices in the Avenida da Liberdade. The terror campaign stretched into 1984 and 1985 when the group held up an armoured car in downtown Lisbon and tried but failed to launch a mortar attack against NATO ships anchored in the Tagus. In September 1985 ten of its arrested members escaped from Lisbon Prison, which sits at the top end of Parque Eduardo VII and looks like a medieval fortress. The group's last victim was a police inspector shot dead while chasing three FP-25 members through Lisbon.

The *retornados* were not the only ones to come from Portugal's former colonies. African immigrants began to arrive in Lisbon, too. They also came with little or nothing and sought out relations or friends already settled in the metropolis. The biggest problem was that there was nowhere for them to live. So they did what they had done at home—

build shacks. Shanty towns sprouted on the fringes of Lisbon. They offered scenes out of Africa: wooden huts with corrugated iron roofs and hard dirt floors. Some of these *bairros de lata*—such as Casal Ventoso, on a hillside above Alcântara, or Pedreira dos Húngaros, which was the biggest and had an estimated 30,000 shacks—became no-go areas that were notorious for crime and poverty.

Sweeping away the shanty towns through slum clearance programmes in the 1990s became possible due to lavish development funds from the European Economic Community, now European Union, which Portugal joined on 1 January 1986. Indeed, the improvement in living standards made Portugal a symbol for the benefits of European unity. Unfortunately, the shanty town residents were shifted into tall, council-owned apartment blocks (identifiable by the absence of balconies) that frequently degenerated into graffiti-splattered sink estates.

The signing ceremony to formally join the EEC was held in—predictably—Belém, on 12 June 1985. On a sunny Wednesday morning, the leaders of ten European countries, along with those of fledgling members Portugal and Spain, posed for a family photo in the Tower of Belém with the tall ship *Sagres* on the Tagus behind them. Around 700 guests attended the subsequent open-air signing ceremony in the exquisite cloisters of the Jerónimos Monastery. "In these 400-year-old cloisters, the past and the future of Portugal meet," Soares, the prime minister at the time, said in his speech. After that, the leaders proceeded down the road to the Palácio de Belém to hear a speech from President António Ramalho Eanes. Portugal completed the bloc's Atlantic border, and Europe opened its arms to the Portuguese who for so long had stood on the banks of the Tagus and devoted their attention to the watery horizon.

To foreign eyes, Lisbon in the mid-1980s appeared to be in thrall to a kind of unfashionable retro style. The cars, the clothes, the cafés had a distinctly 1960s feel. That, too, was part of the New State's legacy. But the city possessed a shabby charm that was seductive. One of its dusty gems was almost lost in 1988. At about 5:00 a.m. on 25 August, a fire started in the Armazéns Grandella department store in the Chiado, the traditional bohemian neighbourhood. It spread quickly, threatening to consume a large chunk of the old downtown. Live television coverage of the menace captivated the capital. Orange rooftop flames and a thick plume of smoke like a volcano eruption could be seen from around the city. Firefighters had difficulty getting their fire engines down the tight streets, just as the revolutionaries had with their tanks in 1974. Narrow stairs and corridors made it hard for them to get through with breathing apparatus. Exploding gas canisters and crumbling walls turned the old buildings into death traps. Nevertheless, by lunchtime the blaze was under control.

Firemen recall that Thursday with a shudder. Two people—a resident and a firefighter—died in the blaze. Around seventy people were injured, 300 left homeless and two dozen buildings gutted. The cause of the fire was never ascertained. In the city's memory, it was a dark day. The Chiado is a pleasant and cherished part of town. "It's a catastrophe," Mário Soares, who by then was Portugal's president, said of the fire. "It's a national disaster." The rebuilding project, masterminded by award-winning architect Álvaro Siza Vieira, took twenty years to complete.

The bountiful European development funds worked magic in Lisbon. More than the rest of the country, the city experienced slingshot development. An intended national symbol of the new era fell flat, however. The Belém Cultural Centre was created to host and to mark Portugal's first six-month presidency of the EEC in 1992, which was a significant national milestone. The building fails because it attempts to be both humble and important at the same time and ends up falling between stools. It is too monolithic to be humble and too bland to be important. It was also built close to the Jerónimos Monastery, in a pointed reminder to the EEC of Portugal's glorious past, but was diminished instead of embellished by the contrast. Low and boxy, in concrete with stone panel cladding, it is a forgettable building and a missed opportunity to say something about modern Portugal.

The memorable emblem of those days of plenty is EXPO '98. The last world's fair of the twentieth century was held in the Portuguese capital, which triumphed over Toronto's rival bid, and it was the cue for what became known as Lisbon's "Big Bang": a torrent of major public works that included the Ponte Vasco da Gama, Europe's longest bridge; a new underground train line with seven stations; and the graceful Gare do Oriente international train station by Spanish architect Santiago Calatrava. EXPO '98 was a symbol of a desired wider retooling of Portugal. The country was bursting with confidence after joining Europe's new shared currency and was determined to show the world what it could do.

The world's fair marked the 500th anniversary of Vasco da Gama's discovery of the sea route to India. Its theme was the oceans and their protection. A massive urban redevelopment project was set in motion, turning a run-down industrial area on the eastern side of Lisbon into a showcase of modern architecture. The area was razed, leaving just a Petrogal refinery tower as a reminder of its past, and then rebuilt. It stood roughly on the site of the Cabo Ruivo Maritime Airport, which received the hydroplane passengers in the 1940s.

EXPO '98, which opened on 22 May for four months, welcomed around eleven million visitors to its riverside pavilions and its long, hard riverside walkways with their bright, white Portuguese paving. On its last night, the fair drew a record attendance of 215,000 people. Many of them went to the venue by car, and the traffic jams caused a tailback which stretched all the way across to the western side of the city. Afterwards, the site became the Parque das Nações, a desirable residential district that includes an oceanarium which is one of the world's biggest, with more than thirty aquariums and 7.5 million litres of water; the city's largest concert hall; and the Lisbon Casino.

The standout feature and abiding reminder of the event is the bridge. It was given a name that would not cause the same problem brought on by the city's older bridge. Nobody could argue with the pick, as Vasco da Gama's feat is one of Portugal's claims to fame in world history. The bridge crosses the Sea of Straw, linking Sacavém on the north bank of the Tagus with Montijo on the southern side. It is roughly where Duarte Pacheco, the former public works minister, had proposed building. The 17-kilometre span took three years to build. Its foundations were designed to withstand the impact of a 30,000-tonne ship travelling at 12 knots.

The inauguration was a very Portuguese affair: a free bean stew for 17,000 people. They were ferried out to the bridge deck in a fleet of buses and seated at one long table that snaked across the brand-new structure. There were 8 tonnes of stew, to be eaten with plastic plates and cutlery. There wasn't enough to go around, however, and some people became hot under the collar about it.

It is hard not to admire the bridge's elegant bearing and the spectacle of its achievement. There is a darker side, however, and it was captured in the 1999 Portuguese film *Tarde Demais* (Too Late). Made while the new bridge was being built, the film tells the haunting story of four fishermen from a poor riverside town on the south bank. Out on the Tagus at night, their old boat with outdated equipment is holed and, within sight of Lisbon and its new bridge, they are fatally stranded on a sandbank. Doomed, they silently watch the city lights twinkle tantalizingly at sunset. These men are so near, yet so far. They, like many others outside the capital, savoured no part of the economic prosperity and well-being concentrated in Lisbon. Seven centuries since the capital was moved there, Portugal's case of macrocephaly, its outsize metropolis concentrating power and resources, still held true.

ACKNOWLEDGEMENTS

Having worked as a foreign correspondent in Portugal's capital for the past thirty years, I wanted to tell Lisbon's story from the inside, joining up the dots between past and present in an enlightening and entertaining way. This is not a linear, historical narrative culled from dusty archives. Even so, studies by Portuguese historians have provided indispensable background and detail, and they are quoted in the text.

Among them are the magisterial *Guia de Portugal* (Guide to Portugal) masterminded by Raul Proença. I found in Proença the same appetite for his subject and the same scrupulousness encountered in Nikolaus Pevsner's architectural guides to the British Isles. Published in eight volumes between 1924 and 1969, Proença's guide has few illustrations but has an enviable literary quality in its prose descriptions. Among its contributors were great writers and academics of the day such as Aquilino Ribeiro, Jaime Cortesão and Orlando Ribeiro. The guide came in a dark green hardback slightly bigger than a hand and with pages as thin as tissue paper so that the exhaustive detail could be crammed in. The volume on Lisbon and its surroundings has 696 pages. Other vital sources were the works of numerous Portuguese experts on Lisbon's history—who are identified by the tongue-twisting designation *olisipógrafos*, after

ACKNOWLEDGEMENTS

Olisipo, the ancient Roman name for Lisbon—such as Norberto Araújo in the twentieth century and José Sarmento de Matos nowadays. Praise must also be given to the resources of enthusiastic and outstanding blogs on Lisbon history, such as aps-ruasdelisboacomhistria.blogspot.pt and restosdecolec-cao.blogspot.pt.

Thanks are due to my wife Carmo for her enthusiasm and my daughter Maria for her eagle-eyed rigour. Equally valuable were the generous assistance and expertise of Sandy Sloop, Gonçalo Couceiro Feio and Frederico Melo Franco.

INDEX

INDEX